John Updike's Early Years

John Updike's Early Years

Jack De Bellis
with David Silcox

LEHIGH UNIVERSITY PRESS
Bethlehem

Published by Lehigh University Press
Co-published with The Rowman & Littlefield Publishing Group, Inc.
4501 Forbes Boulevard, Suite 200, Lanham, Maryland 20706
www.rowman.com

10 Thornbury Road, Plymouth PL6 7PP, United Kingdom

British Library Cataloguing in Publication Information Available

Library of Congress Cataloging-in-Publication Data

De Bellis, Jack.
John Updike's Early Years / Jack De Bellis with David Silcox.
pages cm
Includes bibliographical references and index.
SBN 978-1-61146-130-5 (cloth : alk. paper) -- ISBN 978-1-61146-131-2 (electronic)
1. Updike, John--Friends and associates. 2. Updike, John--Criticism and interpretation. I. Silcox,
David P. II. Title.
PS3571.P4Z635 2013
813'.54--dc23
[B]
2012040811

♻™ The paper used in this publication meets the minimum requirements of American
National Standard for Information Sciences Permanence of Paper for Printed Library
Materials, ANSI/NISO Z39.48-1992.

Printed in the United States of America

Dedicated to the classmates of John Updike,
Most near, most loved, and most far.

Contents

Acknowledgments   ix

Author's Notes   xi

List of Short Titles and Abbreviations   xiii

Introduction   xix

1   Updike's Early Years: Background   1

2   Personal   33

3   Leisure   41

4   Athletics   49

5   Clowning   57

6   Girls and Women   65

7   *Chatterbox:* Cartooning and Drawing   73

8   *Chatterbox*: Poetry and Prose   83

9   Inspirations and Models   89

Appendix A: Updike Chronology   101

Appendix B: Updike's Published Writings Set in Pennsylvania   109

Appendix C: John Updike's Contributions to *The Little Shilling*
    and *Chatterbox*   117

Appendix D: Updike's Classmates, Faculty, and Administrators   131

Works Cited   161

Index   165

Acknowledgments

John Updike's Shillington contact for many years, David Silcox, was helpful in facilitating interviews with the loyal classmates of Shillington High School. In addition, David unlocked many doors and tracked down numerous leads. He modestly has identified himself as simply a "facilitator," but he was much more. His rich knowledge of everything about Berks County added immeasurably to this book. The classmates he introduced me to were exceptionally kind in providing a great many stories, anecdotes, and details about John Updike's life. They were enthusiastically forthcoming in permitting me to examine correspondence, photos, and memorabilia. I thank them all most deeply for making this project so pleasurable. In particular, I wish to thank Ann Weik Cassar, Jackie Hirneisen Kendall, Barry Nelson, Jerry Potts, and Joan Venne Youngerman. They all provided photos and work by Updike never before seen—Updike with his kindergarten class, at birthday parties, playing roofball, and relaxing. Among many happy discoveries was a poem written to Jackie Hirneisen when Updike was ten years old. Many classmates permitted me to examine Updike's inscriptions in their copies of his books and in their yearbooks. Myrtle Council, a leader of the Shillington High School Alumni Association, offered unstinting help in locating Updike's classmates. Mrs. Kathy Hess, of the Reading Public Library, and the staff at Governor Mifflin Middle School enabled me to inspect Updike's contribution to his school newspaper, *Chatterbox*. One of Updike's closest friends, the late Barry Nelson, allowed me to use his indispensable works—an unpublished study of John Updike's life at Shillington High School, a history of the town, and a study of parallels between characters and places in Updike's *The Centaur* and the real-life Shillington models. A special thanks to Mrs. Mary Weatherall, John Updike's first wife, and their children, David, Elizabeth, Michael, and Miranda, for many kindnesses. Lehigh University computer consultants were immensely helpful. Monica Najar of the Lehigh University Press and Jane Mara of Rowman and Littlefield Publishing Group were consistently patient, concerned, and good-humored.

To my encouraging, forbearing wife, Patricia, I say a very loud thank you. Your cheerful support and valuable suggestions made this book (and others) fun to write.

PERMISSIONS

I wish to thank the following persons for allowing me to quote from interviews: Shirley Berger, Harlan Boyer, Ann Cassar, Robert Daubert, Bill Forry, Mahlon Frankhauser, Emerson Gundy, Jack Guerin, Milton Hall, Jacqueline Kendall, Nancy LeVan, Richard Manderbach, Barry Nelson, Bernarda Palm, Edward Pienta, Gerald Potts, Robert Rhoads, David Silcox, James Trexler, Donald VanLiew, and Joan Youngerman.

I wish to thank the following for their generous permission to reprint photographs: Mrs. Ann Weik Cassar, for several photos of John Updike as a child; Richard Manderbach, for a group photo of Updike with friends; Mrs. Nancy Nelson, for pictures of Updike playing roofball; and Peter Windhorst, for a photo of Updike's Shillington home.

Author's Notes

In the interest of facilitating identifications, the first time a female married school friend is mentioned in any chapter, she is identified by her full name; thereafter, only her first name and maiden name appear. But citations to collections of letters owned by married women are listed by their full names. John Updike is referred to as Updike throughout.

Please consult the "List of Short Titles and Abbreviations" to find sources included in the parenthetical documentation. For information about the classmates quoted, please refer to Appendix D, "Updike's Shillington Classmates, Faculty, and Administrators." Quotes without internal documentation were provided in interviews.

To make the copy of the captions in Appendix D exact copies of the originals, I have followed the yearbook's practice and left unitalicized the words *Hi-Life* and *Chatterbox*. However, italics in the yearbook captions have been retained.

The Updike Estate requested that no quotes from unpublished material be used except with very loose paraphrase. This may account for unusual locutions at times.

List of Short Titles and Abbreviations

"Alice"	"Alice McDermott Wins a Top Award for Fiction." *New York Times* 20 Nov. 1998: B8.
Americana	*Americana*. New York: Knopf, 2001.
AP	*Assorted Prose*. New York: Knopf, 1965.
Astor	David Astor. "Updike Is Honored by Cartoonists." *Editor &Publisher* 15 Dec. 1990: 36.
AWCC	Ann Weik Cassar collection.
Bay	John Updike. *Bech at Bay*. New York: Knopf, 1998.
Bech	Henry Bech. "Henry Bech Redux." *New York Times Book Review* 14 Nov.1971: 3.
Book	John Updike. *Bech: A Book*. New York: Knopf, 1970.
"Bookish"	John Updike. "A Bookish Boy." *Life* Oct. 1990: 101.
Bragg	Melvyn Bragg. London Weekend Television. June, 1990.
Britton	Burt Britton. *Self-Portrait*. New York: Random, 1976.
C	John Updike. *The Centaur*. New York: Knopf, 1963.
Callaway	John Callaway. "John Callaway Interviews John Updike." WTTW Chicago 26 Nov. 1981.
CB CNY	"Foreword." *The Complete Book of Covers from* The New Yorker *1925-1989*. Knopf: New York, 1989. v-vii.
CH	*The Carpentered Hen and Other Tame Creatures*. New York: Harper & Brothers, 1958.
"Church"	Linda Grace Hoyer. "Church Attendance in Olden Times." Robeson Evangelical Lutheran Church. Mohnton, Pennsylvania. Unpublished booklet. N. d.
Concerts	John Updike. *Concerts at Castle Hill*. Northridge, California: Lord John Press, 1993.
CP	John Updike. *Collected Poems, 1953-1993*. New York: Knopf, 1993

"Craftsman"	Bruce R. Posten, "Craftsman Weaned on Self-reliance." Reading *Eagle* 25 Sept. 2010. Website edition.
CWU	James Plath. *Conversations with John Updike*. Jackson, Mississippi: U of Mississippi P, [1994].
DC	John Updike. *Due Considerations : Essays and Criticism*. New York: Knopf, 2007.
De Bellis	Jack De Bellis. *The John Updike Encyclopedia*. Westport, Connecticut: Greenwood Press, 2000.
DLBD	"John Updike." *The Dictionary of Literary Biography Documentary Series*. Vol. 3. Matthew J. Bruccoli and Richard Layman. Farmington Hills, Michigan: Gale, 1983. 251-320.
DUC	David Updike Collection.
Dudar	Helen Dudar. "John Updike: The Art of Whittling Fantasy out of Paper." *The Attentive Eye*. Ed. Peter Goldman. Philadelphia, Pennsylvania: Xlibris, 2002. 19-31.
Ecenbarger	William Ecenbarger. "Tracing Updike's Roots." Philadelphia *Inquirer* 10 Oct. 2008: A1.
ES	John Updike. *The Early Stories, 1953-75*. New York: Knopf, 2003.
"Forty"	"Forty Years of Middle America with John Updike." *South Bank Show*. BBC.
Hagan	Chet Hagan. "John Updike: Berks County's Most Honored Writer Now Challenges the New Millennium." *Historical Review of Berks County* Spg. 2000: 57-60, 62-63.
Hartman	Susan Beth Hartman. "The Role of the Berks County Setting in the Novels of John Updike." Diss. U of Pittsburgh, 1987.
Heer	Jeet Heer. "Dear Orphan Annie: Why Cartoon Characters Get All the Best Mail." *Boston Globe* 25 Sept. 2002: Ideas.
Heizmann	Louis J. Heizmann. *The Library That Would Not Die: The Turbulent History of the Reading Public Library*. [Reading, Pennsylvania]: The Reading Public Library, [1971].
HF	John Updike. *Hub Fans Bid Kid Adieu*. New York: Library of America, 2010.

HG	John Updike. *Higher Gossip*. New York: Knopf, 2011.
Hoerr	Dorothy Lehman Hoerr. "Shillington Native, World-renown Author John Updike." *Berks County Living* May-June 2005: 48.
HS	John Updike. *Hugging the Shore: Essays and Criticism*. New York: Knopf, 1983.
IBL	John Updike. *In the Beauty of the Lilies*. New York: Knopf, 1996.
JHKC	Jackie Hirneisen Kendal collection.
JPC	Jerry Potts collection.
JVYC	Joan Venne Youngerman collection.
Kreider	Dusty Kreider. "The Class of 1950 at Shillington High School Remembers John Updike and He Remembers Them." *Susquehanna Magazine* 3 (Jan. 1978): 19.
LL	John Updike. *Licks of Love*. New York: Knopf, 2000.
Mandelbaum	Paul Mandelbaum. Ed. *First Words: Earliest Writing from Favorite Contemporary Authors*. Chapel Hill: Algonquin Books of North Carolina, 1993. 420-71.
MFT	John Updike. *My Father's Tears*. New York: Knopf, 2009.
Miller	Larry Miller, "C. F. Boyer– Retiring Teacher." Reading *Eagle* 30 Apr. 1969.
MM	John Updike. *More Matter*. New York: Knopf, 1991.
"Mother"	"Mother of Updike Dies at 85." Reading *Eagle* 12 Oct. 1989: 22.
MS	John Updike. *The Maples Stories*. New York: Knopf, 2009.
NelsonJUSHS	Barry Nelson. "John Updike at Shillington High School." N. d. Typescript.
NelsonUT	Barry Nelson, "The Updike Terrain: An Identification of Places the Author Writes about Locally." Bound at Reading, Pennsylvania: August, 1996. Typescript, eleven pages.
OF	John Updike. *Of the Farm*. New York: Knopf, 1965.
OJ	John Updike. *Odd Jobs*. New York: Knopf, 1991.
OS	John Updike. *Olinger Stories*. New York: Vintage, 1964.

"'Pleasing'"	"John Updike: 'Rabbit' Books 'Pleasing to Write'." Roanoke *Times*7 Feb. 2005.
Posten	Bruce R. Posten. "Berks-born Author John Updike Dies." Reading *Eagle* 28 Jan. 2009: A2.
PP	John Updike. *Picked-Up Pieces*. New York: Knopf, 1968.
RA	John Updike. "Introduction." *Rabbit Angstrom: A Tetralogy*. New York: Knopf Everyman, 1995.
"Remembering"	"Remembering Updike." Reading *Eagle* 15 Mar. 2009: E1.
SC(K)	John Updike. *Self-Consciousness*. New York: Knopf, 1989.
SC(F)	John Updike. *Self-Consciousness*. New York: Fawcett, 1990.
SD	John Updike. *The Same Door*. New York: Knopf, 1959.
"Seeing"	John Updike. "Seeing Norman Rockwell." *The Wilson Quarterly* 15 (Spring 1991): 136.
SMN	Sydney *Morning News* 23 July 2006.
Story	*The Shillington Story: 100 Years in the Making*. Shillington, Pennsylvania: Shillington Centennial Committee, 2008.64-65.
Taylor	C. Clarke Taylor, *John Updike: A Bibliography*. Kent, Ohio: Kent State U P 1968.
"TFP"	"The Family Panel." John Updike Conference. Alvernia University. 1 Oct. 2010.
Thomas	Heather Thomas. "For Linda Updike, Reclaiming the Farm Came before Writing." Reading *Eagle* 17 Jan. 1982: 25.
TKL/DSC	Mrs. Thelma Kutch Lewis and David Silcox collection. Alvernia University. Reading, Pennsylvania.
TM	John Updike. *Trust Me*. New York: Knopf, 1987.
"Toast"	David Updike, "A Toast to the Visible World: Remembering John Updike." This eulogy by David Updike was read at the New York Public Library's Tribute to Updike, March 19, 2009.
Trapani	Beth E. Trapani. "Pastor Revs up Fun." Reading *Eagle* 23 July 1994 B1, B4.)

"View"   "View from the Catacombs." *Time* 26 Apr. 1968:
                66-68, 73-75.

Weber   Bruce Weber. "As Good a Writer's Mother as One
                Could Ask For." *New York Times Book Review* 14 Jan.
                1990: 11.

Introduction

INCEPTION

This project originated shortly after John Updike's death in 2009 during discussions with Professor James Plath. It seemed best to start where Updike started, with the town and the people he loved. Since many of Updike's classmates still live in Shillington and nearby, personal visits were possible, and the same voices that spoke to Updike spoke to me. So, with David Silcox's help, I conducted two dozen interviews carried out over many months, fruitful interviews which taught a good deal about Updike's teachers, Reading, Shillington, and Plowville. I discovered that Updike had honed his creative talents in high school, that his early life was more complex than anyone had otherwise noted, and that he was very adroit at transforming material at hand into art. Updike repeatedly journeyed to Berks County to see his parents and his friends and to reawaken his awareness of all aspects of early life. He kept his first years green from his earliest stories to his deathbed poems. Every trip to Shillington replenished Updike's creative consciousness, as attested by the "Rabbit" saga, *The Centaur*, *Of the Farm*, and a host of stories and poems set in Berks County, not to mention his memoirs, particularly *Self-Consciousness*. Updike said Shillington was his incubator, and the dedication I have chosen shows that his Shillington High School classmates were essential to his inspiration. This book proposes that John Updike's school years in Pennsylvania were the crucible in which he forged his consciousness, transforming a simple suburban city, Shillington, into Olinger, the world of his creative imagination.

ORGANIZATION

The initial chapters of this book offer necessary background and thus begin with brief biographies of his family and sketches of Updike's Pennsylvania. Afterwards, the chapters focus directly on his classmates. "Personal" shows how Updike, despite being afflicted with psoriasis and stuttering, cultivated a great many friends and became their acknowledged leader; his closest friends were involved in the arts as well as sports. Their loyalty made his physical problems easier to bear. The next chapter, "Leisure," reveals how most of Updike's routine activities, like movie-going, contributed to his dual arts, cartooning and writing. "Athletics" demonstrates how Updike's interest in sports provided the groundwork for the four novels and novella focusing on the once first-rate basketball player, "Rabbit" Angstrom. Chapter 4, "Clowning," discloses how Updike's considerable repertoire of pranks expressed the budding writer's irrepressible zest for wit and surprise in his cartooning and poetry. "Girls and Women" reveals how the maturing Updike came to realize the importance of women in his life; they became the cornerstone of his fiction. Then, "*Chatterbox:* Cartooning and Drawing" shows how Updike's avid desire to draw led him to forms he applied in his work. "*Chatterbox:* Poetry and Prose" explores how Updike as reader and writer of light verse and thrillers polished his artistic abilities in his early writing. "Inspirations and Models" explains how he continuously used his classmates to create many enduring characters.

Because Updike's drawings, prose, and poetry for the Shillington High School newspaper, *Chatterbox*, have not been compiled, an appendix documents those appearances. Other appendices list Updike's use of Pennsylvania, provide an Updike chronology, and reproduce profiles of students and faculty administrators.

CLASSMATES

Since no Updike commentators have systematically mined the classmates' memories or the towns in which he matured, this book adds much neglected information. The letters from Updike to his classmates disclose touchingly specific recollections, revealing his concern for his friends and his continuing affection for Shillington. Many of his friends knew him since kindergarten, and their reunions and correspondence anchored him toShillington for nearly sixty years after graduation.[1] At reunions they admired his talents but also looked to him for fun. Though they might now unavoidably see Updike through the window of his literary celebrity, and memory tends to weed out unpleasant things, these no-nonsense Pennsylvania Germans are realists who see the warts as well as the spirit of John Updike. They also recognize the frailty of memory. As classmate Jack Guerin cautioned, "You have to remember, at my age what I remember might not be accurate." The reader, however, must assume the trustworthiness of their memories when verification is unavailable. The classmates are living history, and history is fragile. In order to place the classmates' comments within the context of Updike's own reflections on his life, I have weaved into their remarks loose paraphrases of Updike's own words drawn from his essays, interviews, and memoir *Self-Consciousness*. And following his practice in that work, I have supplied (mainly in notes) parallels between Updike's life with his published work.

   As class president, Updike never missed a reunion. The parties always featured Updike signing his books and reading from his work. After telling Pennsylvania Dutch jokes, dancing, and singing school songs, he would trade memories with his friends. The reunions enabled him to shuck his celebrity as the writer "John Updike" and just be "Chonny," the Pennsylvania pronunciation of "Johnny." As Barry Nelson quipped, "We put him in his place." In "Updike and I," Updike distinguishes between the writer and his "actual" self, and Shillington offered him respite from his persona (*MM* [757]–58).[2] He must have been grateful for this holiday, for he wrote, "Celebrity is the mask that eats into the face."

   With his classmates he could re-acquaint himself with the world he had physically left behind, but which always remained part of his creative imagination. With his friends Updike shared the everydayness of life in the Depression and world war, but in that mundane world he also glimpsed "God's fingerprints," something beautiful and fathomless for him.

UPDIKE'S CHARACTER

Though no one can control the circumstances of their life, Updike was adept at turning an unfavorable situation into something beneficial. For example, as an only child, he might have felt his parents and grandparents disagreeably vied for his affection, but although he always felt loved, he never felt crowded. Without siblings, Updike might have become antisocial or self-centered, but his classmates report that he was eager to join in all their activities, though he certainly enjoyed his solitary time, "to whittle a fantasy out of paper, all that relates to being an only child" (Dudar 25). If he felt "the only child's tentativeness in the human grapple," his classmates report that they never observed it (*SC* 109). Additionally, since his mother was a reclusive writer and his father a gregarious former athlete, Updike might have felt pulled between their contrasting temperaments, but he easily balanced a love for the arts with an appreciation for sports. Yet as an only child Updike felt "there was little in my life beyond my uncle's annual visits to broaden my definition of 'family'" (*AP*202).

   This only child arrived in 1932, after his parents had been married nearly eight years, when "the claws of the Depression were deep into the hide of the country"(Callaway). The Updikes had been living with Linda Hoyer Updike's parents since their marriage in 1925, and the addition of a child might have strained relations between the families, and in turn could have created a difficult atmosphere for the child. Yet Updike developed empathy for his elderly grandparents, reading the Bible and newspaper to his grandfather, and later employing his realistically affectionate observations of the elderly in his first novel, *The Poorhouse Fair*. Though life in a small town like Shillington on the outskirts of a big city, Reading, could intimidate a child, Updike valued the city for its big stores, movies, public library, and museum. Reading no doubt whetted his appetite for exploring New York, something he achieved only a few years after high school. Until he was a senior in high school, Updike felt no desire to leave Shillington, and, when he did so, he honored it by converting the ordinariness of the town—even its devolution—into enduring literature.

Another way in which Updike turned a problematic situation into a success is shown by his response in 1945 to his mother's relocation of the family eleven miles south of Shillington to the ancestral Plowville farm. He detested the farm but learned to use the new arrangement wisely. Without friends and games to occupy his time, he concentrated more than ever on reading, writing, and drawing. The enforced distance surely made Shillington all the more special in his imagination. The move was a proof of the "strange law" whereby, Updike wrote, "we achieve our desire by turning our back on it" (*ES* 96). Years later Updike would acknowledge the "dizzying depth of life" in that sandstone farmhouse (*MM* 775). A final example of Updike's way of turning a difficulty into an achievement concerns another aspect of the move to Plowville.

Since after 1945 Updike was forced to wait after school in order to be driven home to Plowville by his father, his familiarity with the town and its heroes deepened. One such hero emerged on the Shillington High School basketball court. Wesley Updike sold tickets and tallied the receipts after the game,[3] so his son probably had chances to meet the players. They remained etched in his memory, particularly those who became an inspiration for Harry "Rabbit" Angstrom. The Shillington High School motto, still adorning the wall of Governor Mifflin Middle School, aptly described Updike's ability to exploit his experiences: "Live to learn. Learn to live."

THE LOST CLASSMATES

Regrettably, three of Updike's closest classmates died before this project began: Peggy Lutz, Fred Muth, and Nancy Wolf. Peggy Lutz was a classmate from kindergarten through high school. They were members of the same clubs and accordingly saw much of each other. As one who had caught his eye as a cheerleader with pep and May Queen good looks, Peggy Lutz might have reflected on Updike's crush on her, but she died in early December, 2008. From childhood to his deathbed, Updike was concerned about Peggy Lutz. News of her death, sent to him by David Silcox, prompted the dying Updike to write the poem, "Peggy Lutz, Fred Muth 12/13/08" (*Endpoint* 26–27).

Fred Muth collaborated with Updike on plays and became his rival in a mock-literary feud in *Chatterbox*. Both became valedictorians. According to the classmates, Fred Muth was probably Updike's best reader, so it would have been valuable to know his feelings about Updike's literary work. Unfortunately, as Fred Muth's sons reported, Updike's letters to his friend have vanished. Peggy Lutz and Fred Muth have a teasing resemblance to Updike's own parents: Peggy Lutz shared Wesley Updike's athleticism and social engagement; Fred Muth mirrored Linda Updike's studiousness and discipline.

Nancy Wolf dated Updike steadily during his senior year. At the end of her life, while in assisted living, her home was destroyed by fire, and while she and her husband were hospitalized, their ruined home was looted of whatever remained of her Updike letters and inscribed books. Nancy Wolf passed away on Valentine's Day, 2009, just eighteen days after Updike died. Thus, the deaths of Peggy Lutz and of Nancy Wolf bracketed Updike's passing.

These three friends are lost to this study, and, of course, such gaps in research always leave researchers apprehensive. But even with the contributions of these three important classmates, the authors sense that, inevitably, Updike would elude us. Biographical and historical approaches to literature, like all methods, are limited in what they can reveal. Updike was certain that the facts of his life would be uselessly intrusive in interpreting his work. He insisted that his life was uninteresting and unimportant and that anyone exploring it revealed a "morbid" curiosity. As he stated rather cryptically, "My life is, in a sense, trash; my life is only that of which the residue is my writing" (*PP* 499). Still, I am concerned very much with Updike's "trash," and a very distinguished "trash" it is. Updike's classmates recovered Updike for me as the sensitive, charming, witty, ingenious, daring, energy-laden, fun-filled guy they knew personally. They performed an act that Updike might have called "personal archeology" and rescued his early life. For this I am grateful.

In the following chapters I will provide a factual description of Updike's life to 1950. My sources are two: Updike's classmates and Updike's writing. Since I have relied in many cases upon Updike's fiction where the work is plausibly autobiographically based, I ask the reader's indulgence for my sometimes speculative approach. My intentions are to recover Updike as child and youth, and to shed some light on his developing artistic consciousness, and thus enhance appreciation of his mature work. I hope that I have not violated Updike's axiom, "Biography should not appropriate poetry's license to create truth" (*DC* 12). If I have done so, the reader will dismiss my misappropriation, and other biographers will correct my miscalculations.

NOTES

1. Updike's fictional persona, David Kern, contrasts his classmates' ordinary lives to the joy of the "youthful memories" they bring him, while he recognizes the distance between them (*MFT* 187). Kindergarten may have been a difficult experience for Updike. In a story with autobiographical overtones, a mother enters in her *Baby's Book*: *"September 6, 1938. Off to kindergarten. Donny clung and clung. Heartbreaking"* (*LL* 144).

2. In a playful mood, he converses with "Oppositional Other" about his memoir and playfully yet revealingly shows the underlying tension he felt in writing about himself: "I am weary of *Self-Consciousness* . . . it is indiscreet and yet inaccurate, a greedy squandering of a life's minute-by-minute savings, a careless provisional raid upon the abyss of being." When he debates not publishing his memoir, "Self" counsels him to publish since, "It was written . . . only by Updike; it has nothing to do with *me*"[italics Updike's] (*HG* 472). This work thus shows the victory of nostalgia over restraint, and the recognition that the persona "Updike" is not the "real" Updike.

3. The Updike family was so poor that Wesley Updike borrowed from sports receipts, making Linda Updike fear he was embezzling; yet Updike felt the conversion of tickets to money made his father "magical" (*LL* 50–51), though the story was "frightening to divulge" (*MM* 777). Clearly this reveals Updike's need to believe in his father's respectability, while at the same time delighting in his improvisation.

ONE

Updike's Early Years: Background

MEMBERS OF THE UPDIKE/HOYER FAMILIES

Linda Grace Hoyer Updike (June 20, 1904–October 10, 1989)

Linda Updike felt she was very lucky to have been born, since her father was nearly killed by lightning before he married. Accordingly, she harbored a sense that her life had a special destiny. She was born in her parents' sandstone farmhouse in Plowville, Pennsylvania, the daughter of John Franklin Hoyer, a farmer and teacher at Maple Grove, and Katherine Ziemer Kramer Hoyer. Linda Updike could walk to the Joanna one-room schoolhouse for her elementary classes, and when she was eleven she boarded at Kutztown Normal School, thanks to her father's unusual insistence that she be given the same education that a son of his might have had. The Hoyers's prosperity allowed them to send their daughter to college, a rare thing for a rural Pennsylvania Dutch girl, even one as precocious as she. Linda Updike graduated in 1918 from Keystone Normal School (later Kutztown University, where she and her son would receive awards in 1985), and in 1923 she earned a bachelor of arts degree at Ursinus College in Collegeville, Pennsylvania. Her son would receive a doctor of letters degree from Ursinus in 1964. Her papers are in three libraries: the Myrin library at Ursinus University, Collegeville, Pennsylvania; the Reading Public Library, Reading, Pennsylvania; and included in her son's work in the Houghton Library, Harvard University, Boston, Massachusetts.

John Hoyer encouraged her to take an advanced degree at Cornell University, where she re-connected with Wesley Updike, whom she had met at Ursinus. Margaret Stamm, a Shillington High School teacher, said that Linda Updike in her twenties and thirties was "a model of grace and charm." Wesley Updike must have responded to those qualities, for they

1

Figure 1.1. *John Updike's Kindergarten class. Updike is in the third row, far left.*

married August 31, 1925. After nearly seven years of marriage, on March 18, 1932, they welcomed their only child into the world, and on his first birthday, a drizzling day, Linda and Wesley Updike and her parents planted a pink dogwood tree on the southeast side of their home (*CP* 170). For Updike, the tree came to symbolize "my shadow" (Ecenbarger A1). Surprisingly, the tree still stands in the yard after eighty years. Visitors to the home sometimes take away flowers from it as remembrances. If the family anecdote recorded in Linda Updike's autobiographical *Enchantment* can be taken as fact, after the tree was planted the child was offered, as an "aptitude test," three traditional choices: a dollar, a cake, or a book. He is said to have grabbed, rather ambitiously, all three (*Enchantment* 68–69). Her fiction reveals that after the test, Linda Updike felt she was on a dual mission: to advance her writing career and her son's. Linda Updike was as ambitious for "Chonny" as her father had been for her, and she for herself.

This dual mission proceeded as she cared for her son. She needed to stop him from eating dirt from parlor flower pots when he was about three, something his grandmother thought would promote his health (*ES* 439; *SC* 205n), and nurse him to health when, at age five, he was glancingly hit by a car, his nickel for the Grace Evangelical Lutheran Church collection still held tightly in his fingers (*SC* 205n; 9). Whenever he was sick in bed his mother would bring him cinnamon toast cut in strips. Because she had psoriasis, Linda Updike must have felt somewhat guilty when her son inherited the disease from her after his attack of measles in February, 1938 (*SC* 42, 183).[1]

While nurturing his growth, Linda Updike saw that her plan for her son was succeeding, since in 1937 Updike had a collage published in a children's magazine. Unpublished but more important was the red crayon drawing he produced depicting the "Hill of Life" when he was just six (*CP* 363). Surprising for its grasp of life's cycle, the drawing[2] shows his grandparents, already having scaled the hill and now descending to the bottom. His father is at the hill's peak, his mother halfway up, and he, at the bottom, has just begun his ascent (*CP* 70). At eight he began a short story ("View"73). These early indications of his talent ran smoothly while he was a child, but his mother's frustration with her writing must have clashed with her son's blissful delight with composition, to judge by the speed with which he completed his drawings and writing. For whatever reason, Linda Updike was subject to temper tantrums which frightened the child who witnessed "darts of anger . . . like a crown of spikes . . . in the middle of her forehead"(*SC* 86).[3] Despite such things, Updike insisted later that his mother's "aspiration descended to me," and she was "as good a writer's mother as one could ask for" (Weber 11). Updike was not very demanding.

Although Linda Updike probably didn't imagine that her behavior affected her son's development, she did feel that his association with boys would distract him from the life she had chosen for him. Joan Venne Youngerman, a close friend of Updike who often visited the Shillington and Plowville homes, recognized that when Linda Updike sensed, particularly from boys, that an impediment to her son's life was presented, she could become decisively stern. Linda Updike was troubled by her son's boyhood friends for three reasons: she dreaded her boy might become an athlete, a homosexual, or the battered loser of a fight.

The first fear was unnecessary, since Updike was not dedicated to sports. Still, she protected him from injury and the company of local athletes by restricting his sports activities. Myrtle Council remembered how Linda Updike wouldn't let him play ball, leaving Updike craning his neck down Shilling Street watching the other boys in the playground. Jerry Potts, who starred in basketball, recalled that he was never encouraged to enter the Updike home when he came to seek a playmate. Perhaps, as Victor Kroninger theorized, "I don't think she wanted John to get his hands too dirty."

Linda Updike's second concern, her son's sexual orientation, suggests over-protectiveness, as when she reprimanded him for wrestling with another boy, supposing that their grappling was suspicious (*SC* 84; *MM* 790).[4]

Her third fear, that he might become hurt by being overly aggressive, arose when he came home with blood streaming from his face from a fight. At once, Linda Updike quit her fourteen-dollar-a-week job as a part-time drapery saleswoman at Pomeroy's Department Store in Reading. "Now," she said, "I'm going to stay home–and become a writer" (*SC* 84; "Mother" 22).[5] Apparently Updike was never again involved in such a scrap.

Time has proven Linda Updike's fears unfounded, but her worry that her son might become trapped in Shillington by marrying impulsively was not unwarranted and led her twice to redirect his feelings for girls. First, when Updike was a child he kissed a girl, liked it, and kissed her daily until his mother solemnly told him to stop (*AP* 167). A second, more serious, problem arose when, in his senior year at Shillington High School, her son dated one girl almost exclusively. Linda Updike, fearing, probably, that this attachment might precipitate a hasty marriage and so cause him to swerve from his career goals, told the sweethearts to stop meeting (*SC* 39). She admitted that she intervened because the girl was from Shillington, "this place I found so contemptible" ("View" 73).[6]

Linda Updike had no problem with other female classmates of her son, so long as he expressed no emotional interest in them. Joan Venne, like Barbara Hartz, always felt "welcomed" in the Updike home. Joan Venne declared that after her performance in a seventh-grade class play, Linda Updike told her, "'Joan, you have the best stage presence in the whole school.' I wanted to be an actress then . . . I wanted to go stay in her house forever, the lighting was good—and all those books." Joan Venne added that she was no threat, since Updike did not consider her a girlfriend.[7] Barbara Hartz found Linda Updike to be "a lovely person" who remembered her after graduation, and "she swept me in cheerfully." She could also confide in these school friends. Carl Kendall remembered how she "vividly and movingly" told him about the lonely, "awkward childhoods" she and her husband had suffered. He found Linda Updike "honest and open and witty." Sometimes he swung on the pear tree outside the house. She must have enjoyed the children, since, as Barbara Hartz remembered, Linda Updike had a "circus" for children in front of her home, "and I hung from my legs from a big oak tree in the back yard. She gave me a porcelain box for hanging the longest at her circus."

Apart from shielding her son from the pitfalls that might have deflected him from the path of art, Linda Updike sought to cultivate his interest in the arts. So, she enrolled him in piano and dancing classes, and he was enthusiastic enough to write to his father's mother, Virginia Emily Blackwood Updike, that in the past ten months he had been tap dancing and singing (*SC* 183; he again took up dancing lessons at age twelve, *MM* 36). This may account for his later enviable prowess on the dance floor.

To fortify her son's interest in drawing, Linda Updike arranged painting lessons with Clint Shilling, a highly respected local artist whose ancestors had founded Shillington (*SC* 20). She encouraged his interest in drawing and cartooning, and sometimes joined him on the floor to fill rooster and rabbit designs with crayon colors. Linda Updike took him to the Reading Museum, and two things remained in his memory later: the mummies in the sub-floor and the bronze statue, Drinking Girl, by sculptor Edward McCartan, which still dominates the staircase. Updike used them in *The Centaur*. She also introduced him to the world of books, and her bookcase seemed to him "the door to a secret passage." Updike's teacher Kathryn Brobst Hartman in 1941 said he "always had a book in his hand, even when the class was doing something else." She attributed this to his mother's having taught him to read before he came to Shillington Elementary School. He noticed that Shillington respected books, since his first piano teacher, Miss Schiffner, had the latest John Steinbeck book on her shelf, perhaps *The Moon Is Down*, published in 1942.

While she prepared her son for a fuller acquaintance with the arts, Linda Updike sent her works to *Scribner's*, *Collier's*, *Story*, and *The New Yorker*, and they were rejected nearly always.[8] Meanwhile, she received little support from her father, who "mistrusted writers and thought it was disgraceful for me to try to write" (Thomas 25). But, encouraged by Professor Lane Cooper when she studied at Cornell, Linda Updike began writing seriously, and she later took a correspondence writing course from Thomas H. Uzzell of Texas. As a persistent, disciplined writer, she personified the writer's life and had no illusions about the reversals an artist must face. With her few publications, Linda Updike made enough money to buy herself a Dodge (Weber 11), and this might have demonstrated to her son that hard work eventually paid off, despite the inevitable rejections.[9] The clack of the typewriter was one of the earliest sounds Updike heard, and while she wrote, Updike tongued the letters on his blocks, later asserting that they "marked the dawn of my consciousness" (*SC* 104; Weber 11). Her dogged pursuit of a novel about Ponce de Leon might have imprinted her son with a curiosity about writing, along with its hazards. Updike consciously echoed the explorer's name in locating the Angstrom retirement home in Deleon, Florida (*Rabbit at Rest*).

Linda Updike discovered her subject after her son was born. The thinly-veiled autobiographical story-cycle *Enchantment* centers on an alter ego, Belle Minuit—*linda* and *belle* both mean "beautiful." The theme of the book is Belle Minuit's conviction that her son is destined for greatness. Linda Updike describes the birth of a son to her heroine and persona, Belle Minuit, as the arrival of a genius, and she feels her life "mystically" justified because of this. Considering the protectiveness she took in nurturing her only child, it is probable that Linda Updike shared this conviction when her son was born to her.[10] Her focus, with few exceptions, would always be on her son.

Yet at times Linda Updike's dedication to her craft may have been at the expense of her son's need for attention. As a child Updike felt he had a rival for his mother's affection, her typewriter. Home ill from school, Updike was rebuked when he interrupted his mother as she wrote, and this caused him the painful realization that he was not the only object of his mother's regard (*SC* 105). Conceivably, the source of this discontent rested in her inability to untie the knots in her writing or to find kindly publishers. Such frustration could lead her to over-respond to domestic trivialities(151). But even alterations in Updike's personal appearance, like his cutting off his forelock (because it interfered with his copying a comic strip from the daily paper when he lay on the floor) would make her irate (84). So, in Updike's phrase, Linda Updike harbored "a store of middle-class unhappiness" ("Pleasing"). Since the sources of such unhappiness were Updike's own parents, Updike, at an early age, encountered the theme of the anxiety of middleness that was to become the center of his work.

Linda Updike was also anxious outside her home. For example, she worked as a substitute teacher in Benny Palm's seventh-grade class, but after a few hours she left, never to return (*SC* 27). The seventh-graders were too young to understand that Linda Updike never doubted what was conducive to her development and what offered impediments. She knew she was unsuited to teaching.[11] She imagined the young principal, Charles J. Hemmig, could have eased her life and didn't. This apparent frustration at not being treated with the respect she thought she deserved arose again when, in the 1940s, after gaining some attention through publications, she was invited to join the local Woman's Club of Shillington. Linda Updike came to the initial meeting and later complained to Myrtle Council that, "she wasn't treated right." She never returned. Myrtle Council was bemused since, "No one could understand why she felt that way." Her self-protection was akin to her protection of her son. But she felt at home in the Reading writers' group, where for several years women met weekly to read and discuss their work. One member, successful novelist Roma Greth, found Linda Updike a "gracious, kind person" who always had time to talk as a friend and writer. Far more comfortable among practicing writers than socially adept women, Linda Updike was a proud woman who clearly avoided whatever might distract her from her mission of becoming a writer. With qualifications, the same could be said about her son.

Besides her frustration at not being treated as she wished, Linda Updike must have felt exasperated when she was forced to live in Shillington and not in the Plowville farm where she had been born and where she had spent her first seventeen years. This absence might have intensified her feeling that Shillington was "contemptuous." In their own ways, both mother and son were deeply attached to their childhood. But those who knew her in Shillington as a unsociable writer thought it odd that she decided to relocate the family. Jim and Evvie Trexler, for example, thought it peculiar since she was "too refined to be a farmer's wife." Yet the farm meant more to her than farming. Not only was it her birthplace, but she might have felt that she was restoring her father's pride, since John Hoyer had been forced to sell the farm in 1921 and move to Shillington. (In 1945, the Shillington home was sold for $8,000, exactly what John Hoyer had paid for it twenty-three years earlier.)[12] During the war she served as a spotter for enemy planes, but more importantly she worked in a parachute factory, saving enough money to make the farm's purchase a reality (*MM* 802).

It had been her dream to return to the farm, she said, and even writing was "always secondary" to being on the farm (Thomas 25). She must have felt that the farm would enable her and her son to pursue their arts in a more congenial place. She knew that Shillington had little use for art or artists, but she miscalculated the importance of Shillington to her son.[13] As a child, he could not understand why she disliked a town that he loved, but he could feel his mother's discontent with Shillington and grew fearful of her frustration and her ensuing anger (*SC* 84). To her the town meant "small minds, small concerns, small hopes" (37); to him it was his "idea," even his "being" (41). But to Linda Updike, the move to Plowville provided the added advantage of separating her son from the "small minds" during his impressionable high school years.

Everyone knew she had encouraged Updike's interests in cartooning from childhood drawings to *Chatterbox* cartoons. Margaret Stamm, a Shillington High School teacher, said that Linda Updike took such pride in her son's accomplishments that she "bound and kept everything" he wrote. Ironically, the isolation gave Updike the time to "incubate" as an artist, despite his social deprivation.

The sudden move to Plowville just as Updike was entering high school must have confused his friends, since many of them had seen him almost daily at the playground, in school, at the movies, or at church. For many, he was a fixture in their lives. Some of the students presumed (correctly) it was Linda Updike's "fault." Tony Van Liew guessed that "Linda laid down the law and that was it," but Joan Venne surmised that Wesley Updike was smart enough to accommodate his wife's wish and knew how "to give her the lead" to keep the peace. She had earlier overruled her husband's wish that they move to Florida, since his successful relatives considered giving him a job there. Updike felt his mother's inflexibility senseless, but had they gone to Florida he would have missed his crucial senior year at Shillington High School (*SC* 172).

Life began, she affirmed, when she moved back to the farm (Corbett E-20), but when Linda Updike took the lead, somewhat selfishly, it was costly to others. She liked the proverb, "Take what you want and pay the price for it" (*SC* 209), but her family paid for her choice as well. In the small, poorly equipped farmhouse, her parents were deprived of comfort and privacy, her husband missed proximity to the school where he taught, and her son lost continuous contact with his friends. Updike disliked farm chores, as well as the farm's "musty stillness" that contrasted unfavorably to Shillington's "bright life"(*SC* 25). Perhaps Linda's choice was the seed of one of Updike's basic ideas in his fiction and in his life, the "yes, but" character of life: "Yes . . . to our inner urgent whispers, but—the social fabric collapses murderously" (Plath 33).Fortunately for Linda Updike, she was able to heed her urgent whispers without rending the social fabric.

Barry Nelson surmised that Linda Updike wanted her son "to be smart and make something of himself. His dad wasn't as worried about it." When he was ready for college, Linda Updike needed to find a distant and appropriate school for his talents. She discovered that short story writers in Whit Burnett's anthology, *This Is My Best* (1942), were mostly from Harvard, so she asked Shillington High School's supervising principal, Jack Hemmig, to write a letter of recommendation for him when he applied for a scholarship to Harvard that would enable him to follow his dream of working as a cartoonist for Walt Disney; writing was less important to him at this point in his life. Though Princeton did not accept him, he was offered scholarships to Harvard and Cornell (Updike's parents' alma mater). Updike chose Harvard because there he could contribute to the *Lampoon* (Plath 12–13). In August 1950, he saw a photo of the *Lampoon* staff which looked "inviting" (*MM* 794).

Her son now on his way, Linda Updike could concentrate on her novel about Ponce de Leon and other projects.[14] She was so driven by her writing to the exclusion of all else that it is no wonder that she appeared odd to her son's classmates. An earlier graduate of Shillington High, Myrtle Council noticed that Linda Updike was "strait-laced," supporting Benny Palm's description of her as an "old-fashioned person" who "didn't smile a lot." Bobby Rhoads said bluntly that it was "rare that anyone said they liked her." That may have been because, as Bob Daubert reported, Linda Updike "was a little strange." Barry Nelson found her to be "very quiet, withdrawn," and Jackie Hirneisen identified her with one word: "recluse." Harlan Boyer observed her remoteness later when he saw her at Barry Nelson's celebration honoring Updike's Pulitzer Prize for *Rabbit Is Rich* (1981): "She sat several rows behind us and would have ignored us if my mom hadn't gone over to her." Her writing routine and her dedication to her son's success had absorbed her life and made her unapproachable.

After Updike became a published author, Linda Updike sought his advice about her own writing. She may have used too much of that advice, for, when writing her book, *The Predator*, she feared that she had lost possession of the book. She told Shillington High School teacher Thelma Kutch Lewis that because of her son's assistance, "It's not my book anymore." She must have had mixed emotions in knowing that she had encouraged her son as a writer only to discover he had superseded her. But she did give him important advice when he asked her opinion about a story. Updike was so convinced that he phoned in cuts to *The New Yorker* even though the proof had already been printed (*MM* 781). When asked her opinion about her son's career, she said bluntly, "I'd rather it had been me" ("Forty").

Although Updike's classmates knew Wesley Updike, since he taught mathematics and coached swimming and basketball at Shillington High, they had little knowledge of Linda Updike. Yet their observations of Linda and Wesley Updike made them aware of their dissimilar personalities. Myrtle Council felt "she was on the uppity side and he was down-to-earth," and Benny Palm imagined that since "they were polar opposites" their differences must have created instability in the marriage. Updike corroborated her guess in his memoir, acknowledging that he had to hide under the table during their frequent quarrels. In Benny Palm's opinion, he rejected the anti-social part of his mother and reflected his more outgoing father.[15]

Without question, though, Linda Updike deliberately influenced her son's emerging creative consciousness. Updike recalled his childhood happiness when she allowed him to "tap the keyboard," and he saw "the perfect letter-forms leap up." He felt that her typing rendered his home special, giving it an atmosphere of a "secret, questing life"(*SC* 105). That secret was the life of his mother. Clearly, Updike felt so close to her that he might have wanted to hide this from friends. He felt rebuffed when told by the Rhoadses how much he resembled his mother, because the likeness made him appear to be still a child, but perhaps also because he knew this was true (*SC* 242). He implies that in a way he was dependent for his personal history upon his mother, since without the photos she took of him, he thought his past might have disappeared (*SC* 12). Describing one such photo session, Linda Updike had him model as the "Author in Early Bud." Updike imagined the picture was made "out of sheer hopes for the future" ("Bookish" 101). He seemed to have little choice of a career, since he once flatly told Joan Venne that his mother had decided that he would become a writer. In Linda Updike's writing, she imagined her son a successful writer of nearly mythic proportions. Updike's rich uncle told him he would become important one day because he would "please" his mother, but he added, that to do everything to please his mother would be a mistake (*AP* 204–5). Once launched as an artist, he dedicated some of his books directly to her, at one time calling her his best reader and exemplary guide (Inscriptions to *Picked-up Pieces* and *Problems*. The Linda Hoyer Updike Collection, Reading Public Library, Reading, Pennsylvania).

Updike thus saw his mother in terms that defeat time, but static while he was dynamic. He came to discover that the more his mother aged, the more the image of her in his mind was that of "the young mother in the

Shillington backyard with the fireflies and flowering cherry trees" (*SC* 234–35). But in his boyhood his mother appeared to him to be immobile: whether in her garden or writing, she was retreating from the world (12). She was in fact countering his vibrant urge to explore Berks County. For him, as for his narrator in "A Sandstone Farmhouse," that was where the "action" was (*Afterlife* 135). For Updike, Shillington would always be where the people were, and this is why his very being was tied to the town. For him it was an urban Arcadia. To keep it imperishable in his imagination, he never thought to take up residence in Berks County once he graduated from Harvard.

Ironically, although taking her son away from Shillington to satisfy her own needs was harmful, the separation stimulated his yearning. Since he surmised that only through art can you go home again, since, "No one possesses anyone entirely, except in memory," in his Proustian recollections of Shillington Updike possessed it completely, giving it a realistic yet lyrical reality that recreated the town as Olinger, as indelible an American locale as Sherwood Anderson's Winesburg or William Faulkner's Yoknapatawpha County. Linda Updike's intuition had been right: she had given birth to a star. Capturing her son in her fiction, she fashioned him in fabulous proportions, and he did the same for the town of his boyhood.

Wesley Russell Updike (February 22, 1900–April 16, 1972)

Like others who were born in the early twentieth century, life was cruel to Wesley Updike. Malnutrition ruined his legs so badly he had to wear braces. When he delivered newspapers, hefting the bags on his right shoulder distorted his left shoulder, and the paper route so exhausted him that he had to quit high school. Luckily, a benefactor enabled him to enroll in St. Stephen's Episcopal Boarding School (later Bard College). There he earned his high school degree, and then attended Ursinus College on a football scholarship which he augmented by working in the kitchen (*SC* 173). Once again lucky, at Ursinus he met Linda Hoyer and fell in love (*SC* 201).[16] His stint in the army kept them apart, but after re-connecting at Cornell, they married on August 31, 1925.

Before marriage, Wesley Updike taught at high schools in Florida and Delaware and was also an acting principal, but afterwards he supplemented his income by working as a superintendent for a small oil and natural-gas field in New Waterford, Ohio. His checkered career included working as a desk clerk in Reading hotels and joining an AT&T crew that planted telephone poles around Reading.[17] He never earned more than one hundred dollars a month. His wife traveled with him apparently from 1927–32, but sometime in the 1930s, she moved in with her parents in Shillington (*SC* 177, 208); Wesley Updike had to leave his job to be with her for his son's birth.

Settled in Shillington, Wesley Updike gradually accumulated education credits at Reading's Albright College, and then came a stroke of luck, like the one that had sent him to St. Stephen's Episcopal Boarding School. Linda Updike's cousin, Elsie Kachel Becker, had married Orville Becker, owner of Becker's Garage in Shillington and a member of the school board. He arranged for Wesley Updike to teach at Shillington High School in 1934.[18] To augment his small teaching salary, in the summers he rejoined AT&T as a lineman (*Chatterbox* 31 July 1997, p. 2; *SC* 27, 210n).

Wesley Updike taught for many years quite inventively, and he participated in school and community events (TKL/DSC, Letter to David Silcox, 30 May 2008). In keeping with his patriotic spirit, Wesley Updike paraded as Uncle Sam after World War II in the autumn of 1945 and loved it (*SC* 126; *ES* 216). He also marched in the Memorial Day parade with Luther Weik and J. Allen Richards. A photo, dated by his son, "circa 1940," shows Wesley Updike smiling quite broadly (AWCC, 29 May N. d.).[19] Though he tried, he was not invited to any fraternal organization (*MM* 239). He was an active deacon in Grace Evangelical Lutheran Church in Shillington.[20] According to Reverend Kroninger, after he had preached a sermon about bringing down the "racial wall," Wesley Updike pointed a finger at him, stared into his eyes, and said, "'Victor, listen carefully. You preach like John writes.' That gave me courage. After that I thought, 'I'm going to preach and raise hell.'"[21] Wesley Updike had the ability to empower people, and his nearly four decades of teaching mathematics gave him ample opportunity to affect the lives of his students.

In Wesley Updike's career at Shillington High School he encountered, of course, many of Updike's friends and classmates either as their teacher of arithmetic, algebra, or geometry; as their homeroom teacher; as a speaker in auditorium appearances (Victor Kroninger said that "students cheered when he appeared at assemblies"); or as their swimming or basketball coach. He must have made an imposing figure — tall, with a hawk-like nose, broken many times in his football and baseball days, and bad good looks. Shirley Smith and Barry Nelson said he resembled Abe Lincoln's "sad, horse's face," to which Dick Manderbach added that Wesley Updike "was not as good looking as Abe Lincoln." As one of his students recounted, Wesley Updike was always "neatly dressed with white shirt, coat and tie, and was business-like." Mrs. Mary E. Shupp Huntzinger noted that he was "usually a serious teacher who could reach the back of the classroom in four long strides. He never seemed to have raised his voice. . . . I realized it was going to be a no-nonsense-tolerated classroom" (JVYC, Letter to John Updike from Mrs. Mary E. Shupp Huntzinger, 6 Oct. 2006). Wesley Updike had mathematics so completely in command that Shirley Smith said that he was "too intelligent to be teaching high school math, and should have been a professor in college." Benny Palm also wondered why he wasted his time teaching high school. At times he must have questioned his decision, but he began teaching at Shillington

High School just two years after Updike was born, so he was not going to take any risks.

Wesley Updike often employed unusual measures to keep the students focused and to show his distress with inattentiveness or lack of understanding. Some teachers might consider his devices histrionic, but others could see them as valuable pedagogical tools. He might, for example, use a teasing insult. Bill LeVan remembered how, when he had a test returned with "DD" on it, Wesley Updike said, "This fellow should be a minister. The grades are DD: Doctor of Divinity." He once said of Joan Venne, "This girl is on top of Fool's Hill."[22] Dick Manderbach related that "he told me I discovered 'Manderbach math,' since I had different ways of approaching a problem." Though such remarks delivered the students over to the class's embarrassing laughter, those teased no doubt took some pleasure in getting attention. Using another device, Wesley Updike wrote on the blackboard "Twenty-one forms of escapism," showing the students that their methods of avoiding work were well-known to him.

In the 1940s corporal punishment was permitted, even encouraged, and, like other teachers, Wesley Updike used it. Bobby Rhoads remembered that Wesley Updike used to "flip" a kid's ear if he misbehaved, though he never did this in anger. Harlan Boyer recalled that Wesley Updike once "threw an eraser and just missed a kid." When pushed, Wesley Updike could go further. As Harlan Boyer related, "Charlie McComsey was turned around talking to me. Bam! Wes hits him across the side of the head." Even more shocking, Wesley Updike once told Jerry Potts to hit Charlie McComsey, and, because he "was told to do so," he hit him so hard his blow knocked McComsey off his desk seat and into the aisle. For years at reunions Charlie McComsey and Jerry Potts laughed about the incident. Most Shillington High School teachers were often quite strict. Harlan Boyer noted that Mrs. Showalter would rap your knuckles with a ruler if you didn't do penmanship correctly.

Though Bobby Rhoads proclaimed Wesley Updike, a "great teacher," he was more likely a born entertainer first, and a teacher second. His histrionics might have been extreme devices, but they were often very funny. Shirley Smith cringed when the supervising principal, Charles J. Hemmig, entered the classroom while Wesley Updike was "jumping up and down on the desk." Nancy March LeVan felt that such things distracted from his teaching because, "He knew what he was talking about, but he couldn't convey it." While Ed Pienta thought Wesley Updike the model of the "absent-minded professor," most students confirmed that when he got a few bad answers from his students, he would say, "You guys are trying to kill me," and then would produce a toy gun and shoot himself. Or, according to Harlan Boyer, he would simply stretch across the exit, "lie down, and say, 'Go ahead, walk all over me, that's what you've been doing throughout this class.'"[23] The students must have been mortified with guilt when, according to Milton Hall, their teacher, from sheer disappointment during a trigonometry class, would plead in his usual soft-spoken voice, "Don't you get this?" then "bang his head against the slate backboard three times." Tony Van Liew said that "to get our attention" to his displeasure with his students, Wesley Updike locked himself in a closet.

For other effects, he would use the window as a prop for his theatrics. One tale, repeated by nearly everyone who ever had a class with him, was the "snowball story." When the students failed to put a period at the end of a mathematical formula, Wesley Updike would open the window, fashion a snowball, and then heave it at the blackboard, shouting, "Now do you get it?" The students enjoyed this stunt, so Wesley Updike repeated it for years. No doubt it also sharpened their sense of how badly he wanted them to learn. Peggy White recollected that he threw erasers out the window in her seventh-grade arithmetic class, and Nancy March Le Van remembered, "He would throw things out the window or yell something. Kinda dramatic." Barbara Hartz noted several times how he would open the window, stick his head out and "go WHOOOOO WOOOO." Myrtle Council witnessed such a maneuver, remembering, "When he got impatient with students, he hung his head out the window and pretended to be throwing up." Harlan Boyer and Joan Borner Conrad reported that their teacher would put half his body out the window and say, "I'm going to jump," and once, according to Tony Van Liew, he "opened the window and jumped out," but probably not from his homeroom, 204, since that room was on the second floor facing Lancaster Avenue. Jim Trexler understood his teacher's situation, and anyway, the "kids never minded" when Wesley Updike would shout out the window "these goddamn kids." Such things proved to Jim Trexler that Wesley Updike could have found a more congenial vocation than teaching. Such devices were used by Wesley Updike though he constantly worried about being rehired and knew work was hard to find during the Depression.

When he wasn't teasing, applying corporal punishment, or using outlandish devices, Wesley Updike would digress in class. He once decided to lecture about his wife's family, the Hoyers. This simply confused Mary E. Shupp Huntzinger. "I never learned who the Hoyers were since he never told us. It seemed to me that they were folks with whom he did not always agree, but whose opinions he always had great respect for" (JVYC, Copy of a letter to John Updike from Mrs. Mary E. Shupp Huntzinger 6 Oct. 2006). Clearly, he was an audacious teacher who willingly risked his career by trying to find creative ways to reach his students.

He took his position as a teacher *in loco parentis* seriously. He included personal lessons in his classes, not just math. He was, after all, a deacon after school hours. Myrtle Council felt that Wesley Updike used lecturing to enforce a point, as when, for example, he said, "If you're going to rob something don't rob a loaf of bread, rob a million bucks. If you're to do something, do it right." Yet she felt such moral tales were "way beyond the reasoning of high school kids of our time." They would miss his ironic tone. Wesley Updike never missed showing concern for his students' welfare. When Roma Greth arrived in high school, she felt she "was having a little problem relating to the other kids. . . . I didn't quite fit in there and Wesley Updike was a nice man who stopped me in the hall and talked to me." Shirley Smith noted, "He'd praise kids to other kids," always a good policy. He would also heal an ego when another instructor had bruised it. Overhearing head football coach William Firing tell Bobby Rhoads, "Go play with the girls," Wesley Updike, as assistant football coach, took Bobby Rhoads aside and helped to restore his confidence. Bobby Rhoads, when he became Reverend Rhoads, "retaliated," according to Reverend Victor Kroninger, by ministering at William Firing's funeral.

No doubt some students misinterpreted Wesley Updike's methods, but Shirley Smith recognized his underlying seriousness and said, "I never thought of Mr. Updike as a joke." She thought that many students were too young to appreciate the actions of an adult, and since she was always around older people, she "didn't see anything comical about him." Updike, who lived with elderly grandparents, was also sensitive to "the real struggle" and "the agony of the working teacher."[24]

Wesley Updike understood the sexual stress the students felt and how it interfered with learning. Dick Manderbach recalled how Wesley Updike would spend half the class talking about "boy's and girl's business," as an explanation for a student's lack of concentration. When a couple showed affection in class, Wesley Updike would say, "If you boys are smart enough to marry a homely girl like mine, you'll have no problems keeping her."[25] Reverend Victor Kroninger recalling this remark declared (amusingly) that it helped him find a bride. For such reasons, many students recall Wesley Updike as a wonderful teacher and friend. Shirley Smith felt that he was "a lovely, good, wonderful soul." Jackie Hirneisen stated simply, "Everyone loved Mr. Updike," and Ann Weik Cassar said cheerfully, "Wesley Updike was a wise and precious person." These remarks were echoed by his grandchildren, who visited the Plowville farm every summer and reveled in his warmth and his understanding of how to entertain them. David Updike recalled his grandfather as constantly providing fun when he and his siblings made yearly visits to Plowville. Once Wesley Updike reached into a pit the children had dug to extract clay. Modeling clay kept them happy all afternoon (Reading *Eagle* 15 Mar. 2009).

How did Wesley Updike's teaching affect his star student, his son? Updike had a good opportunity to observe his father for four years as his mathematics and homeroom teacher. Often Updike was asked by his father to step to the blackboard and explain a mathematics problem to the class. He was chosen because he was the class leader, not because he was the son of the instructor. Though Shirley Smith stated that Updike was "embarrassed" by Wesley Updike, Updike said he was proud to see his father perform antics that caused the auditorium to "roar with laughter" (Plath 214).[26] However, like most teenagers, Updike could be made to feel uncomfortable by his father. Emerson Gundy's eyewitness account of Updike's response to his father's driving reveals this. Since he was driven to school from the Plowville area by Wesley Updike, Emerson Gundy saw Updike disrespect his father. He heard Updike "take issue with a lot of things about his dad," particularly his absent-mindedness while failing to stop at traffic signals or turn off the windshield wipers.

Yet there seems little doubt, as Myrtle Council, Benny Palm, and Jackie Hirneisen attest, that Updike acquired his social success from his father. Wesley Updike was brought to life in the caption in *Hi-Life* that described him as a lover of gardening, Harry James, roast beef, George Raft, and Lucille Ball. This sketch certainly suggests a man of public and private interests (*Hi-Life* 1946).The ballpark near Plow Church was named "Wesley Updike Field." (To this date, nothing has been named for his son.) Wesley Updike's many interests and easy disposition must have helped his son endure Linda Updike's reclusiveness and irritability. He declared to a former teacher, Mrs. Margaret Stamm, "I was closer to my father."[27]

Until 1945 Wesley Updike and his son could walk to school, but once they moved to Plowville they commuted in the family's black 1936 Buick.[28] Such moments allowed him to provide his son with realistic advice in the form of axioms. His favorite was, "Dog eat dog." Another one, "Butter toward the edges; enough gets in the middle anyway," was accepted by Updike as his artistic guide (*SC* 209). He also corrected his son's illusory view of the Depression. When his son remarked that he never felt a money pinch as he grew up, his father protested, "Oh, no, Johnny, we were *poor*"(29). Updike later said that his "household" had "a strong undertow of Depression," though he could always find six cents for a Tastykake (*OJ* 68; *DC* 23–24).Wesley Updike would often remark that since the poorhouse was only a short distance from their home, they could walk there when impoverishment finally arrived (*AP* 156). Such exaggerations made strong impressions on Updike, who dreamed he saw his father standing naked in a barrel, pelted and reviled on the steps of the town hall (*SC* 127).[29] Updike thought that he "inherited" his father's fear of living beyond his means (180), and he seems to have made important decisions based on this apprehension. For example, he never had a literary agent, and he handled all his financial affairs with a bookkeeper's care.

Updike and his father led oddly parallel lives. Each was extricated from a difficult situation by a college scholarship, and both found wives in college. Each hated the Plowville farm and found ways to escape it: Wesley Updike "rubbing elbows" even with strangers, or always going to church meetings or Lions Club get-togethers (*AP* 202; *PP* 499); his son drawing cartoons, writing, and reading. As Wesley Updike was tormented by his "useless compassion" for his father's failure as a minister (*SC* 202), so his son planned to avenge his father by satirizing those who disrespected him.[30] Both father and son were called "Uppy." Since his father had several siblings and Updike had none, he thought he should give his children many brothers and sisters, so he fathered four children in five years. Father and son were born in one state but lived out their lives in another. Clearly neither father nor son feared appearing foolish, and Updike's pranks seem strangely similar to those of his father, though far more risky. But like his father, his apparent foolishness allowed him to be who he was (250). Both father and son had unhappy marriages, though Wesley Updike's did not lead to divorce. (Updike did not divorce until his father died.) Years after his father's death, Updike felt that his father was with him, as he walked through Shillington on a soft spring night (23). Although the watch cap his father wore irritated him when younger, Updike began wearing one later in life, despite his second wife's objections.[31]

Evidently Updike and his father were tied closely together. So it grieved him to see his father unappreciated. He tried to set things right in *The Centaur*. For example, since his father was disappointed not to have been named George (he had been born on George Washington's birthday), Updike named the character inspired by his father in *The Centaur* George Caldwell (198–99). Also, Wesley Updike was paid poorly, treated condescendingly by the school staff, insulted openly by the students, and mocked when his name was uttered.[32] Such abuse led his son in *The Centaur* to attack the principal and others who had belittled him.

Fictional representations of Updike's father reveal Wesley Updike's playful qualities, as well as his naiveté. While learning to understand his father from the perspective of 1963 when he wrote *The Centaur*, Updike attacked those (including himself) who, in 1947, misunderstood him. He reveals his father's devotion to his wife when Caldwell refuses a sexy proposition from another teacher, his perseverance when he teaches despite a raucous class, his kindness when he gives a stranger a ride, his patience when conferring with a dull student, his humanness when he fears cancer and death, and his heroism when Caldwell dies (metaphorically) for his family. Meanwhile, the principal is made to look lecherous and petty; the faculty to seem indifferent to students, immoral and irreligious; and his wife apathetic to his need for sympathy. In *The Centaur* Wesley Updike is not only a realistic, if undervalued, teacher, but also an ideal mentor; in creating mythical analogues for every character, Updike makes George Caldwell's analogue Chiron, the teacher of Prometheus. Peter Caldwell corresponds to Prometheus, Chiron's best student. Through the dual presentations of realism and myth, Updike redeems his touchingly pathetic father by making him altruistic and heroic. For example, frightened of death as the high school teacher George Caldwell, he overcomes death as Chiron when he dies for Prometheus. On the realistic level, George Caldwell achieves a kind of "everyman heroism" by working every day for his family. Updike has thus used his novel to re-valuate his father and re-imagine the short-sightedness of his younger self.[33] The older Peter Caldwell has written a recognition of the human failings both he and father experienced.

Katherine Ziemer Kramer Hoyer (1873–1955)

John Hoyer's wife, Katherine, was Updike's maternal grandmother.[34] The youngest of a dozen siblings, she married a man ten years older than she, and, after great pain, gave birth to Linda Updike in 1904 in the Plowville farmhouse. Katherine Hoyer watched over Updike while his mother worked, and once brought him down from a tree (*OJ* 64). Twenty years later, she held in her arms Updike's first child, three-month-old Elizabeth. She knitted sweaters and embroidered shirts for her grandson, and she projected the image of "always serving" (*OJ* 64). Her first language was Pennsylvania "Dutch"—a dialect of German: "Deutsch" = "Dutch." She was among the first women to drive a car in the county. She believed firmly in the afterlife, feared becoming a "little debil," and often said she saw her dead brothers. Perhaps this contributed to young Updike's fear of ghosts. Updike describes how as a child he demanded she guard the door while he "did toidy," and once, when she fell asleep and failed to protect him, he "pounded on her hunched bony back" (*HG* 26). The story is repeated virtually unaltered in "Kinderszenen" (*MFT* 224–25).

In a story by Linda Updike, Katherine Hoyer always lived in the present ("An Arabian Beauty" *Enchantment* 121). In a nostalgic story, "The Blessed Man of Boston, My Grandmother's Thimble, and Fanning Island," Updike recalled how with adolescent gusto he had swept up his little grandmother, "who had carried me." "Shaped like a sickle," as she seemed to him, "her life whipped through grasses of confusion." Though he thought of her as always serving, he quoted his mother as saying that she served her husband until he could do nothing without her (*OJ* 66). In 1953 she gave her silver thimble as a wedding gift to Updike and his bride, Mary Pennington, and Updike reported this in the story "The Blessed Man of Boston, My Grandmother's Thimble, and Fanning Island" (*ES*91–101).

Katherine Hoyer fought a long battle with Parkinson's disease, and Updike's observations helped him describe the affliction of Mary Angstrom in *Rabbit Redux*. During his childhood and adolescence, he witnessed Katherine Hoyer's strength and her enfeeblement. So he witnessed the physical unraveling of a life, a dominant theme in Updike's work.

John Franklin Hoyer (1863–1953)

Updike's maternal grandfather, John Hoyer, was born in Berks County, just after the battle of Gettysburg, to a long line of Lutheran farmers and to Pennsylvania Dutch Democrats who were involved in county politics. Since the 1780s, the Hoyers had occupied a seventy-acre area near Plowville southeast of Reading. John Hoyer, like his father, preached for several years and then devoted himself to farming. He retired before Updike was born (*HG* 439).

A summer storm nearly killed John Hoyer. On June 2, 1895, he and other men had gathered at Plow Tavern. Because an approaching storm made their horses restless, they stepped outside to quiet them. Then as they stood on the porch, a lightning bolt struck the building and two men were killed instantly.[35] John Hoyer was stunned, and when he recovered he took this as a sign that he should marry Katherine Kramer, with whom he had been engaged for years (*Reading Tri County Shoppers News* 3 Feb. 1987).In 1904 their only child, Linda, was born, and she gave birth in 1932 to a son named for her father.[36]

John Hoyer helped to pave the "snug grid" of Shillington streets (*MM* 807). More importantly, he participated in building the steeple of the Robeson Lutheran Evangelical Church about 1904 (*CP* 196). As Linda Updike recounted in 1970, "my family and nearly all of the neighbors had shared in the adventure. He had wheeled stones as high as the belfry and carved his name there. He spoke of the dangers that had to be faced—not only in the handling of the heavy masonry but in the minds of the men—working there."[37] He is listed as contributing eight dollars toward the building of the church, probably a little above the average gift ("Church" [4–5]).

John Hoyer prospered and could afford to send his daughter to college despite his feeling that he "distrusted women." With money made in the stock market he purchased, for $8,000, a large white house in Shillington with a tiled chicken coup in the back at 117 Philadelphia Avenue (JPC, 18 Dec. 2000). It was to be the town house, since the family lived at the Plowville farm most of the year. The Hoyers, their newly wedded daughter, and her husband, Wesley Updike, lived together in this home from the mid-1920s until 1945, and then in the farmhouse. The Hoyers died there in the 1970s.

After Black Friday, 1929, John Hoyer was forced to sell the farm and live exclusively in Shillington (Hartman 19),[38] where his impressionable grandson grew up. John Hoyer helped to repair roads and lay out the "Speedway," site of a former racetrack. (The Shillington High School sports teams were called "The Speedboys" in remembrance of past horse races.) John Hoyer read the Bible daily and enjoyed orating to family members with antique rhetoric. He spoke "elocutionary English" as well as Pennsylvania "Dutch" (*SC* 86). Updike compared his grandfather to

President Buchanan, since both were Masons who knew the Bible well, and because women played an important part in their lives.

Updike said *The Poorhouse Fair* was a memorial to John Hoyer, who inspired the character of the ninety-four-year-old history teacher John F. Hook (Plath 47). Updike included in his novel the only political story he recalls his grandfather telling. It concerned the Pennsylvania Quakers' exploitation of runaway slaves. Whether as admiration for his grandfather or his mother or both, John Updike often remembered his Hoyer side, signing his cartoons for the Shillington High School *Chatterbox* and the *Harvard Lampoon*, "John Hoyer Updike," or "JH." Oddly he signed "HH" for his Ipswich *Chronicle* music reviews (*Concerts* 3).

Hartley Titus Updike (1860–1923)

Updike's paternal grandfather was born in Pennington, New Jersey, but moved to Berks County.[39] Hartley Updike graduated from Pennington Seminary in 1879, orating on "Moral Courage." He attended Princeton University, 1879–83, and Princeton Theological Seminary for two years, and then Union Seminary in New York. Ordained in 1887, Hartley Updike preached in Presbyterian churches in Missouri, Indiana, Nebraska, and Arkansas. He married Virginia Emily Blackwood on July 21, 1891 (*SC* 179–80).[40] In 1896 a throat ailment in Livonia, Illinois, ended his ministry. Hartley Updike's failures left his son, Wesley Updike, feeling a "miserable helpless pity," which Updike observed, to his distress. Updike thought his compassion for "the put-upon, the hard-working and the battered" united him with his father and Hartley Updike (*SC* 202).

Mary Updike (1898–1985)

Updike's aunt married her first cousin, Don Updike, and thus retained her maiden name and close family ties. A secretary in New York at *The New Republic*, Mary Updike introduced her nephew to the Museum of Modern Art in 1945. She gave the Updikes a subscription to *The New Yorker* at Christmas, 1944, and so helped to direct Updike's passions for cartooning and writing (*SC* 169). He was so impressed by her and her home in Greenwich, an hour from New York City, that Updike thought that he might try to emulate her life.

UPDIKE'S CLASSMATES READ UPDIKE

The classmates were, in general, understandably delighted to see references to themselves in an Updike work distilled by his celebrated talent; such a notice would confer a kind of immortality on them and on Shillington. As a group, they read only what related to Berks County. By the time he wrote *Of the Farm* in 1965, an interviewer noted, "It is probably a mercy that his memory for exact detail is slightly rusty, since he has peopled many of his short stories and two of his novels, *Rabbit, Run* and *The Centaur*, with characters who are composites of the people he knew when he was in school. It has become a game among his former classmates to try to identify themselves in his stories" (Sulkis 10). His first eight novels brought this observation: "The whole corpus of Updike's fiction before *Couples* amounts to a memoir of his boyhood. His mother has called those writings 'valentines to the friends and family back home'" ("View" 53).

Updike's other novels, stories, and poems either did not interest the classmates or were found too difficult to warrant reading, although Ann Cassar Weik liked the imaginative *In the Beauty of the Lilies* and *Gertrude and Claudius* (Ann Weik. Message to Author, 23 Nov. 2009). Most students hadn't acquired the taste or the tools necessary for an understanding of contemporary writing. Literary fiction was probably not taught at Shillington Elementary School or Shillington High School, and they did not seek it out. One classmate recalled reading Dumas; his favorite was the novelist of westerns, Louis L'Amour. But one might recall that even though Updike himself had a well-read mother, his own reading consisted of light verse and humorous novels or thrillers until he began to consider going to college. Probably they were not prepared in high school to read Updike. (Ironically, neither was Updike.)

Nor were Updike and his classmates likely to derive much guidance for serious reading, and even the organization of the grades and classes might have worked against it. Like other schools of the 1950s, Shillington Elementary School sorted out the A and B students, while Shillington High divided its students between those preparing for higher education and those interested in skilled labor rather than professions. To widen this divide, the students separated themselves socially into what one classmate called "the jock strappers" and the rest. This may have created a sense among some students that reading was an impractical, thus unimportant, activity. Such an attitude might also have governed the faculty's selection of texts. The Shillington High School yearbook, *Hi-Life,* reveals that while some students hoped to attend Albright College or the University of Pennsylvania, most others intended to become secretaries or garage mechanics. Some had their education curtailed by serving in the Korean War (25 June 1950–27 July 1953. Updike's psoriasis earned him a deferment.) A few who pursued the professions went on to graduate school and became teachers.

Instead of systematic training in the explication of texts, memorization was the standard teaching method of Shillington High School English teachers. This must have had a lasting impact on some students, for Bobby Rhoads during an interview suddenly recited a *Macbeth* soliloquy. Even those who taught or became librarians did not read Updike, despite his literary prominence. Emerson Gundy said astutely, "He was so far ahead of everybody that half the people couldn't comprehend what he was saying." Joan Venne Youngerman guessed that only Fred Muth read Updike's work seriously.

Yet, Barry Nelson, who said he learned "much" from Updike in science, literature, cartoons etched into mimeograph sheets, and even how to win at pinball and how to smoke, read quite a bit. He "cherish[ed]" the early novels (*The Centaur, Of the Farm,* and *The Poorhouse Fair*),enjoyed all the "Rabbit" novels as well as short stories and essays like "Pigeon Feathers," "A Soft Spring Night in Shillington," and "Lunch Hour." Nelson made the interesting observation that when he wrote about himself through an alter ego he was serious; otherwise, he would deftly expose those around him and "distribute criticism and praise in doses designed to . . . sooth his subjects' feelings" (Barry Nelson, letter to the author, 18 May, 1996).

Jim and Evvie Trexler also read Updike's work, Jim Trexler declaring with awe, "His descriptive powers are absolutely beyond imagination," and Evvie Trexler praising Updike's scrutiny of everything in Hummel's garage in *The Centaur.* Jackie Hirneisen read Updike's *Endpoint,* noting, "I really love this book, especially the first poem ["Endpoint"]." Shirley Smith read through *Endpoint* twice. Bobby Rhoads found the "Rabbit" saga fun to read, since he "knew where Rabbit was going," as he walked the streets of Reading. Though Joan Venne said emphatically, "No one collected his books," the Trexlers did, and many of their books are autographed. They even corrected details to "A Soft Spring Night in Shillington," which Updike incorporated into later printings of the essay.

For many classmates, Updike's serious writing posed many difficulties. But his essays and light verse were accessible and available, though few seem to have read *The New Yorker,* where most of the verse could be found, or explored his volumes of poetry and essays as they were published. Though some classmates attended his readings when he appeared in the area, they were not spurred by them to read his work more extensively. If they were content with the Berks County writings, they also found difficulties there. Problems with Updike's detailed, lyrical style, as well as plots and characters offered obstacles, and the central themes eluded them. Barbara Hartz said jokingly, "In college they ask, 'What's the meaning of this book?' With Updike it's, 'What's the meaning of this sentence'? . .It boggles your mind."

Many considered Updike's subjects too alien. Benny Palm, a teacher for thirty years, complained that she tried to read *Rabbit, Run* but gave up: "The readability was there, but where he was coming from isn't where I was living." Tony Van Liew assented, saying, "I forced myself to read *Rabbit, Run* because I knew they were making a movie about it." Since Updike merely recorded what was already known by Updike's classmates, according to Marvin Waid, he could find nothing new in

Rabbit, Run and threw it away. "I wouldn't read him. I knew too much of what he was writing about. Johnny wrote about people he knew, and I knew the same people." The settings and characters were, to some, too familiar. Harlan Boyer found the novel "ponderous . . . breaking away, winding me down these alleys, to me it was plodding. I'd have to read some passages more than once Like reading a technical manual." Bob Daubert concurred: "I tried to read him, but he was truly beyond me." This is quite understandable, because ten years after leaving school Updike was writing under the influence of writers his teachers probably had never encountered: Marcel Proust, Henry Green, Joyce Cary, and James Joyce.

Other readers had similar problems. Charlie Wilson, assistant city editor of the Reading *Eagle* admitted, "I find a lot of his stories pretty tough going, and often I only read them because John wrote them." Miriam Gruber, the Reading *Eagle* Society editor said, "I read his things . . . and I must admit that the only thing I understood was a poem about a mosquito." Even his journalism teacher and supervisor of *Chatterbox*, Thelma Lewis, conceded that though she taught a class using Updike's writing, "I am among those who can't often appreciate his plots." But she loved his language, as most readers do.

Content posed other problems. While Ann Weik declared the Rabbit books "disturbing, although they are certainly great literature" (Ann Weik, Letter to Author, 23 Nov. 2009, e-mail), Nancy March Le Van found Updike's books offensive, stating calmly, "Many of the things he wrote I wouldn't read as a Christian. Other things are way above my head. Why would anyone want to write that anyway?" The subtext for many of these statements about Updike's difficulty might actually be an aversion to his graphic eroticism, a common stumbling block for readers of both sexes. Ann Cassar Weik, who read widely in Updike, remarked, "*Villages* was okay, but the explicit sex is tiresome. I didn't read *Couples* for this reason" (Ann Weik, Letter to Author, 23 Nov. 2009, e-mail). Nancy March traced her lack of "interest" to "the sexual parts." But she went on to lodge a different objection to *The Witches of Eastwick* and *The Widows of Eastwick*. She remarked, "there is witchcraft, and I don't think it's good to build it up." Could an Updike novel kill? This was the suggestion raised by Marvin Waid, who asserted that Wesley Updike had a heart attack after reading *The Poorhouse Fair*. "A lot of people don't know that, but that's what it did, because it was people that Johnny knew and stories that were known in the town. You gotta know the people in Shillington to know that." The protagonist of that novel was based on Updike's grandfather, John Hoyer, but it is difficult to see what, if anything, could have affected Wesley Updike very much.

Updike loved his classmates even if they came away puzzled or bored. He was not disturbed if they failed to understand his work. Ed Pienta recalled an exchange that made him "crack up." He told Updike at a reunion that he couldn't understand *The Centaur,* and Updike "very jovially" said, "'Eddie don't worry about it. You never will.'" Far from being offended, Ed recognized their different ranks, "me the clown and John the intellect, and a friendship was formed." Eager as the classmates were to welcome their friend when he returned to Shillington for reunions or to visit his mother in Plowville, and proud as they were to know a writer of international importance, they made realistic appraisals of their inability to follow him into the unfamiliar literary world. Certainly, Updike understood their difficulties with his work and didn't miss their readership.

Although the classmates and the author may have shared the locale of *Rabbit, Run,* after 1950 their lives diverged considerably. In the decade between graduation from high school and the publication of that novel, Updike had been to Harvard and England, had lived in New York while working for *The New Yorker,* and had relocated to Ipswich, Massachusetts. Though he was always happy to see his friends at reunions, he never condescended but took them as he found them. After all, they breathed the air he did as a teenager. They faced similar problems finding meaningful work, choosing mates, and raising a family. And they lived in Shillington, the center of his life. That was all he needed from them. As he lay dying, Updike wrote that his classmates were "all a writer needs, all there in Shillington" (*Endpoint* 26). They peopled the world that was his "being."

UPDIKE'S PENNSYLVANIA

(See Appendix B, "Updike's Published Writings Set in Pennsylvania," for a list of Updike's Pennsylvania writing.) At the end of his life Updike declared, through an alter ego, that he hadn't left Pennsylvania, because "that is where the self I value is stored" (*MFT* 207). He explored those values in fictional depictions of Reading as Alton or Brewer, Shillington as Olinger, and Plowville as Firetown. Though commentators have examined the novels and stories located in these towns, they have typically shown little concern for the early life of Updike that gave them birth. *The Dictionary of American Biography,* for example, begins a summary of Updike's life with his graduation from Harvard. But since what Updike called his "value self" was stored in Pennsylvania, specifically in Shillington and Plowville, it seems a description of the world, the Olinger world, in which he grew up would be helpful in understanding what fueled his creative fire.

Interestingly, although Shillington is about fifty miles from Philadelphia, the metropolis seemed "an ominous blob on the horizon" to Updike and hardly appears in his writing (*DC* 666). Though Updike lived on Philadelphia Avenue, he never imagined that his street actually led to "the city of brotherly love" with "the once-sacrosanct altitude of William Penn's hat." (The immense statue of Penn, placed atop City Hall, at the crossroads of Market and Broad Streets was then the heart of the city and everywhere visible.) Yet he thought his visit to Philadelphia in 1949 or 1950 "most crucial" because Wanamaker's Department Store, near City Hall, hosted a high school art competition annually, and he won a blue ribbon. This award signified important approval (667–68) because he hoped to become a Disney cartoonist, and for that he needed a larger endorsement of his talent than Berks County could provide.

Philadelphia was never really in his mind while he grew up because Reading (named for William Penn's birthplace in England) satisfied most of his needs. Updike was born in West Reading Hospital in 1932 when Reading was Pennsylvania's fifth-largest city, boasting a population of 120,000, and prospering under a socialist administration. The red-brick city was for Updike "the master of cities," with its odors of chocolate and violet toilet water, and its "vast velveted movie theaters" (*AP* 162). It was a city that offered him "Big Little Books," and he scoured the five-and-dime stores for them on Saturdays. It was a city that made things, like his father's Trenton, New Jersey (Plath 183). For example, Luden's menthol cough drops, invented by William H. Luden, who built his first plant at Eighth and Walnut streets, were sold by the 1930s in twenty-six countries. Likewise, the clothing manufacturer Vanity Fair created an outlet store for its products in the first outlet mall in the United States. It became Reading's major attraction.

One attraction that didn't succeed was Mount Penn's "The Pagoda," a Japanese-style building constructed in the 1900s as a hotel. Criticized by environmentalists, it faltered and became a tourist attraction, since it affords spectacular vistas of Reading, the "flowerpot city" (*RA* 22). The curving road that reaches Mount Penn bears the name of Charles Duryea, whose Duryea cars were tested on this drive to the Pagoda. Updike describes two memorable climbs to the Pagoda in *Rabbit, Run,* and he charts the two-mile walk from Reading to Shillington in the story, "In Football Season," through good sections and bad, past churches and across bridges (*OS* 188). One such church was Grace Evangelical Lutheran Church, Shillington, where Updike was confirmed when he was fourteen. As he summarized, Reading was "immense, remote, menacing, and glamorous" (*HG* 456). Perhaps the most important aspect of that glamor was the Reading newspapers, the *Times* and the *Eagle*, whose sports and comics pages he devoured when young, and to which he contributed to a column by Jerry Kobrin when working summer vacations from Harvard.[41]

After 1945 the relocation to Plowville heightened Updike's enthusiasm for the energy of the "ominous great city," Reading (*OJ* 871; *MM* 805). He felt that Reading offered him "access to people's real selves" (Sulkis 11). Visits to its library and museum expanded Updike's own "real" self. The Reading Public Library dates from 1763, and it became a public library in 1899 when Andrew Carnegie supported it; thereafter, it flourished (Heizmann).As a building in classical style, it seemed to Updike's twelve-year-old eyes to convey spiritual meaning. Its balconies "cosmically mysterious. . . . A kind of heaven" (*OJ* 837–38).[42] Updike brought home books by the armful by such authors as Nero Wolf and T. S. Eliot. Though he found Eliot's *The Waste Land* pleasantly obscure, he mostly enjoyed the thought that at fourteen he was checking out such a poem (*DC* 859). Bolstered by reading Eliot he tried Joyce's *Ulysses* but was so overwhelmed by its "whiff of death" that he quickly returned to reading unchallenging mysteries. For this he called himself cowardly (*DC* 858–59). Like other authors, he said that such reading fed his creative talent (Plath 219). Also, he found "something glamorous" in the Reading library and imagined his own books someday on its shelves ("Alice" B8). Fortifying this dream was his happy discovery that the librarian, Miss Ruth, was a classmate of Wallace Stevens, one of America's foremost poets. (Updike probably saw the Wallace Stevens plaque adorning the writer's Reading home at 323 North 5th Street, though it might not have meant much until he returned there after being at Harvard.) He researched his Harvard paper on *Heloise and Abelard* at the Reading Public Library (*OJ* 838).

To enhance his appreciation of the visual arts, his mother took him to the Reading Museum.[43] In *The Centaur* he recalls being frightened by the mummies and other funeral artifacts in the basement, but he was captivated by the statue of a nude woman called *Drinking Girl*, by Edward McCartan. She stood (and still stands) at the head of the staircase on the second floor, and Updike's narrator of *The Centaur*, Peter Caldwell, imagined that at night she tasted the water flowing so close to her lips (267–68), and thus inferred that art can improve the human condition. But Reading could not improve, and on his periodic returns, on college vacations, as a copyboy for the Reading *Eagle* during the summers of 1950–1952, and to visit his parents and attend class reunions, Updike witnessed the decline of Reading's railroad, textile mills, and heavy industries, as well as its altering demographics, as more Hispanics and African-Americans came to live in the city. Reading served his imagination, but in Shillington "a precious treasure" lay buried, his sense of "being." This gave him the passion to examine the connections between the particular stores and people to the infinite, as Vermeer "did pictorially for 17th Century Dutch provincial life" (Sulkis 11). Since Shillington was Updike's supreme setting for his work, it deserves extended attention.

Shillington was founded around 1684 by John Mifflin. His descendent, Thomas Mifflin, who, like Benjamin Franklin, was a member of the American Philosophical Society, had his and his wife's portraits painted by John Singleton Copley in 1773. (Shillington High School changed its

name after Updike graduated to Thomas E. Mifflin Middle School.) The
Borough of Shillington was formed August 22, 1860, when Samuel Shilling laid out a plan to develop lots for homes along Philadelphia Avenue,
where Updike would live until October 31, 1945. Three-Mile House, a
hotel and stagecoach stop, was built in 1761 by George Riehm. In 1886
Aaron Einsteing who had owned the hotel, built the "Three Mile House
Track," later Speedway Park, where horses and later cars raced. Benneville H. Hemmig operated a mill; his descendent, Charles Hemmig,
would become the supervisor of all Shillington schools. Afterwards, hat
factories, cigar factories, and hosiery mills were built, and a trolley service to Reading began running in 1891. The Borough of Shillington was
incorporated August 18, 1908, and became a suburb of Reading.

Shillington has small businesses, stores, and row houses with white-
washed facades. Updike's home at 117 Philadelphia Avenue was brick
painted white, with a chicken coup in the backyard, a walnut tree on the
east side, and, in the south front, a privet hedge. On March 18, 1933, a
pink dogwood tree was planted. The house was bounded by a playground a block to the north, small stores and homes to the west, and row
houses and the elementary school across Philadelphia Avenue to the
south. East on Philadelphia Avenue was the poorhouse, the setting for
Updike's first novel, *The Poorhouse Fair*. It was authorized in 1824 and
situated on the former property of Thomas Mifflin along the Old Lancaster Road. It contained 417 acres and was purchased for $16,690. On Octo-
ber 21, 1825, the first poor people were admitted, octogenarians William
and Dorothea Hydecam. Normally the institution housed about 350 prior
to 1885.Other important buildings on the property were the Insane Building (1837) and the Hospital (1871–1874).

Across the street from Updike's home lived Clint Shilling, who gave
him drawing lessons; Peggy Lutz, a lifelong friend; and Jerry Potts, a
sports pal. North of the house and across Brobst Street was the playground, and after school Updike would play roofball tirelessly. He was
so small he would get dust in his eyes from the scuffling feet of the bigger
boys (*AP* 170). On nearby New Holland Avenue Joseph Shverha had
purchased "The Roxy" movie theater in 1935 then changed its name to
"The Shillington Theater." It became Updike's favorite. After going
through several transformations to compete with television, it was sold
twice, first to Grace Fellowship Church 1987, then in April 2005, to Berks
Bible Church. This was fitting, since Updike points to similarities between church and movie house in *In the Beauty of the Lilies*. [44]

Shillington was a curse for Linda Updike but a blessing for her son.
Plowville reversed things for both. Shillington had been the center of his
world, but at thirteen he was exiled to a farm eleven miles from that
world. That distance kept him rooted, unless his father drove him to
Shillington. (Updike earned his driver's license in March 1948.) He disliked the farm labor his mother heaped on him in her effort to transfer her

love of nature to him.[45] Though Updike disliked picking strawberries on humid June days and felt embarrassed selling them to his parents' Shillington friends, the distance afforded by the farm enabled him to turn distress into art. For example, years later he could write about the Plowville barn as lyrically as he had about the Shillington streets (*ES* 29).Sequestered miles from Shillington, the thirteen-year-old read avidly. In his loneliness he produced many drawings, essays, stories, and poetry for his high school newspaper. Plowville thus became what he called his artistic "incubator."

If the Plowville farm has changed slightly (the barn roof has been replaced, and a modern addition has been added to the home) many of the places Updike has reminisced about in Shillington are gone or considerably altered. Shillington High School was demolished, and a shopping center has replaced the poorhouse. Dr. Rothermel's home has been converted into a restaurant. Becker's Garage has given way to a Turkey Hill Minit Mart at Brobst and Lancaster Avenue. The Dives Estate is gone, and the playground at the corner of South Brobst and Waverly Street has become part of Mustang Stadium (NelsonUT 3). Updike's cherished luncheonette at 34 E. Lancaster Avenue, Stephen's, is now owned by Admixtures Inc., a concrete products firm. Offices have been added to Updike's home, now owned by the Niemczyk Hoffman Group ad agency. The new owners were kind enough to allow John Updike Society members admittance to the home during the John Updike Conference in 2010. They have also cared for the healthy dogwood tree, which Updike said was "in a sense, me." The society bought the home in August 2012 and plans to restore it. Shillington has changed, but in Updike's mind it remained immune to time, and for visitors, if you look, he is still there.

NOTES

1. Updike quotes a letter from his mother dated May 2, 1939, in which she provides a detailed description of the ailment they shared (*OJ* 865). The alterego of Updike, Francis, describes how his mother ministered to him throughout his illnesses, imagining that she "blamed herself for his frail health" (*HG* 27).

2. In his poem "Midpoint" Updike admitted that at thirty-five he had reached that "downward side" of the "Hill of Life" himself (*CP* 71). Linda Updike claimed that her son was inspired to draw "The Hill of Life" when he heard his father remark on his thirty-fifth birthday, "After thirty-five, it's all downhill" (Hartman 19). Yet that remark would have been made in 1935, when Updike was nearly three; either his mother's memory faltered or Updike was indeed impressionable.

3. Such an experience may have prompted Updike to write a harrowing scene in which Allen Dow, an Updike alter ego, described how his cowering father had been chased under the dining table "while his mother, red-faced with fury, tried to get at him to slap him again. Allen never forgave her for that" (*Afterlife* 234). She also whipped Allen's legs with a switch made of pear tree suckers if he was a half hour late, her face "red with fury" (*MM* 799). Perhaps her coloration was related to her high blood pressure (*OJ* 867).

4. In "The Lens Factory" Updike describes David Kern's discomfort at a homosexual pass (*HG* [41]–45), and he records that he held such a job and quit after three days ("Early Employments and Inklings" *DC* 665–66).

5. For a different account of the fight, see "Kinderszenen" (*MFT* 216–17).

6. Updike's story "Flight" treats a very similar situation, but after giving up a girl he wanted to marry, David Kern warns his mother dramatically, "All right. You'll win this one, Mother; but it'll be the last one you win" (*ES* [52]–66).

7. Joan Venne felt honored when Linda Updike asked her to pray for her son when he contracted a severe cold in Russia in 1965.

8. Updike describes her perseverance in "My Mother at her Desk." (*Endpoint* 12–13).

9. *The New Yorker* published "Translation" in 1965. Six more *New Yorker* pieces formed the heart of her second story cycle or quasi-novel, *The Predator*, published posthumously in 1990.

10. Linda Updike makes little effort to differentiate Eric from her son, even quoting specific works by Updike as if they were Eric's, e.g., "The Blessed Man of Boston, My Grandmother's Thimble, and Fanning Island," and she includes many details related to her son. According to her autobiographical story, "Locked into a Star," Wesley Updike (as the character George) was opposed to having another child: "Another child? Hell *no*. I've seen *enough suffering*. Haven't *you*?" But the narrator continues, "The . . . . prohibition was my father's, based on a belief that children . . . may cause suffering in innumerable ways." This disagreement might have been the source of the heated quarrels Updike overheard when a child (*Enchantment* 74). In fact, Updike's birth might have been the source of such quarrels. Consider this remark in a story/ essay: the father in the story says he and his wife were knocked "for a loop, we had never figured on ourselves as parents" (*Licks of Love* 58).

11. In the guise of Belle Minuit in "Dropouts in September," Linda Updike remarked that she did not share her husband's "faith in our public school system with doubtful pupils" (*Enchantment* [175]). Considering his mother's experience and his father's negative attitude toward teaching, it is little wonder that Updike shied away from teaching.

12. In 1971 Updike said, no doubt facetiously, that his mother was prompted to repurchase the farm after reading the essays of E. B. White throughout World War II (*PP* 435). In *One Man's Meat* (1942) White recorded his experiences when moving from New York City to a saltwater farm in Brooklin, Maine. In an oddly parallel move, Updike relocated from New York City to Ipswich, Massachusetts in 1957.

13. Linda Updike, her husband, parents, and her grandparents are buried in Plow Cemetery, and though she chose a burial plot for her son, he was cremated in Beverly Farms, Massachusetts. His children, however, in a ceremony in Plow Cemetery, June 14, 2011, placed some of their father's ashes amid flowers next to a memorial stone created by Michael Updike.

Updike later sold the Plowville farm to Emerson Gundy, a second-cousin on his mother's side and a Shillington High School classmate. Updike retained eighty acres, leasing them to a Mennonite farmer.

14. Updike remarks that her novel, "slept in a ream box . . . and like a strange baby in the house, a difficult papery sibling, the manuscript was now and then roused out of its little rectangular crib and rewritten and freshly swaddled in hope" (*OJ* [833]–34).

15. "Rabbit" Angstrom remarks in *Rabbit, Run* that his mother had the most "force" of any person he knew. One can imagine Updike thinking the same thing of his mother, and the consequent strain he must have felt growing up with parents of such dissimilar temperaments.

16. At some point Wesley Updike had formed a relationship with a German woman, but his family—"good conventional Hun-haters"—opposed the match. The First World War was being fought and American chauvinism was pervasive. Although Linda Hoyer was also German, she must have been more acceptable.

17. Possibly Updike reflects upon his father's work when in his poem "Telephone Poles" he observes the cleat marks and electrical debris on the poles (*CP* 16–17; *SC* 58n).

18. In "Locked into a Star," an autobiographical story, Linda Updike has George, a character based on Wesley Updike, say "I'm not a teacher . . . I hate teaching" (*Enchantment* 73).

19. Updike appeared in a parade in Shillington, but unlike his father, he found it "agony" (*OJ* 131–17; Plath 227). Updike provides remarkable portraits of his father, from his ancestry to his development as a man and teacher and his devices for survival during the Depression and war in *Self-Consciousness*, "The Lucid Eye in Silver Town" (*AP* 188–99), "My Father on the Verge of Disgrace" (*LL* 44–59), and "My Father's Tears" (*MFT* 193–211).

20. Victor Kroninger's father, also Rev. Victor Kroninger, baptized Updike in this church.

21. In *Rabbit, Run* Reverend Kroninger served as the model for Reverend Fritz Kruppenbach who preached hell-fire sermons. When younger, Updike had sneered at his father's deacons meetings, but in Ipswich Updike came to emulate his father by serving on church committees and writing a sermon for the rector of St. John's Episcopal Church in Ipswich.

If Wesley Updike saw his son in Reverend Kroninger, Updike, according to his first wife, Mary, theorized that Updike saw his father in President Johnson. She inferred that Updike defended President Lyndon Johnson during the Vietnam War because both father and president were schoolteachers plagued by disorder (*SC*127).

22. Updike uses the same image in a story/essay: "You're on top of Fool's Hill right now, but you'll come down the other side, I promise you" (*Licks of Love* 54).

23. Seniors intending to embarrass Peter Caldwell describe how their science teacher, George Caldwell (modeled on Wesley Updike), would tell the same snowball story and also had asked the class to walk on him. Updike's classmates witnessed both events (*Centaur* 121–22).

24. Updike taught only one summer session of creative writing at Harvard in 1962, and through the success of *Couples* he avoided teaching until he rescued John Cheever in the fall of 1974 by substituting for him at Boston University. John Barth said that Updike "recoiled from Academia," and "quite disliked the experience" (De Bellis, *John Updike Remembered* to be published).

25. Wesley Updike's son thought his father had a weakness for sermonizing: "Entire classes . . . were wasted in monologues in which he tried to impart the lessons that life had taught him" (*Licks of Love* 53).

26. In a story (more likely, an essay), Updike's first-person narrator is clearly upset by his father's appearance in *A Midsummer Night's Dream*as: "a gawky, dirndl-clad lipsticked Thisbe, in a reddish-blond wig with pigtails." He watched his father "reach the chink in the Wall . . . played by the thickset football coach . . . . The screams of disbelieving hilarity around me made my ears burn. I shut my eyes. This . . . was worse than any of my dreams" (*Licks of Love* 54–55).

27. In the autobiographical story "The Beloved," the protagonist, Francis, hits his father in the head with a snowball, and years later is slapped—the only time—for throwing gravel at his father's head. Francis appeared to want to discover the limits of his father's patience and love (*HG* 27).

28. Barry Nelson described the car as having "all the intriguing features of automobiles manufactured just before the war. The body of the car was streamlined with the fenders accenting this sleekness. The hood extended far out in front of the chrome-plated hood ornament, grill, bumper, wheel covers, side panel openings and a beautiful stripe from the front of the vehicle to the trunk mounted just under the line of sight at the base of the windows added a special touch to the car. Shiny door and trunk handles helped finish off the stylish automobile. The final touches were the small wide windows that broke open and allowed air to stream into the front of the car" (Barry

Nelson, "Transportation and Daring," from "John Updike at Shillington High School."
N. d. Typescript, 1).

29. In a "Note" to "My Father on the Verge of Disgrace," Updike admitted that his father's robbing the ticket money to buy food still frightened him to relate (*MM* 777).

30. But in a 1993 review concerning Sinclair Lewis, Updike remembered that when he was quite young he thought writing satirically of "common life" was "wrong, morally and aesthetically" (*MM* 239). Since this didn't dissuade him from including satire in *The Centaur*, his need to defend his father by using satire had changed when he became a serious writer.

31. Although the teenager Peter Caldwell, an alter ego of Updike, in *The Centaur*, felt his father's cap represented "everything obsequious and absurd" about him, Updike himself discovered that when he emulated his father by wearing a watch cap, he found a truth his father knew: foolishness brings a degree of pleasure (*SC* 250).

32. Wesley Updike's name was subject to jeers of "Downdike" or Downditch." In movie theaters the name "Updike" prompted laughter, since it was often given to a stock comic type, the rich snob, an easy target during the Depression.

33. No doubt Updike had his own family in mind when he had Peter Caldwell perceive that his grandfather, his father, and himself represented, "Priest, teacher, artist: the classic degeneration"(*C* 269). True, Updike's grandfather was a failed minister, and Wesley Updike was a frustrated teacher, but Updike (as Peter Caldwell) in narrating *The Centaur* redeems the minister/grandfather and teacher/father through his ingenious use of myth, while he discovers the art by which he can explore his necessarily limited compassion as an adolescent. Updike's end-of-the-line degeneration as artist rescues his father by providing a modernist portrait of him, which only mature art can create.

34. Updike thought her full name was "beautiful" (*OJ* 64).

35. Linda Updike's narrator, Belle Minuit, refers to this incredible "escape" in her story, "A Time of Tribulation," noting that her father "had survived the lightning's thrust at the Plow Hotel" (*Enchantment* 28).

36. Since Wesley Updike planted telephone poles while on the road for AT&T from February 1927 until June 1932, he nearly missed the birth of his son (*SC* 220n). But, according to David Updike, after receiving a telegram on March 17, he went to West Reading hospital in time for the birth of his only child the afternoon of March 18 (E-mail message to the author from David Updike 21 Sept. 2011). Wesley Updike visited wife and child several times, then returned to work. On March 30, mother and child returned to Shillington.

37. Updike describes in "Plow Cemetery" his grandfather's "savoring/ the epic taste the past had in his mouth," as he recounted the story how he worked on the spire (*CP* 186).

38. Charles Hemmig, Superintendent of Shillington Schools, sold John Hoyer the only stock that didn't collapse after the stock market crash (*CP* 359–60). Apparently, however, that stock was not sufficient to keep the Hoyers on the farm.

39. Updike's first wife, Mary Pennington, had the same name as his grandfather's hometown, a coincidence which amused the Updikes.

40. Hartley Updike inspired Reverend Clarence Wilmot of *In the Beauty of the Lilies*. Like Reverend Wilmot, Hartley Updike's collapse ruined him, as if in "some tale by Hawthorne" (*SC* 182). The "bookish" quality of his grandfather would surface in Updike's dedication to deep and broad reading, a rich acquaintance with the domestic and international collegiate world, and the creation of dozens of novels and hundreds of stories, poems, articles, and reviews.

41. Jerry Kobrin's columns could not be found in a search of the Reading newspaper files.

42. This sense of the library as a celestial world is echoed in "Bech Enters Heaven" when Henry Bech's mother takes him to an even grander building, apparently the Academy of Arts and Science in New York (*Bech* 185–203). More prosaically, an alter ego of Updike's, Allen Dow, is taken to Reading where his mother buys him shoes,

and Allen saw "the bones of his feet move in an eerie green space at the bottom of a fluoroscope" (*Afterlife* 238).

43. The museum opened to the public in 1929. Updike may have had his interest in graphic arts stimulated by the museum's art collection, which eventually included George Bellows, Frederic Church, Edgar Degas, John Singer Sargent, and N. C. Wyeth. Updike later reviewed exhibits of the work of Church, Degas, and Sargent.

44. Throughout *Rabbit Angstrom* the downward path of Shillington is underlined through the declining quality of movie theaters and films.

45. In *Of the Farm* the narrator, Joey Robinson, a character similar to Updike, also dislikes farm life, though he mans the tractor and chops the tall grass to please his mother.

TWO
Personal

Whatever he knew his inner life to be, Updike was judged, understandably, by his appearance first. He had been cute enough to win a freckle contest at Shillington playground, but in school he seemed "twerpy" to his classmates (*SC* 150; Hoerr 48). Uniformly, they agreed that Updike was unappealing; primarily because of the way he dressed. Joan Venne Youngerman stated, "his clothes were god-awful, just unbelievable," and

Figure 2.1. *Updike in Mrs. Rothermel's Second Grade class, 1940, second row, second from the right.*

she thought he wore mustard-yellow shoes "just to devil" her. Joan Borner Conrad said, "He was sort of sloppy. His shirts would be buttoned
wrong. His shirt tail would hang out and his hair was such a scraggily
mess, we'd always get him combs and lay them on his desk." Sulkis
notes, "Class pictures show Updike wearing limp shirts with long
pointed collars and outrageously patterned neckties as broad as a man's
hand"(10). But other photos show that his neckties were part of his costume for the senior class comedy, and pictures in *Hi-Life* show Updike in
formal clothes. Apparently, his mother insisted on his "public" dress, but
allowed him to choose his personal outfit.

But even when he dressed well he annoyed one of the kids he accompanied to school, for Barbara Hartz admitted that she couldn't resist jos-
tling and dirtying him, because he "always wore wonderful sweaters. He
would walk the curb. We'd sorta push John and he would slip and get
wet and he'd go home and come back in another sweater, a beautiful
gray with cable stitch." The sweaters were probably made by his grandmother, Katherine Hoyer, who had hand-embroidered many of Updike's
outfits. It would appear that Updike couldn't win: if he was untidy he
aroused irritation, but if he dressed well he produced spite. The adolescent girls in Shillington (like most young girls) were unsure about their
own clothes sense and projected their uncertainties onto Updike. He was
self-conscious enough, for he lost his nerve when he tried to join a pre-
teen party, since he saw through the basement windows that the other
kids were in costume and he wasn't (JVYC, Letter,16 Apr. 2004).

Even if his clothes were passable, Updike presented other personal
problems for some of his classmates. He had a disturbing, boyish laugh,
and, apart from his disheveled hair, according to Harlan Boyer his face
was "full of acne," and he sported a hawk nose (JVYC, Letter to Linda
Updike, 20 May 1951). He labored under the mistaken assumption that
his classmates were all "terribly beautiful" and wondered why he wasn't
(Sulkis 10). Barry Nelson declared Updike was "not too handsome" (Barry Nelson, letter to the author, 18 May, 1996). So his decision to include
his acne in his self-portrait for *Chatterbox* seems to be a strategy for co-
opting criticism by caricaturing himself. Those who looked beneath the
surface, like Georgean Youndt, understood that Updike was clearly a
person who had "something" that "would set him aside" (Kreider 19).

As an adolescent, then, Updike was seen as an unappealing, uncon-
descending "brain" who, like his friends, struggled to find his identity,
but unlike them did not fear appearing strange. He seemed to take pleasure later when identifying himself as "the most awful twerpy little mis-
fit" (JVYC, Letter to Joan Youngerman, 19 Nov. 1983).

His unattractive appearance was one thing, but his stuttering and
stammering were another matter. Jack Guerin said Updike stuttered
"very severely." Harlan Boyer and Bobby Rhoads agreed that it was not
only serious, but that the stutter was "very upsetting" to Updike, even

though his friends were patient. Harlan Boyer thought it originated in Updike's tendency "to talk a mile a minute. Bright people seem to do that, but that was John and we accepted it." Harlan Boyer and Bobby Rhoads noticed that Updike could overcome his stammer when he spoke more slowly, and Milton Hall detected that Updike "talked slower to women, because of his shyness, so less stuttering." With a typical athlete's respect for overcoming adversity, the two ball players agreed that Updike "worked his way through it." Joan Venne felt that Updike dealt with it by making "more fun of himself than anyone else did," as he had with his Chatterbox portrait. Pointedly, he stuttered less when he felt "somewhat known and forgiven," mainly by Shillingtonians (*SC* 85).

Interestingly, when Updike overcame his stutter, his "manners" became "more sophisticated," according to Harlan Boyer and "it wasn't John!"[1] Marvin Waid noticed that Updike didn't stutter on stage during his dramatic performances, and Barbara Hartz found that Updike didn't stutter during television interviews or readings. Yet, at reunions, "you'd find him stuttering among us," confirming his own observation that such gatherings made him so happy he stuttered (*CP* 90). Dick Manderbach alone thought he was "putting it on . . . oh, sure, when he wanted to say something he could say it." The stammerless Updike seemed to have something "like royalty around him," Dick Manderbach declared. Everyone agreed with Jack Guerin that they were amazed that he overcame it.

So, with effort, his stuttering could be controlled, but not his psoriasis. That tormented him. It originated in February, 1938, after he contracted measles. Bobby Rhoads remembered that Updike had psoriasis on his scalp, so he'd let his hair come down to cover traces of it.[2] Still, Updike would not let psoriasis hold him back, and when he joined his buddies in swimming, hardly anyone detected the scales and blotches on his skin. Even when swimming with Jackie Hirneisen and Shirley Smith Berger, his ailment went unnoticed. Shirley said, "I never realized his skin was different from others." She felt that Updike "spent years agonizing over nothing," and Jackie Hirneisen understood, but only after reflection, why Updike wore long-sleeved shirts. Despite this approval, particularly from females, Updike admitted to feeling isolated by his condition, since his only therapy was sunbathing on the eastern-exposure porch of his Shillington home. Jack Guerin suggested that psoriasis "affected his personality" because it conflicted with his love of attention-getting. Unlike acne, which he outgrew in time, or stuttering, which he learned to control, Updike had to accept psoriasis, so he spent his life trying to contain it by soaking up sunshine on Caribbean isles and Massachusetts's North Bay. At last, he resorted to radiation treatments.[3]

Certainly Updike's friends could disregard his sloppy style of dressing, stuttering, and psoriasis because he was such fun to know and because he was so intelligent. Ann Weik Cassar found Updike "brilliant but strange," a judicious response. An English teacher, Mrs. Ernie Rothermel, told Jackie Hirneisen that "his genius was recognized in the first grade" by Miss Tate. Updike was not only the leader in the humanities courses, but distinguished himself in mathematics and science. His father often sent him to the blackboard to demonstrate the solution to a math problem for the slower students. As Jack Guerin said, "He always knew more than the teachers" (Sulkis 10).

Updike amassed straight As en route to becoming a valedictorian, and his pal Barry Nelson was quite impressed, since an A at Shillington High was "difficult to get." He also excelled in argumentation and debating. In her English class, Mrs. Florence Schrack devised a "moot court," and, as Emerson Gundy explained, "I represented the defense for a criminal, and Updike, as prosecutor, literally destroyed me." Norman Shrawder, Updike's debate coach, said, "John never got an argument from the opposition because he was always way over their heads" (Sulkis 10).Dolores Frederick Ohlinger found that Updike "never gave the appearance of an intellect, but we all knew he was, and I loved his smile and humor." Bobby Rhoads commented in awe, "What a mind. What a mind. Unbelievable! He was so brilliant in so many ways, scientific, mathematics, the arts. He was an all-around genius." His science portfolio from senior class shows a systematic, uncluttered mind (Linda Updike Collection, Reading Public Library). Barry Nelson said succinctly, "He was a genius."[4]

Of course grades are the most visible signs of outstanding intelligence, and Updike put little effort into earning them. As Dick Manderbach attested, "He was a genius because he'd get straight 'A's and then goof around with us after class. I never saw John study." So, unlike Fred Muth, Updike didn't need to apply himself rigorously to do superior work. When he took the Senior Aptitude Test as part of his college application, Benny Palm learned that "They called him wrong on one answer, and he debated with them, and he was right." Updike led a high-spirited life in which, among other things, he participated in time-consuming pranks and games. No doubt he cultivated the enviable image of a "brain" who got high grades without hard work, and could participate in many and varied school clubs and activities.

Updike's extra-curricular activities are impressive. He worked on *Chatterbox* 1946, 1947 as an artist, and from 1946 to 1950 published over three hundred items there. He served in 1946 as treasurer of Torch, the Shillington High School chapter of the National Junior Honor Society (*Hi-Life*, 1948). He was chosen for Amulet, the school's chapter of the National Senior Honor Society, because of his outstanding leadership, scholarship, and character. (Updike ranked in the 99.9 percentile rating of 428,446 students in the National Honor Society nationwide test.) Members published the handbook and presented scholarship awards. He also spoke on the topic "Should Communists Be Allowed to Teach in Public Schools?" at the Berks County Junior Town meeting of the Air November

23, 1949. He argued, in "Experience—the Best Teacher?" perhaps facetiously, that "it will not matter to Fate who was the best Teacher, but rather who were the best students" (Editorial. *Chatterbox*, 2 Dec. 1949: 2). Updike graduated as class president and co-valedictorian, giving the address "Morality and Ethics." He had straight As, along with Fred Muth and Ann Weik. No Shillington High School class had ever produced three straight-A students.

For fun after school, Updike took part in baseball, basketball, and football, and, during 1946–1947, he saw every basketball game. He played chess during a party, and he spent abundant time at Stephen's Luncheonette swapping jokes and playing pinball. Above all, Updike was a passionate movie-goer. At home he read the Philadelphia and Reading newspapers, *The Saturday Evening Post*, *Liberty*, *Colliers*, and *The New Yorker*. Barry Nelson noted that Updike liked *The New Yorker* so much that he drove to Dague's printers in Reading to have his copies bound. He maintained a personal reading program that included masters of twentieth-century literature. Updike listened to radio programs, followed the Philadelphia baseball teams, and read the Bible to his grandfather. After moving to Plowville in 1945, he helped with the farm chores, shot pigeons in the barn, and (reluctantly) sold vegetables and fruit. (It may be amusing to know that Benny Palm knew him as "a farmer boy.")

Unavoidably, though, the twenty-two-mile round-trip from Plowville to Shillington, about an hour back and forth, five days a week from November 1945 to June 1950 accounted for nearly one thousand hours of time, time he could have used reading, cartooning, or writing. Still, the fact that for four years he could contribute cartoons, prose, and poetry each week to *Chatterbox*; write skits and plays; and participate in clubs ranging from debate to leadership suggests a person of exceptional intellect, organizational ability, and discipline. His work ethic enabled him to not only do such things, but do them with exceptional attention and care. His literary career, of course, shows the same capabilities.

Updike could talk as well as he could write, though some might be challenged by his larger vocabulary. He was skilled at debating, acted in the lead for the junior and senior classes, and even served as the interlocutor in the boys' glee club minstrel show. Joan Venne thought Updike's refined language was natural for him, and if it seemed to some that he "talked down" to people, she asked, "Where else would he talk?" Joan Venne, of course, did not mean that he was pompous, but that there were only a few students, like Fred Muth, who could understand his wide vocabulary. Milton Hall agreed, and he insisted that, "Because he was brilliant many thought he was 'uppity' but he never showed that to any of us." Bob Daubert was struck by the similarity of the vocabulary of Updike and William F. Buckley, Jr. Jack Guerin noted that it was "Easy to see he had great intellect. . . . The precision with which he used words!" His speech mystified Doris Keffer Wenrich, who said that Updike "seemed to talk in riddles." Bill Forry found this riddling remark especially characteristic of his linguistic inventiveness, "Seeing your own car come toward you is like seeing your own image in the mirror turn and walk away." Because of Updike's reputation for wit, a confusing remark might be taken as clever by those who do not want to appear dull.

So despite the fact that he was gangly, carelessly dressed, unattractive, stuttering, psoriatic, and brilliant, nearly everyone in his high school class wanted him for a friend. But one boy, five years older than Updike and not a classmate, Eddie Pritchard, bedeviled him when he was a child. Eddie Pritchard called him "Ostrich," which haunted Updike for years because it spoke of the "*power* of stupidity" (*AP* 175–76; *SC* 79). As Milton Hall (who probably didn't know Eddie Pritchard) put it succinctly, "Everyone liked him." Certainly, part of the reason Updike was so well-liked lay in his ability to enjoy all manner of persons, from unassuming people like Fred Muth, Ann Weik, and Nancy Wolf to the animated Jack Guerin, Milton Hall, Joan Venne, and Peggy Lutz. Perhaps Updike had been prepared for this catholicity of friendship by living with persons as different in temperament as his studious grandfather, his hard-working grandmother, his cultured mother, and his gregarious father. For whatever reason, none of the classmates could recall a single incidence in school in which he was bullied. Bennie Palm remarked that no one was ever "out to get" Updike, and Jackie Hirneisen added, there was "never any animosity" toward him. Though he was described as the smartest of his classmates, none of them ever seemed jealous. Even when he was cryptic, cynical, or just a "goof," as Dick Manderbach put it, "everybody liked him." His close friend Jack Guerin asserted, "John had no bad friends."

Updike might have used irritating antics, but he remained a popular, even fascinating classmate. He was so well-liked that he bridged the gap between the athletes and the rest of the students. He counted football players and *Chatterbox* writers among his closest friends, and they endured, probably because, as Jackie Hirneisen declared, "Being around him was such a pleasure." No matter how distracting his classroom pranks, he never was really disruptive, and even when he corrected his instructor, he was not reprimanded. Jackie Hirneisen remarked, "Teachers adored him," possibly because he was a model of dependability, hard work, and imagination. So it is no surprise that his popularity made him the easy choice for class president. Updike took the office seriously, never failing to preside over every class reunion, which helped to keep him in close touch with all of his friends, several of whom carried on a correspondence with him for many years.

Eventually Updike would publish over fifty books in every genre, revise some already published; actively participate in the construction of his books by designing the jackets and writing his own blurbs; travel to England, Europe, Australia, Africa, the Middle East, and Asia; lecture in countless venues across the United States; give innumerable interviews; cultivate (and charm) numerous people; accept awards and honors; participate in civic activities; hold offices in professional associations; golf everywhere and in all weathers; answer a massive correspondence; aid aspiring authors; and help to raise four children. These activities reflected the same systematic, inquiring, and uncluttered mind witnessed by his Shillington classmates. His life balanced an unrelenting pursuit of his craft (a day without writing was "doubly damned," he said) and an authentic social presence. Above all, his extraordinary sensitivity and imagination enabled him to see the world through the eyes of others, and so create a wealth of unforgettable portraits of real and fictional persons. When he felt he had ended his youth, Updike's realization arose from his identification with a dead uncle. He attended the funeral in 1948 and entered adulthood "through respect, pity, and wonder" (*AP* 200).

NOTES

1. A similar transformation occurs in the story "From the Journal of a Leper," in which the narrator's artistic talent deteriorates as he conquers his affliction (*Problems* 181–96).

2. In 1972 Updike broke a leg playing touch football, and since he found it difficult to shave while on crutches, he grew a beard (Message to the Author from Mary Weatherall, 7 Aug. 2011. E-mail). As a bonus, his beard covered his psoriasis.

3. Updike described in *The Centaur* how Peter Caldwell attempted, unsuccessfully, to win a girlfriend's love by exposing his psoriatic chest to her. "From the Journal of a Leper" explores the curative power of radiation therapy in treating "leprosy," code for psoriasis. Unfortunately, in becoming "clear" he loses his mistress and his creative power (*Problems* 181–96). The story bears comparison to "The Birthmark," by Nathaniel Hawthorne, one of Updike's greatest influences. Updike's mother, family physician, Doctor Ernest Rothermel, and *Chatterbox* faculty advisor, Thelma Kutch Lewis, all had the autoimmune disease. Updike concluded that psoriasis selected its victims at random (TKL/DSC, 2 Nov. 1999). However, his alter ego, Allen Dow, traces the ailment to nervousness rooted in fear of his mother's rage. That nervousness prompted "skin rashes, stammering, asthma, insomnia," which were only controlled by "decades of living hundreds of miles beyond her reach" (*The Afterlife* 234–41). Much later, Updike wondered if the disease forced him to become a writer because that way he could be where "nobody has to look at me" (Fichtner1). If so, then psoriasis became his ironic muse.

4. Two other accomplishments from his English classes merit note. Updike's recitation of Antony's oration after Caesar's death was praised so highly that he became embarrassed. Also, his report on a book of Mark Twain stories was so perfect that the superintendent of schools asked him to read it before the class, as an example of how a report should be done (NelsonJUSHS, 10).

THREE
Leisure

As a child Updike sent a formal invitation to his grandmother, inviting her to attend a "penny carnival." Attached to the note was the request that she bring five pennies (DUC to Kathryn Hoyer). His letter, no doubt reviewed by his mother, shows Updike's early appetite for invention, and the invitation shows that he could assume his grandmother would appreciate the offer from her beloved grandchild. The penny carnival was merely one of a great variety of distractions that amused Updike. Carl Kendall: remembered how, when Updike was "about five or seven" they carved horse chestnuts. When he was in sixth grade, he preferred to play alone, according to his teacher, Mrs. Kathryn Brobst Hartman. Updike played marbles and the usual board games with Fred Muth. "Monopoly" kept them happy all day long. The game contains squares indicating (among other things) four railroads, one of which, the Reading Railroad, was among the largest corporations in America in the early nineteenth century. (By 1971 it was bankrupt.)

Naturally, Updike played the usual kids' games, like "Mother, May I?" and "Hopscotch."[1] As Barbara Hartz recalled, "We played Kick the Can, Hide & Seek." Joan Venne also recalled that at her parent's house they played "Spin the Bottle" and "she got John but she wouldn't kiss him, and he said 'That's ok with me.'" In fact, Joan Venne reports that Updike used to sit on the curb and throw balls of green moss at her and others, as much to get their attention as to express resentment. Updike recorded this simultaneous attraction and repulsion toward girls from a child's point of view in "The Alligators" (*SD* 21–19; see Chapter 8).According to Joan Venne, near a big clump of bushes the kids called Wake Island (named, perhaps, after the World War II war zone of late 1941), the gang played "Run, Chippie, Run," whose name echoes *Rabbit, Run*.[2]

By the time Updike was old enough to go to school, he became the leader of what Georgean Youndt Bixler called, "a big gang!!" Some of these gang members had known Updike since kindergarten. Dick Manderbach says the members included Bill Forry, Fred Muth, Mahlon Frankhauser, Bobby and Richard Daubert, Nancy March, Jackie Hirneisen, Mary Ann Stanley, Joan Venne, Peggy Lutz, and Barbara Hartz. Shirley Smith added Neil White, Bill Moser, Jack Guerin, and Marvin Waid. Others joined from time to time, like Mary Orf, Ann Weik, Mary Ann Schmehl, Tony Van Liew, Jimmy Trexler, and Georgean Youndt. Such gangs were not unusual. As Joan Venne recalls, "The Second Street Gang didn't include Updike since he lived on Philadelphia Avenue, but instead numbered Barbara Wagner, Harlan Conrad, and Joseph Jasinski." Of course "gang" meant something much less menacing at that time than it does now, more closely related to the band of endearing children in the *Our Gang* films, whose alternate title was *The Little Rascals* (1922–44). Only occasionally did the kids get rowdy. At Halloween, for example, according to Dick Manderbach, Updike would join in piling leaves at an intersection then setting them on fire.

Like many children who try to visualize their futures, Updike amused himself by wondering what it would be like to become a private detective or a test pilot (*CP* 83; "'Pleasing'"). Though Updike never again mentioned becoming a test pilot, his other aspiration developed into a passion for detective novels, prompting him to produce a four-part detective story for *Chatterbox*, though his sly humor reveals that he couldn't take the genre that seriously. He also started a murder mystery in 1946 that was published in 1993 (Mandelbaum 420–71).[3] Updike has said that at this point in his life he "wasn't the greatest young reader who ever was. . . . But I did manage to read enough so that I wanted to do it myself" (Zanganeh).

Gangs were social fun that teased the children into flights of adventure, but the private Updike sought his adventure in movies, and he loved them all his life.[4] The early impression movies made on Updike can hardly be overstated. For example, with Dick Miller, Updike's closest friend at one time, he would make little theaters using paper, cardboard, and wood (JVYC, 10June1983), and when he was eleven he made his own movies out of strips of colored drawings wound on toilet-paper spools (*AP* 177). When he was only three, Updike went to the movies, sitting between his parents. At six he was allowed to go alone (*MM* [641]). Updike's thirty-five-cent allowance easily enabled him to see a movie three times a week, until a penny was added for the war effort.[5] To avoid having to ask for money for a show, Updike, when twelve, distributed folders listing coming attractions of Shillington movies. He was paid with a free pass. By delivering the circulars in another town, he was able to spend his pay (seven cents) on movie candy (JVYC,27 June 1998). The elegant films of the 1930s showed that others were not reduced to "respectable scrounging"(*SC* 29). During the war he could go to the movies by contributing either three pounds of scrap iron or a rubber tire. As he grew, movies became more than a diversion. Seeking his own style as an adolescent, screen heroes like George Sanders and Cary Grant taught him how to assume a debonair attitude; others, unfortunately, showed him how to smoke.[6] In 1998 Updike asserted that movies helped to form not only his values but those of his generation by their "expressiveness and penetration" which provided "aspirations, ethical values, and notions of social etiquette" (*HG* 477). His shift in feeling about films much later in life shows that Updike was conscious of Hollywood's manipulative power.

In Shillington he watched movies at the Shillington Theater, nick-named "The Stinky." It was the only movie house, and as the children left, the manager, Joe Shverha, would give each child a "pecan roll with nougat center," perhaps to reward them for not eating in the theater. Myrtle Council remembers the manager saying at the door, "You leave the chewing gum out here. You don't dare bring in food and you be quiet or out you go." Benny Palm thought Mr. Shverha "a nice guy, just German and strict." Rowdier kids wouldn't pay attention to the films, and if they threw pieces of paper in front of the projector light, Mr. Shverha would shout, "You, out!" Monday and Tuesday nights he gave out free dishes, even in wartime. Mr. Shverha generously provided a free hour of cartoons for the children at Christmas, and then policeman Sam Reich gave them a box of chocolates as they left (*MM* 797–98).

Occasionally, Updike would sneak into the movie without paying. When that happened, Wilma Mae Yoder, the Evangelical teacher who gave him piano lessons, would spy him entering by way of the alley door and tell his parents. For a larger selection of films, a five-cent trolley car ride would take Updike to Reading. Benny Palm burbled, "Oh, my God, he was a nut on movies."[7] After Updike published *Self-Consciousness*, he was delighted to receive an old pass to the Shillington Theater from a friend (AWCC, Letter from Updike, 7 January 1990).

Other diversions provided occasions for lessons in growing up. A carnival regularly appeared in a hollow on Second Street, and Updike would go there with Barbara Yurick or Skip McCoy. At one point he played the spinning wheel and lost fifty cents, probably given to him by his indulgent grandfather. Afterwards the attendant, acting as a surro-gate parent, told him, "Don't you ever come here again." Since Wesley Updike didn't even want his son to cross Philadelphia Avenue, not to mention walk two streets further to the carnival, he got "royal H," Up-dike recalled.[8]

He would certainly have gotten punished had his parents known de-tails of his war games. Updike grew up during wartime, so it isn't sur-prising that some of his activities were modeled on war situations. Up-dike's pal Tony Van Liew indicated that he, Marvin Waid, and Updike often played near the cemetery off Fourth Street in a gravel hole that they called "The Black Forest." Tony Van Liew recounted that the "Black Forest" was "two hundred feet high with woods around it. We were amazed that none of us were bitten by a snake. I'm surprised nobody ever really got hurt." There they would build imitation machine-gun nests and dig fox-holes and tunnels. From these positions they would pretend to shoot at one another. The game turned serious when Tony Van Liew nearly slid down the hill. The drop could have killed him, but, he explained, "Johnny came along and was near the top, and he grabbed me and pulled me up and said, 'You turned several shades of green.' Another time we built a cave and it gave way with just John's feet sticking out. I think he was in six or seven feet and couldn't get out himself. I don't think he ever went up there again."[9]

Less violent were the card games Updike played throughout the summer of 1949. (His uncle had taught him to play gin rummy the year before).[10] He went out of his way to gather players for a foursome. Shirley Smith remembers that "John would pick me up two or three times, and we'd go up to Fred's [Fred Muth, ed.] with another guy, maybe Jack Guerin, Bill Forry or Frankhauser. Just wanted me to make a fourth." In playing pinochle, she found Updike "wonderful company. We all called him 'Uppy.'" Joan Venne remembered that they sometimes played pinochle or poker when Updike was killing time while his father sold asparagus and strawberries from the back of his car. Updike also caught the canasta craze in his junior and senior years, though, according to Joan Venne, "John always forgot to pay the kitty." Years later a sleepless Updike tried (and failed) to recall canasta rules (JVYC, Letter to Joan Youngerman, 19 Nov.1983).[11]

Some of the gang played more adult games, like strip poker. Dick Manderbach remembered that "Peggy Lutz and Joan Venne would go down to their bras," but he hastened to add that "John wasn't involved." Perhaps not then, but Updike recalled playing strip poker in an attic; a girl had to grope "into her sweater" to bring forth her bra (*DC* 84). He was involved, though, in chess games. He, Fred Muth, and others would challenge one another, even when they were guests at parties, according to Joan Venne. Or sometimes, as Barbara Hartz recalled, Updike would just declare, "Let's read Big Little Books." Then she, Fred Muth, and Updike would pop open the books. Barbara Hartz recalls that, "In the time I read a chapter, he read the book. It was phenomenal." He devoured Big Little Books, and sometimes with Fred Muth, Ann Weik, and others he would form a session devoted to the books(AWCC, Ann Weik, Letter to Author,9 July 2009). Even at get-togethers, she noted, Fred Muth and Updike would find books and "just sit down in a corner and read."

On hot days, Victor Kroninger, Updike, and others would ride their bikes to the dam and crawl through the bushes. Victor Kroninger recalled, "We would check around to see if a woman who walked her dog was near, and we had to wait till she was out of the field to strip." When she passed, they would cut the vines off and "swing naked out over the dam about fifteen feet," and then drop into the cool water of the Porgy. Victor Kroninger, who would later follow his father into the ministry, remembered Updike saying about the feat, "Your Dad's the holy man, so I guess we can risk it." Otherwise, as Marvin Waid related, they might try the Wyomissing quarry, where they would "scoot around on planks." Swimming in the Porgy and the quarry must have been quite a triumph for Updike, since when he was about five years old, his father tossed him into a swimming pool to familiarize him with the water, and this shock distressed him for much of his life (*DC* 82–83).[12]

Shillington must have been the dull "Sunday-stunned town" Updike described in *Rabbit, Run* (*RA* 84), since beyond going to the movies, playing war games, or swimming, there wasn't much to do on Sunday.[13] The usual routine on Sabbath began with going to church or an afternoon movie, and then Updike would lead his gang to Ibach's drug store where, Benny Palm remembered, "the milkshakes were out of this world." After this they would go for a long walk. Jackie Hirneisen recounted how they "hiked out to the Reading Airport, and had umbrellas, and the boys threw them over a big, high fence, but we got them." On another occasion, "Harlan, Joan, I, and John we'd walk along the old Shillington Road by the museum." This jaunt took a surprising turn because "we walked all day. Joan Venne took pictures of us, and there was no film in the camera, which she knew. We almost strangled her."

By far the most popular place to enjoy leisure time the rest of the week was "Stephen's Luncheonette," also called "Stephen's Malt Shop" or "Stephen's Sweet Shop." Sometimes Updike and others even cut class to go to nearby Stephen's, because it was a place where you could be "rowdy." Updike had a favorite booth, and he usually sat with Fred Muth or Bill Forry. Updike would eat hamburgers and smoke in what he later jokingly called "a den of opium"(JVYC, 1Aug., N. d.). Apparently, no one used marijuana, but, Barry Nelson disclosed, "Kids would take aspirins and 7-Up, but not me or John." Instead, some would show off by drinking a beverage called "Around the Fountain," or "Triple on the Fountain," in which one of everything was mixed into a glass. Nancy March called this "a horrid drink, but people drank it." Harlan Boyer could be found "raising Cain," and Nancy March admitted that dancing on the table to the juke box "would have been one of my tricks." The manager of Stephen's might have been lenient because he rented the shop from Barbara Hartz's uncle. Updike played the pinball machine endlessly, like a character in *The Centaur*, Johnny Dedman. "If I had not wanted so badly to be Vermeer, I would have tried to be Johnny Dedman," Updike remarked (Sulkis 11).

Smoking cigarettes was permitted at school and in some homes.[14] Shirley Smith was given a cigarette lighter at graduation, though Peggy

Lutz had to conceal her habit from her strict parents by throwing her cigarette butts out the window; they were eventually discovered. Smoking was an easy way to assume the pose of adulthood, since its dangers, tragic in Updike's case, were not established until the surgeon general's report in 1964.[15] When he was about fourteen, Updike bought his first cigarettes at the Reading train station, as part of his effort to become "more 'popular'" (*SC* 225). A cigarette sagged from his lip as he played pin ball at Stephen's Luncheonette. Joan Venne recalled seeing him dangling a Kool from his lips while tossing a basketball at an outdoor backboard (Kreider 19). He would strike poses with his cigarette similar to those of his film heroes Humphrey Bogart and Cary Grant. Jack Guerin said that Updike would "smoke like a fiend." Apparently, Linda and Wesley Updike did not reprimand their son for his habit.

Updike's greatest use of his leisure time was undoubtedly his discovery of reading. He pillaged the Reading Public Library for Ogden Nash's light verse and P. G. Wodehouse's novels.[16] As a Christmas present, his parents gave him James Thurber's *Fables for Our Time*, which he later reviewed for *Chatterbox* in November 1945. By the time he was fourteen, Updike began to experience the power of books even in the escapist thrillers of Ellery Queen, Agatha Christie, John Dickson Carr, Ngaio Marsh, Erle Stanley Gardner, Eric Amble, and Graham Greene.[17] But when he was about fifteen and tried James Joyce's *Ulysses* and George Orwell's *1984*, Updike became "badly shaken" on realizing that those "suffocating, literary worlds" might become his own (*DC* 291).[18] Updike's reading, as well as his fear of not being able to match the literary backgrounds of other Harvard entrants, had taken him slowly into the richer, disturbing world of serious literature. His wartime fears of oblivion were shown to be universal, and he would shortly confront those fears directly in stories like "Pigeon Feathers" and "The Astronomer," and novels like *Rabbit, Run* and *The Centaur*. Updike focused his leisure activities of reading, drawing, and writing into his vocation. They became unbreakable links in the chain he forged to the last days of his life.

NOTES

1. See "Midpoint" (*CP* 83).
2. Updike's choice of his novel's title might have been related to *Run Rabbit Run*, a song by Noel Gay and Ralph Butler, written for Gay's show *The Little Dog Laughed* of 1939. Updike remarked that his use of this source was "unintentional" (*RA* xii). He derived his motifs of traps, clothing, and running from Beatrix Potter's *Tale of Peter Rabbit*.
3. In 1998 he started and completed an unusual arrangement in which he wrote the initial segment of a mystery on a website, others competed to continue it, and then Updike supplied the final section (*MM* 835–38).
4. Peter J. Bailey argues that by the time Updike wrote *In the Beauty of the Lilies*, he had shifted his feelings about film, since film fails to provide "self-forgetfulness" for his characters. Film also presents the seamy side of life, and skims only the surfaces of

life, thus producing "images like a colorful mountain of compressed and rotting garbage" (Bailey 84;*IBL* 465).

5. Updike notes that when he turned thirteen and had to pay the adult price, twenty-seven cents, that "was too much for me to go twice a week" (*Licks of Love* 49–50).

6. Perhaps a character speaks for Updike, when he asserts that in the theater he "learned to dream and to pose" (*TM* 143). Owen, of *Villages,* learned his "sexual etiquette" from the movies (68).

7. His passion for movies is evident throughout his work. His first prose for *Chatterbox* was a review of Laurence Olivier's *Hamlet* (25 Feb. 1949: 5). Updike's plan to work for Walt Disney continued into maturity, praising him in "Midpoint," and in "The Old Movie Houses" he wrote, "To create motion, frame by frame, appeared Godlike" (*MM* [641]–43). His mature work would treat all aspects of the movie world, from movie theaters and film stars to hundreds of references to films and film personalities, and from extended treatments of single films (*2001: A Space Odyssey*) to films that deepened his personal exploration of selfhood (*Being There*). He conceived of *Rabbit, Run* as a movie and hoped to write its screenplay. In his novel *In the Beauty of the Lilies,* Updike examined in rich detail the life of a Hollywood star. He even used cinematic devices like montage in novels like *The Poorhouse Fair* and *The Centaur* (De Bellis 173–75). Oddly enough, when he entered Harvard in September 1950, Updike listed as his interests: "Basketball, Writing, Art, English Lit, Mathematics, Jazz, Poker, Chess, Cartooning," but not movies ("The Harvard Freshman Register 1954").

8. Updike used these events as the basis for "You'll Never Know, Dear, How Much I Love You" (*ES* [3]–6).

9. Many years later Updike developed asthma, and his description of an attack contains spatial images that recall the collapsed tunnel. Unable to catch his breath, Updike felt, "two walls drawn closer and closer, until they are pressed together" (*SC* 94). The image is strikingly similar to his description in the early 1940s of a childhood claustrophobia attack when he listened to a radio drama featuring a fat man's entombment in a crawlspace (91).

10. "He played to win, and I loved him for that. So many adults refuse to give a child the compliment of a contest" (*AP* 202).

11. At Ipswich much later Updike held poker nights each week. Beginning in December 1957, the game went on for over fifty years. Updike loved its "rapid renewals of opportunity" and its singularly "human" aspect (*DC* 85). In 1984 he published "Poker Night," a touching story of a man who has learned he has cancer but cannot tell his card-playing buddies (*TM* 182–89).

12. The event is vividly recalled in "Trust Me," with the emphasis placed not on the realization that the boy couldn't trust his father, but on his mother's awareness that she couldn't trust her husband (*TM* [3]–12). At the YMCA pool he was "nearly asphyxiated" with fear, and when he was a pre-teen, putting his face in the water was "like sticking my hand into fire." Naval war movies produced suffocating nightmares of drowning (*DC* 83). Updike was obligated to learn to swim before graduating from Harvard and so took lessons and "managed two lengths of the pool—an achievement he seemed as proud of later as graduating summa cum laude. But for the rest of his life he swam with what I would describe as a rather studied dog paddle" (David Updike, "Toast").

13. A reason why Sunday "stunned" Shillington was the existence of Pennsylvania Blue Laws, laws enacted to keep Sunday holy by restricting shopping or certain entertainments. As late as 1950, baseball games could not begin an inning after 6:30 P.M. in Philadelphia, which often curtailed the second game of a doubleheader.

14. Possibly Updike could not smoke around his parents, if the autobiographical stories "Friends from Philadelphia" and "Home" can be taken as factual. In the former, John Nordholm refuses a cigarette since his mother would smell it on his breath, and in the later, Robert remarked that he had to smoke outside to avoid offending his mother who hated it (*ES* [34]–35; 219). The dangers of smoking were not concealed

from Updike. His uncle Ed had been warned by his doctor not to smoke, but he did and died of a heart attack. Updike even questioned his uncle's smoking (*AP* 206–08).

15. An Updike character remarked, "You couldn't get anywhere, in the high-school society of the late Forties, without smoking," and at fifteen he smokes in the car as his father drives him to school (*LL* 58). Thirty tobacco-related surgeon general's reports have been issued since 1964. Updike did not quit smoking until about 1977.

16. Considering his love for the writer and for cartooning, Updike might have seen the film, *Piccadilly Jim*, based on the Wodehouse novel about a cartoonist. One of Updike's favorite writers, Robert Benchley, also appeared in the film.

17. Much later he explained the allure of thrillers as offering the reader a "contract," in which no matter how violent the book you will return to your secure world when you close it. The contract also assured the reader that the two worlds of book and life would always be separate (*DC* 291).

18. Since he had such boundless hope for his future, Updike might have felt this passage from *1984* (which he quoted in his "Introduction" to *The Poorhouse Fair*) as especially unsettling: "Posterity will never hear of you. You will be lifted clean out from the stream of history" (*HG* 431).

FOUR
Athletics

Those who imagine Updike as a stereotypical "artsy" because he cultivated his passions for writing and drawing and because he looked frail even by age fourteen, will be surprised to learn that he participated in a wide variety of sports. From his very early days in grammar school he joined his playground buddies from dawn to sunset in a vigorous game called "roofball." He also enjoyed football, baseball, and basketball, often over his mother's disapproval, and he played with star athletes like Jerry Potts

Figure 4.1. *Roofball action in the Shillington High School playground.*

Figure 4.2. *Lining up for roofball in the Shillington High School playground in 1944. Updike is second in line.*

and Barry Nelson. This enthusiasm for sports was not confined to his school days but would continue after he moved to Ipswich in 1958 and met young couples who participated in golf, tennis, volleyball, skiing, and other sports.

Although Harlan Boyer, who played track and football, stated bluntly that Updike, "was not coordinated . . . maybe that led him to the literature thing," Barry Nelson records that although Updike was, in his junior year, a five-foot-nine, 127-pound, skinny kid with green eyes who wore horn-rimmed glasses, he was a "tough competitor" in gym class and on the playground. Barry Nelson also noted that Updike was "a great supporter" of athletes, though he "poked fun at them too" with his comical drawings in *Chatterbox* and *Hi-Life* of athletes from every sport Shillington High offered.

As a child Updike enjoyed a variety of athletic games. At Shillington Elementary School he played soccer and heard a cascade of screeches as the ball was kicked—against the rules—to the girls' side (*SC* 14). He remembered fondly the street next to his home that led to the nearby playground, tennis courts, and softball field, and he recalled the great teams that played there. As the tallest of the lighter boys in high school, he climbed to the top of a human pyramid, standing shakily at the apex atop "Fats" Sterner's shoulders (46). While in Reading working at a lens factory when he was sixteen, Updike found that during lunch breaks his skill at quoits[1] made him the one to beat, probably because on the Plowville farm he did well throwing horseshoes (*HG* 41–45; *DC* 665–66). Such prowess shows that Updike had good eye-hand co-ordination. At the playground he was the master of box hockey, as well as his favorite game, roofball.

Updike seldom failed at roofball. In his memoir, he explained that the game was played with a red rubber ball which, after it rolled down the roof from a previous hit, was launched back onto the roof, sometimes with spin or clever placement, so that the next player in line couldn't hit it back. Failure to return the ball eliminated that player. The last man standing, usually Updike, was the winner. The game never bored him, and he often played until the park closed at four o'clock. Tony Van Liew noted that Updike had "a good instinct" for the game, and he could even defeat much older, serious opponents (JVYC, 11 Mar. 1996). He honed his skill under the watchful supervision of the playground guardian, Mrs. Thelma Kutch Lewis, his *Chatterbox* supervisor. Shown photos of his friends playing roofball many years later, Updike excitedly identified his playmates (JPC, 8 July 2001). Since girls and boys could play, whether tall or short, husky or thin, roofball came to symbolize for Updike a "perfect democracy" (*AP 170*). He declared he was close to heaven in his playground.

In Shillington, Updike insisted he had all the sports equipment any boy would need, a sled, a baseball glove, and a bicycle.[2] Sledding, though, was hazardous. While sledding on Shillington's steep streets at the age of nine, Updike swallowed a cough drop and nearly choked to death (*SC* 91). Maybe that is why, as Barbara Hartz remembered, "We took our sleds to Chestnut Hill, but John didn't participate much."[3] Well into adulthood Updike reminded a former teacher that barricades were set to protect him and other sledders (TKL/DSC, 29 Mar. 1999). Sledding was dangerous enough, but, considering his mother's hovering protection, it is surprising that Updike would be allowed to ice skate (31).

Second in the sports equipment trio, and most important, was Updike's baseball glove. No doubt his interest in baseball was supported by his athletic father, Wesley Updike, who played catcher at Ursinus and was eventually honored by having a Plowville ballpark christened Wesley Updike Field. Updike's mother resisted his playing ball, and Myrtle Council remembered feeling sorry for Updike because "he couldn't play with his friends. His mother wouldn't have allowed it." Myrtle Council still visualizes Updike sitting on the curb watching kids play baseball. To Linda Updike, baseball was "too rough," and it put her son in the hands of what she considered dubious company. She feared, naturally, that he might be hurt, but she also thought that even the association with athletes might pose a threat by misdirecting her son from his talents as a cartoonist and writer. Updike was unbothered by such contamination, but he did experience the danger in baseball, for, in an essay praising the courage of ball players, he recalled that as a child he prayed a softball wouldn't be hit his way. In a "hardball" game he thought the ball looked like "An imperfectly aimed bullet" (*HG* 474).

Linda Updike did allow her son to faithfully attend his school baseball games. He could also listen to radio broadcasts or read newspaper accounts of Philadelphia's American League Athletics and National League Phillies.[4] And she allowed him to go to Philadelphia to watch ball games. Linda Updike must have looked the other way when Updike played fungo in the lot next door with Tony Van Liew, a superior ballplayer from Shillington High. That Tony Van Liew played with Updike at all might suggest the quality of Updike's ability, even though, in Tony Van Liew's judgment, his friend "wasn't really an athlete." Still, he was with him when they played at the "Orchard" and Tony swatted a ball four hundred feet to Updike's amazement. Undoubtedly, though, this contact with baseball kindled a spark in him for those ballplayers that could turn the sport into an art. The athlete who accomplished this was Ted Williams, and at a double-header in Philadelphia's Shibe Park, Updike watched Williams hit several home runs, one of which cleared the high wall on a rising trajectory (Gordon102).[5] Updike followed him and his Boston Red Sox march to the 1946 World Series. (Updike "well might have" cried when they lost [*OJ* 91].)

From this time forward Williams became for him, as he later expressed it, not just a great hitter but one who could "always *care*" about every detail of his craft, and who made the tissue-thin adjustment between just doing a job and doing it well, something exemplified by Updike's writing in this essay (*HF*12). Updike may have seen his love of baseball and of his passion for writing embodied in Ted Williams. In Ipswich he enjoyed knowing that he was close to the "Splendid Splinter," and could follow his exploits. Updike was in the park when Ted Williams homered in his last at bat of his last game, September 28, 1960, the year that Updike published *Rabbit, Run*, a novel about the problems of a former star athlete (*SC* 57). Shortly before he died, Updike revised the preface of *Hub Fans Bid Kid Adieu*, a detailed account of Williams's last ball game. The essay has remained a fixture in baseball anthologies.[6]

As Harlan Boyer recalled, Updike's third necessary sports item, a bicycle, was a "girl's rattle trap of a bike . . . his wheels were going wild, and he liked to go fast." After school Harlan Boyer and others would ride their bikes down Philadelphia Avenue to Updike's house, where he would make peanut butter and jelly sandwiches for them.[7] The bike rides might have also helped to imprint the features of Shillington on Updike's mind, paving the way for "Rabbit" Angstrom's similar rides by car or bus, as he watches his town change over the course of thirty years. As he discovered in *Rabbit at Rest*, even basketball had changed.

Perhaps Updike's excitement about basketball was a natural transition from his passion for roofball. Joan Venne observed him many times playing basketball by himself. She might have seen him shooting baskets at a hoop nailed to a telephone pole in an alley on property belonging to Jerry Potts's grandparents at 112 Philadelphia Avenue (*SC* 35). This was the same area depicted in the first scene of *Rabbit, Run* (JPC, 29 Feb. 1996). Certainly, he rooted enthusiastically when watching nearly every game of the entire 1946–47 season. Updike told Jerry Potts that he saw him score fifty points, and in another game saw this 1948 team captain total forty-four. He was also there when Jerry Potts broke the county discus record (JPC, Letters to Jerry Potts, 20 Aug. 1993; 16 Nov. 1958). Saying goodbye to basketball players in a poem for *Chatterbox*, "On the Last Day of the Season," Updike affectionately named fifteen classmates he had watched over the years (17 Feb. 1950: 8).

How good was Updike as a player? Opinions vary. Bob Daubert, who played basketball, football, and track, said Updike "was not very good at it" when they played by the ice house from his sophomore to senior years. Barry Nelson, who was named to Shillington High School's "Olympus" for outstanding scholastic and athletic achievement in baseball, football, and basketball (as Jerry Potts had been in 1948), thought Updike was "a bit too awkward . . . to have the moves and balance of an athlete." Yet he enjoyed teaching his friend how "to shoot over his head," and later was delighted that Updike became "pretty good. . . . He could put them in." He relished remembering how he taught Updike "how to hold the ball for the hook shot." Updike's favorite shot was from sixteen feet, banked off the backboard. Thanks to Barry Nelson's help, Updike was able to play forward and center for his homeroom team in intramural games.

Updike improved his game by playing "21"and "Horse"—in which a player copied the previous player's shot, and missing three times put him out of the game. Buthe was eliminated from the tenth-grade tryouts for the junior varsity, which he felt was "an embarrassment to remember" (*MM 817).* Updike would have made the team at a smaller school according to a friend (Nelson JUSHS 11). Jerry Potts agreed, suggesting that elsewhere Updike might have even made the varsity. Had he made the varsity in some other school and become a star athlete, the course of his life might have been very different. Had he become successful enough to become a professional player it would have been, as Jack Guerin believed, "a loss for the country." Perhaps because he saw athletes who failed to adapt when they were finished, Updike was able to project his imagination into those athletes who were lost when their playing days ended, and this alter ego became his most famous character, "Rabbit" Angstrom ("Introduction" *RA* ix-xxiv).[8]

As Updike cheered on his school basketball team, so did he faithfully attend the football games, enthusiastically rooting for the "Speedboys." No mere spectator, Updike played touch football with friends like Leroy Hill, Dick Manderbach, and Fred Muth on "a little patch of grass" in Fred Muth's yard.[9] As an example of his empathy for an injured athlete when he was about sixteen, Updike accompanied Barbara Hartz's cousin Dick Behney, a football player who was on crutches with his ankle in a cast, the three miles from Reading's Albright College stadium to Shillington. The trip is described in "In Football Season" (*ES* [122]–25).

In 1972, in Ipswich, Updike played touch football with such abandon that he broke his leg and had to have it operated upon (*SC* 76). Such gusto typified all of Updike's sports efforts. He played Sunday volleyball with passion, knocking people over as he dived to make a save, or leaping high at the net to spike the ball into the face of a female opponent (78). He played tennis at the Chilmark Community Center, skied in Vermont, and overcame an earlier fear of swimming sufficiently to dive into towering waves at South Beach (61). As Barry Nelson said, Updike was a "tough competitor."

But team sports posed a problem, for although Linda Updike's husband was an ex-football player and a football and swimming coach at Shillington High School, she resisted her son's interest in sports. She considered her son "an academic from the start," in Myrtle Council's persuasive opinion, and though Updike, as we've seen, did participate in sports and came to love them enough to incorporate them into highly successful stories, novels, poems, and articles, Linda Updike's fears directed him away from the camaraderie of men on sports teams. Jerry Potts felt Updike's mother was unwelcoming when he came to her home, guessing that Linda Updike feared he might provide her son with an athletic role model. Jack Guerin also identified Linda Updike's difficulty, conjecturing that, "She may have looked at all of us as a distraction from what he should be doing."[10] But without question Updike showed he could form lasting friendships and find mentors among athletes, just as he could among artists and writers.

Probably the social context of sports helped to stimulate Updike's latent ability, since after moving to Ipswich in 1958 and becoming acquainted with couples who enjoyed all sorts of sports, he performed well. In the late 1950s, he was given a set of golf clubs, took up the sport, and eventually played at the prestigious Myopia Golf Club. His sons, Michael and David, called him a fierce competitor who insisted on golfing with them only weeks before he died. Updike won the match ("TFP" 1 Oct. 2010).[11]

NOTES

1. Quoits is a game requiring hand-eye co-ordination similar to horseshoes. In quoits the object is to toss rings around a stationary spike.

2. The first edition of his memoir identifies the bike as a Schwinn, but the Fawcett publication changes the name to Elgin, illustrating Updike's willingness to correct a faulty memory (*SC* [K] 29; *SC* [F] 28). He kept the correction in (*MM* 800).

3. The sledding meant so much to Updike that in "Midpoint" he wrote: "No snows have been as deep as those my sled/caressed to ice before I went to bed" (*CP* 101).

4. Later he went to Philadelphia to watch the teams play. The Athletics finished fourth in 1948, and the Phillies won the pennant in 1950, the year Updike graduated from Shillington High School. While at Harvard he and his roommate, Christopher Lasch, often went to Fenway Park to see the Boston Red Sox. When both were working in New York, they watched Boston-New York Yankees games.

5. The description of that lofty homer might have been on Updike's mind when he described Williams's last homer: "the ball climbed on a diagonal line . . . less an object in flight than the tip of a towering, motionless construct like . . . the Tappan Zee Bridge" (*AP* 146). The homerun Updike saw in Philadelphia also resembles the perfect golf shot of "Rabbit" Angstrom since the ball seems to gain height as it gains distance and nearly disappears (*RA* 116). Possibly all of these things blended to the image he selected to confirm that he could ride "a thin pencil line" out of Shillington into "unseen . . . hearts" (*AP* 185).

6. When Ted Williams died, *The Boston Globe* reprinted *Hub Fans Bid Kid Adieu* in full.

Updike used baseball in *Rabbit Redux* and *Rabbit at Rest*, in the former to signal the violence and racism sometimes lying beneath sports competition, and in the latter to show "Rabbit" Angstrom's admiration for the Phillies' future Hall of Famer, Mike Schmidt, a latter-day Ted Williams. In *Rabbit at Rest*, "Rabbit" also kept alive his memory of the Phillies' 1950 "Whiz Kids," despite the disparagements of Ronnie Harrison.

7. Bicycling around Shillington made such an impression on Updike that years later he could recall his bicycle in enough detail to use the chain as a metaphor in the poem, "A Bicycle Chain." The kinesthetic feel for the chain's metal coil suggested to him a relation between the shape of the chain and "language's linked lines." As the greasy chain is put into motion by the bike rider, so the poem derives its power from the writer's finding the structure that drives the poem (*CP* 108).

8. What Updike loved and understood about basketball is clear in the "Rabbit" saga and his most anthologized poem, "Ex-Basketball Player" (*CP* 4–5).

9. In "The Road Home" a character resembling Fred Muth is described as having a backyard big enough for fungo practice (*MFT* 188). Possibly Fred Muth is the friend referred to as "C" in "The Dogwood Tree." Updike describes "C" as playing quoits even when his appendix was ready to burst (*AP* 179).

10. Perhaps Linda Updike's careful screening of athletes who might cause him to swerve from his artistic goals made her son wary of close association with writers in New York. If so, this might have led to his resigning from *The New Yorker* and seeking the relative anonymity of Ipswich.

11. Updike might have been inspired to play golf by the fame of Betty Fehl Fegely, a Shillington High School graduate (1940) who won the Central Pennsylvania Championship in 1950, Updike's senior year. Updike made his ex-basketball star, "Rabbit," a golfer, as well as Tom Marshfield in *A Month of Sundays*. The golf stories, poems, essays, and segments from the novels collected in *Golf Dreams* reveal the depth and breadth of his enthusiasm for the game, since they range from fictional realism and fantasy to light verse, and from personal essays to instructional tips. Updike published golf articles so extensively that he chided his 1993 bibliographer for failing to find them.

FIVE

Clowning

While mastering Shillington High School's courses in the sciences as well as the humanities, and perhaps fearing that he might be perceived as nothing but a brain by his classmates, Updike developed various entertaining attention-getting devices, most of which were carefully planned

Figure 5.1. *Updike at 14 with Barry Nelson, and Barry Styer on Shillington High School grounds.*

and required an audience. In class he would declare, according to classmate Joan Venne Youngerman, "John would say, 'O.K., everyone, chairs
to the back of the room' [or] 'upside down chairs today,'" and they
would eagerly comply. Dick Manderbach recollected that Updike would
"take a piece of paper, and write a poem, and do a cartoon of someone in
class and send it around." The effect on Joan Venne was electric; she
would laugh so hard when Updike sent her a note in class that she
"couldn't hold a pencil." Possibly Updike was imitating the success his
father had in class when Wesley Updike did similar things. Like father,
like son?

Joan Venne recalled pranks Updike played in English class on Miss
Showalter, an old maid in her seventies with a no-nonsense style earning
her the nickname, "The Gritzer." One day, while a supervisor observed
her class, Updike removed one of his mustard-colored loafers and passed
it to the student behind him. The shoe traveled from hand to hand until a
classmate placed it on the windowsill at the back of the room. After the
supervisor left, the loafer was passed back, and Miss Showalter never
realized what had happened (Kreider 18).

Certain that Joan Venne could take a joke, Updike executed another
daring maneuver. As star athlete Tony Van Liew remembered, Joan
Venne had a nervous habit of unfastening and refastening the top button
of her blouse when she stood before class to recite. So when it was Updike's turn to deliver Macbeth's "Tomorrow and Tomorrow" soliloquy
from memory, he decided to parody her. Since he was positioned in front
of his teacher, Miss Showalter couldn't see him slowly toying with the
top button of his shirt, unbuttoning it and continuing with the others, as
if preparing to strip, while simultaneously giving a perfect reading of
Macbeth's despair. Miss Showalter couldn't understand why the students were laughing and falling out of their chairs. Then Updike began to
play with his belt. "Whether he was actually going to drop his pants I
don't know," Tony Van Liew wondered, "but I wouldn't have been surprised." Marvin Waid had been in on the gag, since Updike had told him
before class to watch him imitate her.[1] Updike repeated the prank in
another English class, and his buddy Barry Nelson recollected that Updike undid his shirt and belt while reciting Samuel Taylor Coleridge's,
"The Rime of the Ancient Mariner." Surely Tony Van Liew was right to
call Updike, "scholarly but not a geek."

Updike seemed to have the ability to concentrate on two things at
once, for, Jack Guerin remembered that "In English class he used to stare
out of the window and seemed to be worlds away. The teacher would
call on him and John would launch into a long, intricate answer to the
question" (Sulkis 10). Similarly, Joan Venne recalled that a teacher would
ask Updike a question and "he'd stand up and talk for ten minutes on
absolutely nothing." This was sure to draw laughs, and Updike kept it in
his repertoire. She also remembered that he would make some small

sounds to draw attention to a lisp of a teacher, or he would pass "amusing notes and hilarious caricatures" of them. Updike, Tony Van Liew summarized, could "always find ways to break up the class." Some thought that Updike got away with such clowning because his father taught mathematics at the school, but this seems unlikely considering his father's difficulties with the principal, Charles J. Hemmig. More likely, his teachers ignored his antics because, as Joan Venne explained, "he already knew everything that you needed to know." Apparently Updike was never reprimanded, for, as Van Liew said, "Johnny was Johnny, and they left him alone." It is a bit curious that Updike did these things while insisting that teachers were insufficiently compensated for their work, and witnessing for four years his father's classroom frustrations. Close to home, apparently, he empathized with teachers, but in the classroom, responsiveness from classmates counted more than distressing teachers, the timeless adversary and an easy target.[2]

Updike's clownishness was part of the atmosphere at Shillington High School. Marvin Waid reports how he, Updike, and others took the screws out of desks so the next class using them would fall over when they sat down. Also, when Joe Jazinski started blowing his nose, Marvin Waid would blow even louder. He watched as Nancy White and a friend drove Miss Showalter "nuts" by pointing to their throats as if they couldn't speak. Principal Luther A. Weik (his initials spelled "Law") was called in, and the girls promptly recovered their voices. Milton and Clarence Hall, identical and mirror twins, would swap with each other at detention, and Supervising Principal Charles Hemmig never noticed. They would also switch dates, confusing the girls and amusing themselves. According to Milton Hall, Charlie McComsey was great with a whoopee cushion.

Shenanigans were rife at Shillington High. For example, Charlie McComsey and Harlan Boyer once took potassium nitrate, sulfur, gun powder, and phosphorous from a restricted cabinet, placed it all in a mortar and ground the volatile mixture with a pestle to see what would happen. The explosion burned McComsey's hands and sent ceramic shards flying, luckily without further damage. Milton Hall remembered that students from two labs "came running out screaming from the terrific smoke." This occurred *during* class. An item in *Chatterbox* 7 Mar. 1947 stated: "Karl Kemp alias The Human Torch. Moral: Never play with chemicals."

Then as now, school loyalty required playing tricks on another school during athletic contests. Probably the most memorable caper was the whitewashing of Ephrata High School. Jim Trexler recollected that after the football rally, kids in two cars stopped at La Rue's hardware store, and Charlie McComsey was sent into buy white wash, only to return with unwashable paint. Unwittingly, and ignited by the excitement of the coming football game, the classmates raced about thirty miles to Ephrata

High School, where they coated several walls white. Since the paint could not be hosed down later and had to be professionally removed from the walls, Luther A. Weik required each student involved to pay $4.85 to cover the costs. Naturally, the school's students relished the prank and admired everyone involved. According to Benny Palm, Updike instigated the caper. "Yes, of course," she said, "that was a John joke."

Apart from the school pranks, Updike had many other devices in which clowning of a non-subversive sort amused him as well as others. He often fell down the stairs to provoke laughter and to catch girls' eyes. He surprised Tony Van Liew by hanging upside down on a railing which he knew his friend would have to pass under. After school the antics would continue. In the fifth and sixth grades, Updike and others would ride their bikes to his house, where he would make them his favorite sandwich of peanut butter and jelly on toast. But one time, Harlan Boyer recalled, Updike put the already slathered bread on the wire toast rack and turned on the heat, "to get a rise out of me." At a party at Joan Venne's, Updike spent time role-playing with Peggy Lutz. Joan Venne described how "Peggy played me and John played Gary, my boyfriend, and everyone watched like it was a play. He was very funny." He continued his clowning after leaving Shillington. Updike has explained that in 1951 he had planned to intercept art student Mary Pennington by falling down the steps of Harvard's Fogg Art Library. It worked and she became his wife.

If falling down the steps brought Updike a wife, two literary pranks brought him notoriety. First, Updike staged an apparent feud with his buddy Fred Muth, associate editor of *Chatterbox* for four years and contributor to the literary page, "Pen and Ink." With stinging, but fake, sarcasm, they carried on a mock duel in the pages of *Chatterbox*, exchanging barbs about everything from editorial content to grammar. Attacked by Fred Muth for the "humiliating disgrace" of having a poem appear on the feature page, of which Updike was the "unscrupulous proprietor," Updike replied with a nice allusion to William Jennings Bryan's "Cross of Gold" speech.[3] In another poem, "To Fred," Updike chastises Muth for writing, in a previous issue, of his dissatisfaction with the four seasons. *Chatterbox* offered Updike a forum for the public expression of his feelings, and he used it perhaps for the only time in his poem to his friend, "On FM," his last work for *Chatterbox*. The poem reveals that the feud was only a joke, and he ends it with an expression of love ("On FM" *Chatterbox* 28 Apr. 1950).[4]

In his most sensational high school literary prank, Updike pressed the limits of censorship. The senior class of 1949 had poked fun at the junior class's hats. In retaliation, Updike wrote an "Ode to the Seniors," apparently praising the seniors while attacking them. The *Chatterbox* advisor, Mrs. Thelma Kutch Lewis, proofread the poem and "thought it was fine." She surely would have squelched it had she read the first letter of each line downward. Read that way, the letters spelled out an insult (*Chatterbox* 14 Apr. 1949: [7]; Sulkis 10–11). Mrs. Lewis told Updike to apologize, so he produced another poem, "Apology," but again the irrepressible Updike arranged the words so that the first letter of each line, read downward, spelled a slang dismissal ("Apology." *Chatterbox* 22 Apr. 1949: [8]; Sulkis 10–11). This request for forgiveness must have been acceptable, since Updike faced no consequences. Neither Mrs. Lewis nor Supervising Principal Charles Hemmig responded to the dare (Kreider 18).[5]

A prank in which Updike failed to read his audience correctly was not resolved so easily. In 1954, as he left his job as a copyboy and gofer at the Reading *Eagle*, Updike typed a farewell letter which included all the names of the *Eagle* staff. Tony Van Liew, who followed in Updike's job at the newspaper, thinks the lighthearted piece irritated the humorless managing editor who refused to publish the letter and may have destroyed it. According to Tony Van Liew, "No one has seen it since." Probably it contained the same satiric tone as the writing directed at Fred Muth. But that time Updike's pal was in on the joke. Updike sometimes seemed determined to use his gift for wit as a weapon against authorities, whether his father's tormentors in *The Centaur*, the senior class, or his employers at the Reading *Eagle*.[6]

In high school Updike's antics were clearly just hijinks, harmless clowning prompted by his excess ingenuity; his reputation for unusual, funny ideas; his need for attention; and perhaps his realization that his father also clowned and was applauded for it. But tricks with cars were another matter. Ever since childhood, Updike had enjoyed watching the cars go by on Philadelphia Avenue, to his mother's dread, because that was where "the people" were (*SC* 23). He came to know the danger of the vehicle when he was struck by a car on the way to Sunday school. Thinking that the police were arresting him for causing an accident, Updike begged not to be put in prison (9). If this filled him with fear, he outgrew it, as he had his fear of water, and his self-consciousness about his skin, his teeth, and his stuttering. Apparently the nausea Updike had experienced in his parents' car when he was a child also vanished with time. For him as for most adolescents, the car was not a dangerous machine but a passport to fun. Part of that fun lay in the excited responses of girls.

Like most of his friends, Updike had failed his driving test once, but after he got his license at sixteen, he experienced more than freedom. He recognized "the power of death" as he blithely drove along (*SC* 244). But he must have coupled this recognition to a sense of his indestructibility, which he extended to his friends when he piled as many classmates as possible into his father's boxy Buick and went for a joyride at lunchtime. One such trip with Barry Nelson included spinning the car on gravel or snow at intersections, double-clutching, and working the choke. Nelson was so impressed he noted, "he maneuvered the auto as well as he handled the stylus on the mimeograph stencils" (Barry Nelson Letter to the

Author, 18 May, 1996). Throughout the summer of 1949, according to Tony Van Liew, the classmates believed that nothing could go wrong no matter who drove the car, but such common adolescent need for excitement with friends drove Updike to clowning which might have had tragic results. On various jaunts Updike would, according to Harlan Boyer, cause his riders to "return shaken," because, as Tony Van Liew explained, "All of a sudden he'd take his hands off the wheel to see who would grab it." The game was "Chicken," and the men, of course, would hold back. But the women in the backseat like Shirley Smith or Joan Venne would "chicken out" and lunge for control of the car. The thrilled passengers would yelp as they hurtled along Route 222 toward Adamstown. More thrillingly, Barry Nelson remembered playing "Chinese driver" in which, as the car sped along, Updike would slide onto the running board from the driver's seat and, since the back doors opened toward the rear in the old car, he would slip adroitly into the backseat while the rider in the passenger seat would lurch into the driver's place, and the rider behind the passenger seat would tread along the running board, then leap into the vacated front seat. Pals who went driving with him in his father's old car down Cough Drop Hill on Route 10 were thrilled when he steered while standing on the running board.[7] As Barry Nelson softly observed, in the fun-challenged town of Shillington, "It was something to do."

Updike extended his adolescent clownishness much too far into parenthood when, during the summer of 1974, he drove his green Mustang convertible while under the influence of wine and marijuana. "Stoned" to the "point of non-attachment," Updike drove with his children and so many of their friends that they had to stand (*SC* 153).[8] Updike's high school experiences had exhibited his love for pranks, and he never lost his zest for clowning, even when he had no audience.[9] In 1954, a classmate saw Updike bouncing a paper bag on Reading's Penn Street. Only when he drew close did she realize that enclosed in the bag was, naturally, a basketball.

NOTES

1. Miss Showalter was a kindly teacher who once asked Bobby Rhoads after he recited the "Tomorrow and Tomorrow" soliloquy, "Why do you like this?" He recalled replying, "It all fits together." "Then don't you ever stop," she replied.

2. Interestingly, in one of his rare short stories set in a classroom, "Tomorrow and Tomorrow and So Forth," Updike shifts his viewpoint of a classroom prank to the teacher's reaction (*ES* [152]–60). Updike explores a teacher's refusal to believe a mischievous classroom incident is an actual prank. While students recite Macbeth's soliloquy, teacher Mark Prosser intercepts a note and is surprised to find it contains a student's confession of love. Though Prosser learns later from another teacher that the pupil was a noted practical joker, he chooses to believe the note is sincere. The story may represent Updike's acknowledgment of the possible hurt pranks more mischievous than his might have inflicted on his instructors.

Certainly, the most flamboyant illustration in Updike's work of how a teacher fails to control his prank-filled class is the first chapter of *The Centaur*. Hilariously, a class goes completely out of control when George Caldwell, a teacher modeled on Updike's father, tries to explain the history of the universe while the supervising principal observes his class. As Caldwell describes how evolution created a tragic foreknowledge of death for human beings, the lunch bell rings and the class races for the exit, leaving Caldwell overwhelmed. So Updike has it both ways, he enjoys the fun of the pranks while he empathizes with the beleaguered teacher.

3. In a literary duel Updike and Fred Muth wrote poems modeled on "Casey at the Bat," by Ernest Thayer. Updike imagined that the fabled slugger had popped out or walked, and he accompanied his effort with a drawing in which the ball nears Casey's head as he doffs his hat and bows to the crowd—underlining the arrogance which led to Casey's strikeout. The appearance of Disney's 1946 animation film, *Casey at the Bat*, read byJerry Colonna, may have inspired this contest.

4. Together they wrote the class play, "Murder at Blandings," in which Updike played Detective Hemlock Rutts and Fred Muth, Lord Oswald Blandings. In a school assembly, presentations by Latin classes included "Some Times with the Delphic Oracle," narrated by Fred Muth with Updike as a "Sibyl."

5. A Boston Red Sox fan, Updike had earlier written another poem in which a vertical reading of the first lines insulted a ball club from New York. At a class reunion Updike gave seventy-five classmates presentation copies of his poem, "To the Juniors from the Seniors," a gracious work with all names of the class of 1950 included.

6. Updike's determination to push the limits of authority emerged again, more seriously, when he challenged the rules regarding obscenity in *Rabbit, Run*. Alfred Knopf demanded that he excise many offending passages from the novel or go unpublished. Such miscalculation later produced some negative responses to his treatment of African-Americans in *Rabbit Redux*, *Brazil*, and *Terrorist*, as well as Jews in the Bech books, and women in *Rabbit Angstrom, SC.*, and *The Witches of Eastwick*.

7. David Kern drove his car in the same way: "he had a trick, safer than it looked but infallibly producing shouts and screams from his passengers, of putting the car in neutral at the crest of a hill and getting out on the running board and steering through the window" (*LL* 23).

8. The automobile is pervasive in Updike's work. He observed—twice—that Americans "make love in their cars, and listen to ball games . . . small wonder the landscape is sacrificed to these dreaming vehicles of unitary personhood" (*ES* 108). The second time, however, Updike revises the last phrase, adding gender and speed, thus personalizing the fleeting joy cars bring: "our ideal and onrushing manhood" (*DC* 87). Updike's first *New Yorker* poem celebrated the meeting of Mr. Rolls and Mr. Royce ("Duet with Muffled Brake Drums," *CP* 258). In his first novel, *The Poorhouse Fair*, a careless driver precipitates a crisis. In *The Centaur* George Caldwell's '36 Buick ferries the teacher and his son Peter from Firetown to Ohlinger, its smashed grill the result of a clash with one of his student's cars. More hearse than auto, the Buick stalls in a blizzard, and this leads to Peter Caldwell's fever and hallucinations. Probably the same ten-year-old car is described as having flat tires and broken axles (*Licks of Love* 57). "Rabbit" Angstrom performs oral sex in a car, and he makes his dash for freedom in a '55 Ford. In West Virginia, when he hears another auto start up in a "petting grove," he heads back to Mt. Judge. "Rabbit" inherits part of his father-in-law's car business and thrives when selling Toyotas during a gas shortage. His drive to Florida in *Rabbit at Rest* takes him to his death. In the story "Elsie by Starlight," David Kern nearly loses his virginity in a car, and Richard Maple commits his first infidelity in a crashed Corvair (*Villages*; *ES* [618]–23]). Sarah Worth gives up her Mercedes in order to join an ashram in which she mans a fork-lift truck. Updike testifies to the incalculable importance the automobile has for young men in the last chapter of his memoir (*SC* 244). Driving a car is a rite of passage and a rite of flight. Finally, in *Terrorist* a bomb-laden van nearly creates a catastrophe in Lincoln Tunnel. Possibly the only

novels in which automobiles do not appear are the historical fictions, *Memories of the Ford Administration* and *Gertrude and Claudius.*

9. Updike was clearly a born clown, something many readers miss, and he would continue to be after leaving Shillington High School's *Chatterbox* for Harvard's *Lampoon*, and then *The New Yorker.* At the *Lampoon* pranks were rife. His sense of humor is most obvious, of course, in his light verse, but his novels often exhibit it too. A few examples: *The Centaur's* first chapter abounds in pranks, surrealist juxtapositions, and cognitive dissonance; verbal comedy enlivens *A Month of Sundays* in Tom Marshfield's footnotes; a touch of post-modernism enables Henry Bech to write a letter to his creator and compile a bibliography listing works by his author's friends and critics; hilarious dark pranks flavor *Witches of Eastwick*; a shaggy dog joke structures *Memories of the Ford Administration*, since Alfred Clayton admits in the last sentence that he remembers nothing about the Ford administration; and self-reflexive comic irony pervades the letters of *C.* Inter-textual irony, at times comic, appears between the "Rabbit" novels, and also between Shakespeare's *Hamlet* and Updike's prequel, *Gertrude and Claudius.* His most elaborate prank concerned *Rabbit Is Rich.* Updike persuaded Dr. Robert McCoy, vice president of communications at Kent State University, to have the name of Nelson Springer Angstrom put into the commencement program of the College of Arts and Sciences class of 1981–82. Nelson's name was read aloud.

SIX

Girls and Women

More than most of his friends, Updike grew up among women. At home were his mother, Linda Updike, and grandmother, Katherine Hoyer. They make an interesting contrast: the independent, domineering artist who had "force" (as "Rabbit" characterized his mother), and the doting

Figure 6.1. *John Updike's birthday party in the yard of the Updike home on Philadelphia Avenue. The girls on the ground: Ann Weik (left) and Nancy March (right); second row: Fred Muth; unidentified girl; Mark Wenrich; and John Updike; Back row: unidentified girl; unidentified girl; and Joan LaRue.*

**Figure 6.2.   *The steps of Stephen's Luncheonette, favorite gathering place for
Shillington High students. Left to Right: Nancy March, Richard Smith, Donald
Schwartz, Peggy Lutz, Bill Moser, John Updike, Doc Daniels, and Pat Eisenbise.***

grandmother who knitted him sweaters and toddler's outfits, and who
guarded him from monsters. As polar opposites, they exhibited dual pos-
sibilities for women: pursue a career or embrace domesticity. His playmates on Philadelphia Avenue were primarily girls, like Joan Venne
Youngerman, Mary Ann Stanley, Jackie Hirneisen Kendall, Joan Conrad,
Joan George Zug, Peggy Lutz Roberts, and Barbara Hartz Behney. An
athletic friend thought that had Updike been raised in his neighborhood
where girls were scarce but boys abundant, Updike might have participated more seriously in male-oriented sports and been less interested in
writing and drawing. Updike's *Chatterbox* sports cartoons and "Hub Fans
Bid Kid Adieu" argue against a separation of sports and the arts in his
life. Would he have responded to peer pressure by other boys, and thus
honed his ability in basketball and experience the heady popularity that
goes with sports stardom? No one can know, but it does seem unlikely.

Clearly, being raised among females aided Updike's maturity. His
mother gave him opportunities to learn how to dance and play the piano,
under the direction of women. His playground activity, and his writing
and cartooning for *Chatterbox* were supervised by Mrs. Thelma Kutch
Lewis, whom he often called his first editor. She admitted, "I can forgive
anything because of the beauty of his word blending" (Sulkis 11). His
lifelong novel editor at Knopf was Judith Jones.

Half of Updike's schoolteachers were female, and he responded to their knowledge of the arts and humanities. His interests in art, writing, and dramatics led him to work closely with English teachers Florence Schrack and Kathryn Showalter. Classmate Ann Weik Cassar, now a professional editor, spoke highly of both teachers of eleventh- and twelfth-grade English, respectively, asserting that they furnished, "an excellent background that has been invaluable over the years," adding, "I'm sure John also appreciates their influence" (Ann Weik Cassar to the author 25 May 2005 E-mail). He did, for Updike wrote to Ann Weik a few months later, "I often thank Heaven for Mrs. Schrack, who . . . inculcated the basic principles of English grammar in me." Perhaps that is why he added, "It was a good school" (AWCC, Letter to Ann Weik Cassar, 23 Oct. 2006). He took four years of Latin from Mrs. Estella Pennepacker, and would later write that students with her usually wrote beautiful "idiomatic" English. Updike participated in activities requiring graphic and verbal skills that put him in the company of women, who are generally more adept with language than men.

Although girls composed 50 percent of the 118 students at Shillington High School, Updike was the lone male among four females on the debating team; one of only eight boys among the twenty-seven staff members of the school paper, *Chatterbox*; and one of seven males of forty staff members on the yearbook, *Hi-Life*. So Updike had ample opportunity to work and socialize with women. He got to know their features and interests, their idiosyncrasies and wit, their inventiveness and intelligence, their problems and values. He also observed their athletic ability when he played roofball with girls. A person as perceptive as Updike would have found much to consider, remember, and record. Images of women in the movies (like Jean Simmons, Lauren Bacall, and Dorothy Lamour) or encountered in his reading (Molly Bloom of James Joyce's *Ulysses*) also shaped his understanding of women and helped to produce indelible female characters in his books. He did, however, shun standard women's fiction.

But being around so many girls did not necessarily allow them to become more than friends. Jackie Hirneisen found him "plain looking," and though her parents urged her to date Updike she "couldn't see it." A lone voice decrying Updike's "unpopularity with girls," Jackie Hirneisen declared that Updike had an unattractive "physical appearance." Apparently she eschewed boys who dressed carelessly, seldom combed their hair, and stuttered. Despite her response (or because of it?), Updike was attracted to her, and when he was in fifth grade, he wrote her two love poems titled "Song" and "Mush," describing his feelings for her with extravagant comparisons. Decorating another page with a crude drawing of her face, he praised her "soft beauty," superior to "shimmering moonlight" (JHKC, "Jacqueline"). In 1958, Updike used her arrival in 1943 in the fifth grade at Shillington Elementary School for his story, "The Alligators" (*Early Stories*7–12). Bob Daubert and Barbara Hartz guessed that he liked her. Updike admitted in a story through his alter ego Francis, "The brassy girls he adored barely notice him" (*HG* 29). In fact, Jackie Hirneisen was so repelled that, despite testimony to the contrary, she thought Updike a poor dancer. Dancing to her was very important because, as she said, "the last dance was with the guy who walked you home, and that's when you got the kisses." Clearly, she wasn't sufficiently interested in Updike to risk even the smallest romantic incident. However, she once asked Joan Venne bluntly, "Did you ever think of John as sexy?" (The fact that Jackie Hirneisen raised the question is suggestive.) Joan Venne thought it over and decided that Updike "certainly wouldn't have been repulsive to me."

Later Joan Venne admitted that, though he resembled the film actor Richard Gere, "He wasn't a ladies' man." Jackie Hirneisen did not think that four years at Harvard had improved Updike's desirability. "He looked terrible," she said, "wrinkly sweater and pants down under his heels, and he never tied his shoes." It would seem that clothes unmade the man. Yet she accompanied him to Whitner's Tea Room for lunch and discovered that Updike "was wonderful, so stimulating, so jolly, and witty always." Jackie Hirneisen was not as perceptive as her parents, who had urged her to take an interest in Updike.

Besides Joan Venne, Updike enjoyed being with Mary Ann Stanley. Updike named Ann Weik Cassar "most studious," and Mary Jane Potts "my first good friend" (JPC, Letter to Jerry Potts, 18 Dec. 2000). He enjoyed them, as well as Peggy Lutz, probably because they were bold and playful. Pretty and clever girls, like Jouette Eifert Chick later attracted him. He acquired the girls' interest by going with Jerry Potts on Fridays to dances at the Recreation Center, usually with Peggy Lutz and Joan George (JPC, 6 July1996). At the frequent school dances, often chaperoned by his father, Updike would show off the latest steps, to the envy of the athletes. In fact, Milton Hall attributed Updike's popularity to his being, "one of the few guys who knew how to jitterbug."

Fraternizing at movies brought the students closer together. Jackie Hirneisen recalled that in seventh grade the kids would sit in the back row of the movie theater and "pair and snuggle and kiss, and it was wonderful." But she could not recall ever seeing Updike at the movies with a date. Updike was a fellow she just couldn't see. But he was there with Joan Borner Conrad, as well as Joan Zug. After their movie date in Reading, Joan Conrad was asked "Who was that crazy kid you were out with Saturday night?" Updike had earned the adjective by leap-frogging over parking meters on their way home (Kreider 19). Joan Conrad saw in Updike what Jackie Hirneisen had missed when she explained, "I knew even then he'd be famous . . . and I'd be able to say that I went out with him. My father thought he was absolutely crazy, but when I looked at

Johnny, I didn't notice that his hair was uncombed or that he wore funny clothes" (Sulkis 10).[1]

School trips put him in proximity to other girls. Updike's art class made trips to Wannamaker's Department Store in Philadelphia, which he thought "most crucial to his development" (DC 668) because his cartoons were displayed with other student art work. He and Joan Borner, a junior, were often together on those trips. He later told one of his teachers that he thought Joan Borner quite appealing (TKL/DSC, 24 Aug. 1994). Joan Conrad and Peggy Lutz were fellow debaters, and Updike would have been on long bus rides with them when visiting other schools for contests.[2]

Dating (going to parties or the movies) in Shillington was quite safe and "fluid," according to Jack Guerin, with most students "playing the field," at least until their senior year. Since Updike knew many of his female classmates from kindergarten to graduation, it would have been natural for him to become interested in many of them. Perhaps for this reason, his name was linked to girls he had known over the years. Barbara Hartz thought Updike might have dated Joan Venne. The code of the times dictated that couples never went "all the way." This has been termed "consensual repression." Nice guys respected girls who didn't.[3] Two women who did were pregnant when they graduated; neither attended commencement ceremonies. One of them married the father of her child, and the marriage lasted.

Updike and Peggy Lutz saw each other quite a bit, not only as children playing on Philadelphia Avenue, while occupied on *The Little Shilling* in elementary school, and certainly when working for *Chatterbox* and *Hi-Life*. Barbara Hartz noticed that Updike "admired Peggy who was good looking." Shirley Smith said Peggy, "wasn't drop dead gorgeous but had reddish-brown hair and green eyes, so peppy and so full of life." Several of Updike's alluring female characters (Penny Fogleman of *The Centaur* and Pru Angstrom of *Rabbit Is Rich*, for example) have Peggy Lutz's red hair and green eyes. They were on the debating team and other student groups. As class president Updike would have regularly conferred with his secretary, Peggy Lutz, and he would have relished her cheerleading at numerous basketball and football games. Like him, she was a regular at Stephen's Luncheonette, and a photo shows eight students standing on the steps, Peggy talking to two boys, her back to Updike who stands a few feet away, a hand in his pocket, staring in her direction (*Hi-Life* 1949, 69). Two 1950 yearbook photos show them seated side by side for the *Hi-Life* picture of the debating team, and Updike stands behind her for the picture of the senior class play (*Hi-Life* 1950 42, 76). Yet despite their proximity, Updike only yearned from afar, lacking the social confidence to approach a girl who played hockey and became the May Queen. Though Milton Hall assumed that Updike dated Peggy Lutz, since he saw them together so much, Updike must have realized that physically he did not appeal to her, nor would falling down the stairs turn the head of the most popular girl in his class.

Updike wasn't alone in his inability to approach Peggy Lutz. Years later, meeting at a class reunion, Peggy Lutz asked Tony Van Liew why he never asked her out. "I was scared to death," the accomplished athlete answered. Updike must have been intimidated too. Witnessing her dating others must have made him even more reluctant to approach her. To deceive her strict father when she double-dated, she created cover stories that sometimes became comically tangled. So vivacious was she that Bob Daubert reported that his "claim to fame" was dating her for an entire summer, probably between their junior and senior years, because by the time she became a senior, Peggy Lutz dated a Shillington High School 1948 graduate, Tjaden ("Jady") Roberts, whom she married and remained with until her death six weeks before Updike's passing. Peggy Lutz is described in *Hi-Life* as one of the "peppiest" girls in the class, and, touchingly, Updike uses the same adjective in one of his last poems, "Peggy Lutz, Fred Muth12/13/08," calling her a "peppy knockout," while admitting that she was "too much girl" for him (*Endpoint* 26–27).[4] Had she been more accessible, though, she might never have been perpetuated in this poem.[5]

Perhaps when Peggy Lutz became committed to Tjaden Roberts, Updike felt the need to replace her in his feelings, for at the same time, Updike began dating a junior, Nancy Wolf. She was nearly Peggy Lutz's opposite, "plain, even matronly," according to Shirley Smith. Her photos in the high school yearbooks support this characterization. Nancy March described her as a "sweet gal." If Peggy Lutz never condescended, perhaps Nancy Wolf seemed to because, in contrast to provincial Shillington girls, she was cosmopolitan. Her father, an army chaplain with the rank of colonel, was posted to several places, so his daughter was educated in different schools. Finally, he placed her with his Shillington parents and enrolled her in Shillington High School. Updike, who imagined himself destined to live in New York, must have felt far more comfortable with her.

Like Updike, Nancy Wolf was an intellectually gifted only child who grew up with grandparents, and both adolescents were intellectually gifted. Like Updike, she was well spoken, to the consternation of some classmates. Joan Borner recalled that Nancy Wolf spoke so "intelligently" that Joan "couldn't hold a conversation" with her. Like Updike, as her *Hi-Life 1951*caption noted, Nancy Wolf led a very busy life. Her interests and Updike's often placed them together. *Hi-Life 1950* notes they were members of Amulet (the honor society), associate editors of *Chatterbox*, and cast participants in plays written by Updike. It may also be worth considering that Nancy Wolf, a quiet, bright, "matronly" girl may have suggested comparisons in Updike's mind to his mother. For whatever reason, they became close in their senior year, and perhaps the attachment became more important because their families disapproved. His mother pressured him to dissolve the relationship, fearing she would mire him in Shillington, which she "despised." Although Updike loved Shillington, writing that his "being" was there, he knew his mother was right. So he gave up his sweetheart, but she made a mark on him. To him, Nancy Wolf may have represented the world of Manhattan he perceived in the pages of *The New Yorker*. In fact, as will be shown in a later chapter, she may have even appeared in *The New Yorker* in various guises in his stories.

So Barbara Hartz must have been right in thinking that Updike "seemed to like her a lot." Such speculation is bolstered by one of Nancy Wolf's daughters, Lisa Jauss Peters, who explained that a "deep relationship" did exist between them, possibly leading to an engagement. Mrs. Peters feels that Updike's parents (his mother, particularly) may have felt that Nancy Wolf was not suitable for Updike. Although their relationship dissolved late in his last year in school (perhaps explaining why he wasn't at the senior prom?) and ended by the time Updike enrolled at Harvard and she at Lebanon Valley College, they corresponded for a while and so remained connected even after Updike married in 1953 and she in 1955 (Lisa Jauss Peters, telephone interview with Author 12 Aug. 2009). As late as 1990, Updike inquired about her intention to attend a reunion. Since he couldn't be there, he asked Joan Venne, a bit mysteriously, to give Nancy Wolf his love, if she "shows up with her married name"(JVYC, 6 Aug. 1990).

Updike's literary uses of girls he knew in school needs further investigation, but the fact that Peggy Lutz and Nancy Wolf inspired him suggests that the seeds of other female characters can be traced to his first acquaintance with other women. The vivacity of Peggy Lutz can be discovered in Alma Wilmot (*In the Beauty of the Lilies*); the artistic ability of Jackie Hirneisen in Hope Chafetz (*Seek My Face*); the spiritual seeking of cellist Ann Weik in Jane Smart (*The Witches of Eastwick*); and the multiple talents of Janice Angstrom (*Rabbit Angstrom*) in Joan Venne.[6] They were the first, and he did not forget them.[7]

NOTES

1. In her 1965 interview with Joan George Zug, Ellen Sulkis wrote that Updike took her to the senior prom, but she dated Updike to the junior prom, according to Larry Yocum. As for the senior prom, only Joan Venne of the classmates interviewed in 2009 remember him being there, and as president of the senior class he would have been unmistakable. Yet it is nearly certain that in his senior year he did not go to the prom, not even with Nancy Wolf, a junior he had dated all year. Ellen Sulkis also noted that Joan George was described as "peppy" in the 1950 *Hi-Life* (10), but the *Hi-Life* caption does not use that word, as the transcription of it in Appendix D shows. However, Peggy Lutz is so described not only in her caption but also in Updike's poem, "Peggy Lutz, Fred Muth" (*Endpoint* 26). Joan George was given the nickname,

"Pudge," and a similar nickname was assigned to Peggy Lutz. As Updike remarked in "The Dogwood Tree" about a girl nicknamed "Pug," "Everything I did in grammar school was meant to catch her attention," a clear reference to Peggy Lutz (*AP* 168).

2. A similar debating trip in "Flight" takes place in the fall of Allen Dow's senior year. During their stay at the competing school, Allen and Molly dance and kiss innocently. Allen's mother recognizes this as possibly leading to a hasty marriage and intervenes (*ES* [52]–66). Updike gives the story autobiographical resonance when he includes aspects of it in his memoir (*SC* 37–39).

3. In "Elsie by Starlight," David Kern and Elsie strip but decide against intercourse because they are realistic enough to know they will never marry. Elsie wants to give her virginity to her husband and David fears that entanglement with a local girl will interfere with his career (*Villages* 61–77).

4. Updike may have modeled the character "Queenie" of his most famous story, "A & P," on the former May Queen: "Queenie," = "Queen" (*ES* [596]–601). Also, comments in a memoir about her recur in his fiction. For example, Updike wrote in "The Dogwood Tree" about a girl nicknamed "Pug," (no doubt Peggy Lutz), "My love for that girl carries through all those elementary-school cloakrooms" (*AP* 168), and David Kern uses similar words to describe his feelings for Sandra Bachmann: "his love for her had been born in Kindergarten . . . it was impervious to bodily change" ("The Road Home" *MFT* 186).

5. Peggy Lutz became a nurse, had two boys and two girls, and moved to Delaware, where *In the Beauty of the Lilies* is set. Was she the model for film star Alma Wilmot? Was she the inspiration for nurse Annabelle of *Rabbit at Rest* and *Rabbit Remembered*? Peggy Lutz recurred in Updike's creation of fictional women.

6. Updike used at least one female teacher for inspiration. He told Thelma Kutch Lewis that he thought she resembled Thelma Harrison, Ronnie Harrison's wife and Rabbit Angstrom's mistress in *Rabbit Is Rich* and *Rabbit at Rest*. Mrs. Lewis was not pleased, perhaps because she did not grasp that Updike often made composites of people he knew, not literal records.

7. John Updike is among very few male writers of American fiction who have been able to inquire deeply into the nature of women within a masculine-centered culture. They were brewed in Updike's creative cauldron from some women he had known in his adolescence.

SEVEN

Chatterbox: Cartooning and Drawing

CARTOONING

"Have I ever loved a human being as purely as I loved Mickey Mouse?" Updike asked rhetorically in his memoir (*SC* 256). This may be no exaggeration, since his experience with the fabled cartoon character appeared to set him on the road to cartooning and then to writing. Even before he could draw, Updike was excited by Disney films for their design and style. His parents took him to Disney films from the time he was three, and he saw *Snow White* (released, December 21, 1937) when he was five (*DC* 619). He also saw (at least) *Bambi* and *Make Mine Music*, but only Mickey Mouse would leap from the screen in an explosion of delight, and Updike wrote an essay to try to explain the cartoon character's "mystery" (*IBL* 243; *MM* 202–10).[1] He found a link between the Mickey Mouse animated films and the cartooning that occupied so much of his creativity. For Updike, the panels of the cartoons were "like a separate door into the same magical large room" (*MM* 787). He told a correspondent (facetiously?)that his fiction relied on Disney.[2] In high school he decided he wanted to do animation for Walt Disney, and he chose Harvard because the Harvard *Lampoon* could provide an opportunity to refine his drawing. Fortunately, Updike's dream never materialized.

In the opinion of Harlan Boyer, Updike had an innate gift for cartooning. "I don't think he learned it from anyone. I think it came from John." He may be right, since neither his parents nor grandparents worked in any of the graphic arts.[3] Updike was precocious in learning how to draw. As soon as he could grip a pencil, drawing made him a "rapturous child" (*PP* 33). Sometimes his mother joined him, and in 1937 they completed a coloring book filled with images (DUC). That same year he published in *Children's Activities* a drawing of a jack-in-the-box that had to be cut out and arranged as a puzzle (Hagan 57). When he was about six his eager pen copied the Philadelphia newspaper cartoons, such as "Popeye," "Alley Oop," "Barney Google," "Dagwood," and "Dick Tracy" (*SC* 105–6; *MM* 788). He explained his lifelong devotion to cartoons: "I can't remember the moment when I fell in love with cartoons . . . their faces so curiously amalgamated of human and animal elements, that drew me . . . into a world where my parents and other grownups were strangers" (*MM* 787–88).Cartooning was a private, alternate world.

Updike's early enthusiasm for drawing came from two sources: cartoon-rich magazines and newspapers, and his training with the local artist Clint Shilling. In 1939, after his grandfather's cataract operation, Updike read newspaper cartoons to him (*OJ* 3), and the budding cartoonist was deeply stirred by the pictures he saw in the local newspapers. Updike made the startling remark that, "Illustrations affected me more strongly than reality" (*SC* 8). For him, drawing was a "pre-pubescent inkling of cartoon bliss" in which reality "always seemed a little thin" (*MM* 787).

No doubt his childhood love of Mickey Mouse and his exposure to "Little Orphan Annie" and other cartoon strips accompanied his desire to draw. As adolescence approached, his fervor for consecutive square panels with words inside "talk balloons" stimulated his decision to concentrate on drawing one-panel cartoons for *The Little Shilling* and *Chatterbox*. He collected these in scrapbooks and later had his *Chatterbox* drawings bound, just as he had bound his *New Yorkers*.[4] Barry Nelson also collected those cartoons and kept them for sixty years. Jackie Hirneisen kept a drawing Updike had done when he was ten, explaining, "I don't know why, but I just couldn't part with it." Barbara Hartz treasures an Updike cartoon that *The Saturday Evening Post* rejected.

He steeped himself in the more sophisticated drawings in the slick magazines, *Collier's*, *The Saturday Evening Post*, *Liberty*, and, especially, *The New Yorker*; memorizing the styles of the artists. He amazed his friends at Ibach's drug store by swiftly identifying the artist of every cartoon glimpsed by him, even when the drawings were held upside down. Updike could easily spot the work of Gardner Rea, Chon Day, Garrett Price, and John Ruge (*SC* 19, 107).

In 1944, Wesley Updike's sister Mary gave his family a subscription to *The New Yorker*, and Updike enjoyed everything about it, from font to format, and he particularly liked the "spot drawings" within the columns of type. These graphics included the work of Abe Birnbaum, James Thurber, and Edna Eicke. Though Updike admitted he grew up, "within *New Yorker* cartoons," (*MM* 787) the magazine never accepted his own spot drawings (*SC* 107).

This did not deter him. He asked artists like Thurber and Saul Steinberg for original drawings, and Thurber sent him a dog sketch, which Updike hung on his office wall in Ipswich. It stayed there for many years

(Plath 164). Steinberg sent him two inscribed drawings, one for his sixtieth birthday (*DC* 608). On September 6, 1947, Updike asked Milton Caniff, creator of "Terry and the Pirates" and "Steve Canyon," to send one, sweetening the request by calling him a great cartoonist.[5] In 1948 Updike wrote a fan letter to Harold Gray, the creator of "Little Orphan Annie," calling it, "my favorite comic strip." Updike astutely celebrated the cartoonist's draughtmanship, clarity of his drawing, and treatment of light and shadow, which were "as artistic as you can get." When he saw the letter years afterward, Updike was slightly embarrassed at "shamelessly courting the venerable Harold Gray" (Heer).[6]

Updike routinely stayed after school to draw cartoons. He found cutting his drawings into the blue mimeograph paper a satisfying task, since he was deft with pencils, knives, and the coated mimeo paper (*SC* 16).[7] When he was about twelve, Mrs. Eisenberg, *The Little Shilling*'s advisor, selected Updike as one of the art directors. In his first year at Shillington High School, he became a member of the *Chatterbox* staff. One of his cartoons was given the entire cover to depict a disgruntled fledgling on a branch who watches falling raindrops that postpone its first flight (*Chatterbox* 29 May 1944).[8] That would be followed by a drawing of basketball players (30 Nov. 1945). Updike was initially assigned to the sports page, and he drew nearly thirty cartoons of basketball players and other sportsmen. His first such graphic shows rather static figures with "S" and "F" (for Shillington and Fleetwood High Schools) competing for a basketball held aloft by a muscular figure from the Shillington team (30 Nov. 1945). According to the account below the drawing, Shillington emerged victorious. Updike had used scale to stress the greatness of his school's team.

The pages of *Chatterbox* are sprinkled liberally with his drawings that were later called "wonky" by his friends. As the football team goes winless, he finds whimsical ways to reveal the ineffectiveness of the team which didn't score until the third game. A huge footballer's cleats hover dangerously over a tiny prostrate figure. But when Shillington High wins a game, a helmeted hen cackles and lays a happy egg. Updike's caption explains that the hen's cackle meant that this was the first win of the year. Gradually he learned to give his figures life and movement, evident in each *Chatterbox* drawing of every football game. Or, again, a baseball player is shown catching one ball but dropping two others to demonstrate how the team won one game but lost two. The player is cleverly encircled by a huge baseball glove (21 May 1948). Updike's characters were drawn with simple lines and little detail, allowing the images to speak without clutter. No doubt his intentions would have been clear to any reader, since the modesty of the drawings, as Barry Nelson said, "sketched the themes of pride and victory and of gloom and doom, as such were the performances of the Speedboy athletes throughout the year" (Nelson JUSHS 1).

Not all his drawings highlighted sports, though. Updike's cover page for Valentine's Day, 1947, reveals the smile on Cupid's face as he shoots an arrow at a fellow who eyes a passing girl. Another of his Valentine's Day covers shows a smiling clock watching as a young student shyly presents a valentine to a blushing girl (13 Feb. 1948). In another full-page drawing from 1948, Updike used comical stick figures with various musical instruments which surround a band program, with a conductor spanning the stage as he conducts students who disclose their receptiveness by their wide eyes, mere circles with various marks. At the page's foot, a janitor sweeps away discarded musical notes, an amusing touch.[9] Updike knew his audience appreciated witty drawings, and he supplied them in abundance.

Updike could create entertaining drawings on any subject for *Chatterbox*. He could caricature luminaries and friends. He skillfully depicted President George Washington in a few strokes, and he showed President Franklin Roosevelt giving one of his radio addresses, attended by his apparently sleepy dog, Fala (30 Jan. 1948). Updike's delightful Santa Claus hides his face behind his beard and moustache (6 Jan. 1950). Naturally, he caricatured his friends. These are affectionately satirical. Updike drew the likenesses of senior officers, including Fred Muth, Peggy Lutz, and Ann Weik. He did not overlook himself, and his self-portraits are revealing. One shows him in three-quarter profile as a long-jawed, glasses-wearing, acne-spotted, big-eared class president.[10]

By the time he graduated, Updike had developed an unmistakable style, and Barry Nelson said that Updike hardly needed to initial his work since, "As soon as you saw it you knew it was his . . . his style was as familiar [and] . . . as identifiable as Norman Rockwell's paintings" (Nelson6).[11] Not surprisingly, his classmates recalled Updike's cartooning with relish. Sports star Bob Daubert said that Updike's cartoons were "better than the cartoons you read in the paper." Updike's fidelity for putting line to likeness made it easy for Jimmy Trexler to identify himself as "the guy with the long chin." (Some, according to Marvin Waid, "were risqué," though such drawings have not been seen.) Carlton Boyer noted, "John could have become a very successful cartoonist instead of a writer," and Benny Palm concurred, believing that "in his heart he was a cartoonist" (Miller). These compliments may have been paid because of the immediate effect of cartoons compared to Updike's prose and poetry. Updike's classmates immediately responded to his gifts, and they looked forward to the next *Chatterbox* for more installments of his graphic skill. Some are still convinced that his cartoons were accepted by *The Saturday Evening Post* and *Collier's*, though none have been discovered. He received rejection slips from *The New Yorker*, but undaunted, signed them and gave them to friends. The fact that the rumors of his publication persist, though, testifies to their belief in Updike's remarkable artistic ability. Updike created his own "publication" by having his cartoons bound to look like the Reading Public Library's volumes of magazines. Updike's volume of cartoons was, so to speak, the first of more than sixty books he would produce (*OJ*837).

For the 1950 Shillington High School yearbook, Updike included a great number of drawings and designed the cover (TKL/DSC, Letter to David Silcox, 28 Oct. 2004). He sketched twenty-four cartoons for organizations, sports teams, and class plays. To make his work look professional, Updike worked with pen and ink on drawing paper. Done in bold lines, the caricatures accompanied all sports. His baseball player, wielding an oversized bat, was a left-handed hitter. (Did he have lefty Ted Williams in mind?) Two figures decorate the twenty-one pages dedicated to senior pictures: on the upper corners of the even-numbered pages, a graduate in cap and gown clutches a diploma and strides away from a weeping schoolhouse as the sun emerges from a cloud; and on the lower-right corner of the odd-numbered pages, the "world" runs toward him (despite its bandaged foot) with a welcome sign. The planet's head is stuccoed with bandages. Besides all of the drawings, Updike's presence in the yearbook was pervasive: his photo appears six times, most attractively as the class president; and he penned a farewell, the class song, and the "Footnote to the Future." As Shirley Smith, a *Hi-Life* staff member, said, "All I did was type copy. John practically did the whole yearbook." Yet this does not indicate that he wrote the captions of his classmates.

For the senior issue of *Chatterbox*, Updike composed a full-page drawing showing a worried graduate thinking about the trouble ahead (the atom bomb and the Korean war). But in his last editorial, Updike attested that the seniors had the fortitude to overcome these tests. This was a clever and amusing way for Updike to subtly inject a comment upon current political situations, while depicting the confidence of the students and the enthusiasm with which they welcomed the solving of world problems. In 2005 he told Joan Venne that their school was one "whose like we shall not see again." No other school could be "harder" to leave, Updike declared.

FORMAL TRAINING

While Updike was still in kindergarten, his mother persuaded artist Clint Shilling, grandson of the town's founder, Samuel Shilling, to provide painting lessons. A painter and sculptor, Shilling specialized in mural painting. He had done drawings based on his experiences in the Mexican border campaign of 1916–1917 against Pancho Villa, and during World War I. Shilling had earned an international reputation as an art restorer, and he worked on the renewal of the Reading Museum (*SC* 21). Since Clint Shilling lived across Philadelphia Avenue from the Updikes, they must have met informally many times. Updike honored him by describing one of his lessons to his "Kindergarten eyes" in his memoir and by noting his importance to his development in his philosophical poem "Midpoint" (*SCn*21; *CP* 66). Barbara Hartz felt that Shilling took Updike "under his wing" during his high school years and showed him his own "great big oils."

Updike's talent became refined under the tutelage of Carlton F. Boyer in Shillington High art class. Carlton Boyer had students work in different media, from charcoal to oils, but when he taught cartooning Joan Venne could see that Updike preferred to draw. Benny Palm explained that the teacher would bring Updike's cartoons into class and "they'd do critiques and then he'd redo it." Barbara Hartz thought that Carlton Boyer treated Updike "pretty special. I always thought, and Mr. Boyer too, that John was a very good artist."

Notice of his talent spread beyond Berks County. According to Joan Venne, Updike had art shows "quite frequently" wherever Carlton Boyer had influence, such as Wanamaker's Department Store, one of the first in the country to sponsor student art exhibits. Art students from the eleventh and twelfth grades took the train from Reading to see the shows, Joan Venne sometimes sitting next to Updike. Though Nancy March Le Van won the senior art award instead of Updike, she admitted that his cartoons were more deserving, and so did Barbara Palm, who insisted Updike's "WAS the best." He received "An Achievement Key" in Philadelphia on January 21, 1948. On February 15, 1950, he won an award for the best cartoon in the Scholastic Regional Exhibition of Art at Gimbel Brothers in Philadelphia. During this program he gave a talk about five distinctive types of art students.[12] Perhaps unsurprisingly, Updike was not just drawing, but painting in oils, putting into practice what he learned from Clint Shilling and Carlton Boyer.

POETRY AND DRAWING

Since Updike had seen language combined with drawing in Big Little Books and the stories of James Thurber, it was natural for him to blend drawing and poetry. The impact of drawing upon his poetry is seen most skillfully in a *Chatterbox* poem-with-drawing, "Ode on a Pin Ball Machine." On the same page two drawings depict a disconsolate boy in short sleeves looking at an empty bag with the words "tilt" in several styles surrounding him. But in another drawing above the ode the same boy sports wide-mouthed glee as he drags huge bags marked "nickels." The drawings stand right and left, top and bottom of a twenty-eight-line poem describing how the boy wins game after game. Updike was an avid player, and, as Barry Nelson points out, "He scored very well, often scoring enough points to win free games, so ten or fifteen cents kept him going for a long time. This certainly made him popular with the pinball crowd . . . Playing the pinball machine ranked next to his love for shoot-ing baskets at a net back of the high school" (Nelson JUSHS 4). The poem and drawings suggest that the pinball machine is a stand-in for congenial company (14 Apr. 1950: 10).[13]

Another poem, "Frank Advice to a Young Poet," counsels an early death as best for poetic immortality, and he illustrates this idea not only by indicating young poets like Byron and Keats who are considered greater than the elderly, but he also provides drawings of elderly writers like George Bernard Shaw (12 May 1950: 22). As a bonus, then, the draw-ing provides some insight into young Updike's literary taste. These drawings could probably not be effective on their own, as those accompa-nying "Ode on a Pin Ball Machine," so the integration of the illustrations with the poem was essential in "Frank Advice to a Young Poet."

Updike might have hoped to catch Disney's eye by gathering awards for his cartoons, editing the Harvard *Lampoon,* and placing drawings in various magazines.[14] But perhaps he had gathered too many rejection slips. More likely, as Joan Venne guessed, "When he learned what real cartoons and cartoonists were like he couldn't plan to be a cartoonist." Of more importance, probably, was his realization that he wanted to write more than draw, a decision made easier by *The New Yorker* accepting a story in 1954, "Friends from Philadelphia." By the late 1950s he had given up any plans of becoming a cartoonist, and by 1968 he didn't even doo-dle, and he described this as "a sadness" for him (Plath 24). Yet Updike still enjoyed drawing, sometimes replying to a request for an autograph with an inscription accompanied by a small illustration, and late in his life he drew original Christmas cards for friends. He sent Joan Venne one in 1995 with a picture of Santa Claus and a note expressing his pride in demonstrating he could still draw (JVYC, 22 Dec. 1995). He drew a fine Santa for a University of South Carolina appearance.[15]

As he declared in "The Dogwood Tree," the pencil enabled him to bring into existence what had not been there before and to ride his pencil line "into an infinity of unseen and even unborn hearts" (*AP* 185). He never lost his faith in that possibility. His art began as a child's doodling and was honed in the schools of Shillington.[16] His cartoonist's pencil would be laid aside for the writer's pen, but it is likely that this experi-ence with the visual arts helped to shape his writing style, described as "painterly" by several critics (Broer 209).[17]

NOTES

1. Updike praised Disney (along with Barth and Vermeer) for "dissolving Goofy's stride/ Into successive stills our eyes elide" ("Midpoint" *CP* 96). He discovered in Mickey Mouse's ears the "ideal realm" of "pure signs, of alphabets and trademarks" (MM 202). An enormous number of Disney films were produced between 1935 and 1950, many no doubt seen by Updike. Updike was given a Mickey Mouse bank after

winning a spelling bee in the third grade; the winning word was "lonely" (*SC* 150; *DC* 25). A *Chatterbox* item proclaimed him heir to the master animator (7 Mar. 1947:3). Mickey Mouse was an important part of the popular culture, along with coloring books and movies that made Updike catch "the bug" as "another would-be practitioner in the arts" (*OJ* 87). As a resourceful, basically good "Thirties proletariat" who symbolized America—"plucky, put-upon, inventive, resilient, good-natured, game" (*MM*, 204–205, 209). Little cause to wonder why Updike cried when he lost his "playmate" due to a need to conserve paper during World War II. After the war, Updike felt that animation by Disney, MGM, or Warner Brothers never really produced work of Disney's pre-war quality (*DC* 619–20).

2. Letter to Richard Davison in "Brief Encounters with Updike." *John Updike Remembered*. Ed. Jack De Bellis. Tuscaloosa, Alabama: U of Alabama P, date to be announced.

3. Updike's artistic sense, along with that of his first wife, artist Mary Pennington, was passed on to his children. Miranda is a painter, Elizabeth is an artist and art teacher, David is a writer and photographer, and Michael is a sculptor, designer of tableware, and maker of Updike's tombstone in Plow cemetery.

4. This collecting instinct served him well when he preserved all phases of the composition of his poems, stories, essays, and books, from first inception (notes for *Couples* were written in church) through tear sheets, proofs, and finished and even reprinted work. This permitted him to make corrections for later printings, and it enabled him to amass quickly his poetry, essays, and fiction into omnibus editions. Unfortunately, and to the consternation of librarians and collectors, he thriftily reused the computer disks on which he wrote his novels in the 1990s.

5. Jeet Heer suggests that the impact of Caniff is traceable to descriptions of China in *The Widows of Eastwick* ("Updike and Caniff" 10 Feb. 2009. Blog).

6. "Spiderman" was the only comic strip Updike read late into life (*SC* 255), and he complained when *The Boston Globe* considered cutting the cartoon. "CUT THE UN-FUNNY COMICS, NOT 'SPIDERMAN,'" he demanded (Letter to *The Boston Globe*, 27 Oct. 1994).

"Bech Noir" is a rare instance of Updike parodying cartoon characters, blending Henry Bech and Rachel "Robin" Teagarten to Spiderman and Batman's partner, Robin. Updike noted, "Robin, like Spiderman's wife, Mary Jane, worked in a computer emporium" (*Bay* 152–209). Updike's fellow cartoonists took him seriously enough to give him an award, the National Cartoonists Society's ACE Award for "Amateur Cartoonist Extraordinary" (Astor 36).

Updike made an unusual television appearance as the voice of an animated caricature of himself. In the November 12, 1999, season 12 episode of *The Simpsons* ("Insane Clown Poppy"), Krusty the Clown plugs his children's book, *Your Shoe's Too Big to Kickbox God*. The book had been ghost-written for Krusty by John Updike to inflate the book's sale. Updike, with one sentence in his own voice, supports the clown's story. Updike could certainly take a joke, since the writers suggested that his extraordinary creative activity even admitted time for ghost-writing.

7. He describes this process in detail in the story, "A Sense of Shelter" (*ES* [41]–51).

8. Seen in retrospect, the image connects to other uses of the motif of flight and its impediments found in Updike's story "Flight," the novels of the "Rabbit" saga, *SC.*, and *Terrorist*, among others.

9. Interestingly, the same image of a janitor sweeping up notes was used in the syndicated "Peanuts" cartoon strip, August 29, 2011.

10. About twenty years later, Updike drew a full-face self-portrait, with his nose beakishly elongated and his eyes thrust to the top of his head. The illustration is zany and grim (*DLBD* 267). Another self-portrait once again features a deformity. Retaining the large-eared, hawk-nosed earlier likeness, he portrayed his always troublesome teeth with his name upsidedown in bold type. While suggesting that every word Updike uttered found its way into print, the drawing seems sinister. But it also disarms those who knew he had continuous problems with his teeth. The image is quite

unlike the self-amused portrait he created for *Chatterbox* (Britton 8).Both drawings are clever, with extended lines and attention to eyes. Another, more conventional, school drawing was chosen to be the John Updike Society membership pin (*The Paris Review* 45 [Wint. 1968]:85).
The artist David Levine did many caricatures of Updike from photographs, all, of course, focusing on an unusual physical trait and usually related to an Updike novel.

11. Updike applauded the work of Norman Rockwell ("Seeing Norman Rockwell." *The Wilson Quarterly* 15 [Spring 1991]: 136).

12. After graduating from Harvard, Updike studied painting at the Ruskin School for Drawing and Fine Art in Oxford, and he was so proud of this, that this notice appears in all brief biographies attached to his books and dust jackets. Mary, Updike's first wife, has retained several photos of his paintings, including a portrait of her. She, in turn, did drawings of him, one of which is in the Linda Grace Hoyer collection in the Reading Public Library.

13. In *The Centaur* one of Peter Caldwell's "idols," Johnny Dedman (inspired by Charlie McComsey?), repeatedly wins free pinball games (122).

14. Updike did place four drawings in *The New Yorker* attached to four of his essays, but he never published a stand-alone cartoon there.

15. The Santa appeared on the exhibition catalog of Donald Greiner's Updike collection at the Thomas Cooper Library, University of South Carolina, November, 1998–1999; Updike attached a talk balloon to Santa's lips, saying, "Yes, you may display me! Ho Ho!!" Ample evidence of Updike's talent is revealed in the delightful jesters adorning a dozen poems reprinted from the Harvard *Lampoon* in his *Jester's Dozen*. In 1996 Updike published thirty-nine drawings in one magazine ("Reminiscences of My Cartoons." *Hogan's Alley* Spring 1996:124–34; *MM* 787–89).

16. Updike always admired artists who verged on cartooning, like Arnold Roth, who did the three cover illustrations for the Henry Bech books. Updike wrote introductions to books of drawings by David Levine, Saul Steinberg, Arnold Roth, Ralph Barton, Al Capp, and William Steig. He reviewed exhibits by Roy Lichtenstein, a show of celebrity caricatures, and an installation of *New Yorker* cartoons (*PP*3–7, 80–82; *MM*210–13, 740–49; *JL* 131–53). As late as 2004, Updike published an essay on James Thurber for *Cartoon America*. His novels contain remarks on Captain Marvel (*In the Beauty of the Lilies*) and *Apartment 3-G* (*Rabbit Redux*).

17. The impact of drawing upon his poetry is also seen in his "shaped poems," in which the poem's form resembles its subject. Shaped poetry interested Updike because it enabled him to use the printed page's space imaginatively, as in "Nutcracker," "Letter Slot," and "Pendulum" (*CH* 70–82). "Nutcracker" includes the word "nut" within its jaws, and Updike said that it was as good "in its way" as the seventeenth-century poet George Herbert's "Angel's Wings" (Interview Plath 24). Updike even improved these three poems' appearances when they were reprinted in *Hoping for a Hoopoe* (1959), *Verse* (1965), and *Carpentered Hen* (1982). These poems were included in the author's exhibit of "Visual Poetry" (Jack De Bellis, curator. Lehigh University, May 1978). Updike told the author that he admired the shaped poems of John Hollander.

Updike's autobiographical poem "Midpoint" gave the eye a "treat," as he said, not only by altering the size and appearance of type, but also by including photographs enlarged so that the white and black dots ("benday" dots) comprising the pictures became part of the photo (*CP* 72–77, 86–95). As a result, the reader is acutely aware of the artificiality of the representations of the world—and this creates what the speaker calls an "eye/I" pun, in which the viewpoint creates the world. Updike supplied a paragraph about the letter "V" as a companion to David Hockney's illustration of that letter.

EIGHT

Chatterbox: Poetry and Prose

POETRY

Updike entered Shillington High School in 1946, and by the time he left four years later he had published over three hundred works—drawings, prose, and poetry. Unlike other drawings in the magazine, Updike's show movement, comedy, and daring in the use of the figure and face. A feature story notes, with understatement, that Updike "is good in drawing." It would be no understatement to say that his poetry, essays, reviews, editorials, and fiction for *Chatterbox* are clearly superior and not only already publicized Updike's discovery of his style, especially in poetry, but afforded the magazine a sense of identity as well. The quality and quantity of his work were so superior that in 1948 he received "An Achievement Key" in Philadelphia on January 21, 1948. His *Chatterbox* pieces show the high productivity and polished craft that would characterize the professional writer he would become, and they also disclose in embryo some themes he would later explore. Though this is clearly apprentice work, it foreshadows his polished productions.

Updike could compose poetry on sports, holidays, names of magazines, animals, or newspapers. For example, Updike had a keen interest in the magazines of the day, and in a series of poems he examined *Quick, Newsweek, Vogue, Time, Life, Esquire, The Saturday Evening Post, National Geographic, Colliers,* and, of course, *The New Yorker,* which he rated the best ("The Mags IV–*The New Yorker." Chatterbox* Feb. 17, 1950: [8]). In "The Mags IX–*Quick,*" (21 Apr. 1950: 6), Updike puns on the names of several slicks (21 Apr. 1950 [6]). He wrote poems of praise, apology, morality, and the weather. His work is imaginative, humorous, and written with obvious enthusiasm.

At the same time that he decorated his "Ode on a Pin Ball Machine" with witty, thematic illustrations, he was developing an enthusiasm for trying out different poetic forms. As shown in chapter five, Updike enjoyed making clever acrostic structures, in which the first letters of a line read vertically produce clever attacks on a ball club and the senior class. In "To a Serutan" he obviously enjoyed testing his wits in a tour de force, for "To a Serutan" reverses the letters in the words of each line in order to mirror "Serutan," which is "Natures" (or "Nature's") spelled backwards (1 Apr. 1950: 2).[1] Clearly, Updike's facility with rhyme and structure shows ingenuity and an eager inventiveness.

Updike was quick to adopt the methods of his favorite poets from *The New Yorker*—Ogden Nash, James Thurber, Roger Angell, and Don Marquis. Acknowledging a mentor, Updike titled one poem, "Ballad Before the Newsreel (with a curtsy dropped to Ogden Nash)." He used funny off-rhymes in the manner of Ogden Nash and employed a long suspended line whose eventual rhyme brings the reader a pleasant surprise. Surely reflecting his reading of Nash, is "Child's Question." The child asks whether "q" ever follows "a" in an English word, squirming at the effort. Without realizing it, he hits upon the name of a Middle Eastern country which is also a homonym for his struggle(*Chatterbox* 12 May 1950: 16).[2]

Choosing *New Yorker* writer Roger Angell's "Greetings, Etc." Christmas poem as a model, Updike strews couplets with the names of prominent persons, along with his friends Bill Forry, Barry Nelson, and Fred Muth, as well as literary, film, and political celebrities, like his heroes, E. B. White and Ted Williams ("Greetings, Etc." 6 Jan. 1950: [8]).[3] Other modestly experimental poems in *Chatterbox* feature a ballad in Southern dialect, flanked by two drawings, a solemn description of a Wednesday night church service, and buying shoes. If he was quick to emulate light verse poets he admired, Updike took polite jabs at the poetry of Gertrude Stein, e. e. Cummings, T. S. Eliot, and free verse in general ("It Might be Verse," 7 Jan. 1949: [5]). He could hardly know in 1949 that his books one day would include experimental poems side by side his light verse.[4]

Updike certainly had an ear for the musicality of verse. He describes a solemn Wednesday night church service in Southern dialect. Also, it is impressive to see on the same page "Ode on a Pin Ball Machine" and "Sonnet on Chaucer." The latter ends with a nicely turned compliment to Chaucer's adroit knack for words. Since Updike obviously displays great verbal facility, the compliment is self-reflexive. On the same page as his twenty-eight line mock-ode to pinball, he includes a Petrarchan sonnet praising Chaucer, and the two octave pun-filled series of poems on "The Mags." This single page would be enough to indicate that Updike could embark confidently on a writing career.[5]

When he wrote seriously, Updike could create interesting gradations of tone. With black humor, a page-filling poem, "Frank Advice to a

Young Poet," counsels an early death as a good exchange for fame, pointing out that the short-lived Byron and Keats are considered greater poets than Wordsworth, who lived embarrassingly long. "The Moment Called Now" contains enjambment in nearly every line of the last stanza, as if racing toward the disturbing prison image at the end (20 Jan. 1950: 6). Updike could be deeply serious. As Don Marquis in *archy and mehitabel* had Archy, a roach, type messages on his typewriter, so Updike had a lemming write a letter asking humans why they don't all drown themselves ("From a Lemming,"20 Jan. 1950: [6]). A wicked seriousness characterizes "Laugh, World, Laugh," which promotes the alleged curative power of laughter to assuage the horrors of the Holocaust (28 Jan. 1949: [5]). "The Moment Called Now" captures the fear of time passing with a tone of dread beyond mere adolescent melancholy, similar to the existential anxiety of such early works as "Pigeon Feathers," "The Astronomer," and *Rabbit, Run*.

By his senior year three of his *Chatterbox* poems ("It Might be Verse," "The Season of Mud," and "The Rise and Fall of the Sunday Newspaper") won him the first place award at the Pennsylvania School Press Association (*Chatterbox*11 Nov.1949: [1]). Such success allowed him to anticipate acceptance by Harvard's *Lampoon*. When he published his first book, a collection of light verse, *The Carpentered Hen*, Updike included a high school poem, "Why the Telephone Wires Dip and the Poles are Cracked and Crooked."[6]

PROSE

Updike began publishing prose for his school paper only after he had submitted drawings, and several months before his poetry was accepted. When he was thirteen, "A Handshake with the Congressman" appeared (*Chatterbox* 16 Feb. 1945: [5]), and two years later, as the editorial writer of *Chatterbox*, he churned out editorials, among which were ruminations about why people like the movies and praise for President Franklin Roosevelt. Interestingly, he also wrote an article about Ponce de Leon and the discovery of Florida, a subject which preoccupied his mother but which she left unfinished ("Gentleman from Spain" 4 Apr. 1947: 5).[7] Such literary apprenticeship in non-fiction provided a foundation for the hundreds of essays and reviews Updike would later produce. His obvious passion, though, was reviewing films.

At fourteen he appraised Olivier's *Hamlet*, which he considered so perfect it might never be superseded. He found Shakespeare so cinematographic that it seemed to Updike that he was somehow anticipating the movies ("[Hamlet Reviewed: An orgy of superlatives]" 25 Feb. 1949: 5). He was so sure of his evaluations that he could judge Olivier's co-star Eileen Herlie as only adequate.[8] Such certainty in a boy so young rests in a thoughtfully derived critical sense rather than adolescent egotism. He also reviewed light fare like the Bob Hope, Bing Crosby, Dorothy Lamour vehicle, *Road to Utopia*, which he found "silly" ("*The Road to Utopia*," 10 May 1946: [10]). He judged the music in *The Kid from Brooklyn* as passable, but applauded Danny Kaye's flexible face and gave a prize to Jimmy Durante. Reviewing *The Big Sleep*, Updike characterized the mutual attraction of Lauren Bacall and Humphrey Bogart as going together like the food on a well-known breakfast platter. Their eyeing each other could "blind an old, well-seasoned potato" ("The Big Sleep." 25 Oct. 1946: 5). In an editorial, he lobbied, unsuccessfully, for the use of movies to supplement school assembly meetings.[9]

With his drawing, poetry, essays, and school activities taking most of his time, it is a wonder that Updike had time to read, but when he did he plunged into murder mysteries. Such reading must have prompted him to try his own hand at a thriller in 1946, though he left it incomplete (Mandelbaum 469).[10] Very much influenced by his success in writing light verse, his thriller for *Chatterbox* is an entertaining parody. In four installments, Updike traces how a Chinese detective, Sing Hoo, works ("Sing Hoo's Last Case," *Chatterbox* various dates 1947). In essays for the magazine, Updike warned that the murderer is usually someone least suspected, and that that the hero will survive and society will be restored ("Whodun It?"12 Nov. 1948: 5).[11]

In the last issue of the 1950 student paper, Updike declared that his *Chatterbox* work had been stimulating and enjoyable (Nelson [9–10]). He bid goodbye with his usual modesty. In evaluating the quantity and quality of Updike's work for *Chatterbox*, Barry Nelson, who won the Olympus award as a scholar-athlete, said of Updike, "The time and talent he invested in the school paper easily matched the efforts of a three-sport superstar" (Nelson JUSHS[7]). Such energy and discipline would drive Updike for the next fifty-nine years.

NOTES

1. "The Jack Benny Radio Show" 1944–1945 season created jokes about Serutan, at one point offering "Sdrawrof Cream." "Sdrawrof" spelled backwards is "forwards." Updike might well have heard the program.

2. The May 23, 1950, *Chatterbox* announced that the poem would be published in *Annual Anthology of High School Poetry*.

3. Four years later, E. B. White offered Updike a job at *The N ew Yorker*, a magazine that in1960 would publish Updike's essay on Ted Williams, "Hub Fans Bid Kid Adieu."

4. In a review of a book by Max Beerbohm, Updike wrote that rhyme, by making expected, if surprising, effects "eases our everyday seriousness" (*AP* 259). This may explain why Updike's poetry collections always contain light verse. His first book, *The Carpentered Hen* (1958), contains only light verse, and his last book, *Endpoint* (2009), provides a section of light poetry.

5. Later he would dazzle readers by using the outmoded Spenserian stanza in "Dance of the Solids" (*CP* 78–81). He delighted in expanding or mocking the sonnet form ("Spanish Sonnets," *CP* 147–51; "Love Sonnet," *Midpoint* 66).

6. Updike notes that it was written under the influence of science fiction (*HG* 427). The poem has not been seen among contributions to *Chatterbox*.

7. Some articles foreshadow later writing. A piece on "Jackals" anticipates several "People One Knows" for *The New Yorker*. "Cellophane Wrappers" looks forward to Updike's most popular article for *The New Yorker*, "Paranoid Packaging" (*Chatterbox* 2 May 1947:[5]).

8. Ann Weik Cassar reports, "I remember studying *Hamlet*, probably in Mrs. Schrack's 11th grade class. . . . We did *Merchant of Venice* in 9th grade, probably *Julius Caesar* in 10th, and *Macbeth* in 12th" (Ann Weik Cassar. Letter to the author, 23 Nov. 2009).

9. As with so many of his other youthful diversions, Updike's love for the movies would later lead him to write essays on film personalities like his favorite, Doris Day ("Suzie Creamcheese Speaks" *HS* 791–801). In many poems and novels Updike alludes to films and movie personalities. He even considered transforming a few of his novels into screenplays (De Bellis *Encyclopedia* 173–77, [501]–11).

10. When the website *Amazon.com* suggested in 1998 that Updike begin a work of his choosing on the internet and have contestants offer segments that would continue it, he chose to write the first chapter of a detective story, "Murder Makes the Magazine" (*MM* 835–38). Nine years later Updike brought to a boil his simmering interest in thrillers with *Terrorist* (2006), and the Chinese detective was transformed into a Muslim fanatic, and the humor into tragedy.

11. Later, Updike would write novels and stories with thriller elements—*The Coup*, *The Witches of Eastwick*, *Brazil*, *Gertrude and Claudius*, and "Bech Noir," for example—apart from his greatest success in this genre, *Terrorist*. In all of these the hero survives and society is restored.

NINE

Inspirations and Models

Although Updike told an interviewer that a "submerged thread" of auto-biography ran through his work, he also insisted, somewhat defiantly, "I disavow any essential connection between my life and whatever I write" (Plath 27).[1] Embracing the anonymity of the author, he proclaimed, "My life is . . . only that of which the residue is my writing" (Plath 31). Up-

Figure 9.1. *At a party at Dick Manderbach's home, possibly December 29, 1952. Updike sits on the floor. From left to right: Dick Manderbach, Mahlon Frankhauser, Fred Muth, Bill Forry, Updike, and Janet Hettinger.*

dike's use of his own experiences as the ground for his work is incontestably significant for the classmates, since it adds a level of enjoyment and understanding. They would discuss with one another the possible models for Penny of *The Centaur*, Nora of "A Soft Spring Night in Shillington," and, of course, "Rabbit" Angstrom. They turned over virtually every detail concerning the setting, names, places, and people of Updike's fiction. By making such associations, the classmates were thus able to show how Updike often relied upon real people and places as the basis for his creative process. Since they had been students of Wesley Updike, they instantly recognized connections to George Caldwell of *The Centaur*. Barry Nelson produced a systematic study of specific parallels between places in the novel and venues in Shillington (Nelson UT).

Joan Venne Youngerman identified herself as a real participant in Updike's first *New Yorker* story, "Friends from Philadelphia." In that story, the Lutzes decide to send John Nordholm for wine in order to entertain their guests. In reality, Updike's mother's two friends, Karl and Caroline Houck, who lived in Berks County, paid a visit to the Plowville farm. They had known Linda Updike at Ursinus College, and Karl Houck had become a contractor (*DC* 667). Joan Venne was there when these guests arrived in the spring of 1950. She remembers that Updike's parents sent their son to Shillington in his father's Plymouth to get wine, but, since he was only eighteen, Updike was too young to purchase it. So, Joan Venne related, "they went up to my house and asked my father if he would buy it." In the story, John must ask Thelma's father to buy the wine. Joan Venne also recalled that Updike even included the brand of her mother's cigarettes, Herbert Tarrytons (*ES* [34]–40). Updike had compressed the two people into one friend, and moved their home to Philadelphia (*SC* 93).Of minor interest, but instructive for showing how Updike used the names of his friends for his characters, Joan Venne's character is named "Thelma Lutz," probably after two persons Updike knew very well—Mrs. Thelma Kutch Lewis, his playground monitor and high school journalism teacher, and his friend since kindergarten, Peggy Lutz, although "Lutz" was a common Shillington name.

Joan Venne was only one of several students who inspired Updike's characters. As Jackie Hirneisen Kendall said, Updike was kind enough to assure her that she was "the one on whom he created Joan Edison," in "The Alligators" (*ES* [7]–12). Jackie Hirneisen noted, though, that only "70% of this was true," but declined to elaborate. Updike had been in the fifth grade among A-level advanced students when she arrived at Shillington Elementary School. In the story, Joan Edison arrives from Baltimore and a character perhaps based on Updike, Charlie,[2] instantly dislikes her but later comes to love her. His infatuation with Jackie Hirneisen began in his poems to her and his affection continued. In a *Hi-Life* caption Jackie Hirneisen is identified as running "the gamut of adjectives from attractive to zealous." Of course, the literary worth of the story and the character of Joan Edison—that "30%" that "was not true"—resides in Updike's artistry. Tempting as it may be, we should not assume, and I do not, that having found a link to a real person who modeled for a character somehow demonstrates the value of the work. My intention is to reveal the links between living persons and Updike's work, not to explicate it.

One of Updike's best stories, "The Happiest I've Been," was modeled directly upon a classmate's New Year's Eve party held in 1952.[3] As Dick Manderbach explained, it was common for the gang—Updike, Peggy Lutz, Joan Venne, Mary Ann Moyer, Fred Muth, Malon Frankhauser, and Bill Forry—to suddenly say, "Let's have a party at Dick Manderbach's." His tolerant parents were always ready to provide the house, and the gang would dance, drink, and play Ping-Pong. Though the parties elsewhere almost never featured liquor, Dick Manderbach's parties did, since he knew his father kept a bottle of spirits under the attic floorboards and that he never asked if it had been removed, even when he detected some had disappeared. On this particular night, Updike stopped off at Dick Manderbach's with Bill Forry (see fig. 9.1, which may have been taken at that party). After drinking and dancing, Bill Forry's date from Hyde Park fell asleep on Updike's shoulder. Updike and Bill Forry then left for Chicago in a snowstorm, Updike driving his friend's car, while his pal slept. Updike intended to visit Mary Pennington in Chicago and propose marriage. The date of the party would thus appear to be December 29, 1952, since Updike and Mary Pennington were wed in June, 1953.[4]

In the story, Bill Forry becomes Neil Hovey, and Updike is John Nordholm (as in "Friends from Philadelphia"). Updike's given name is undisguised, but his last name suggests his Dutch ancestry, with Nordholm echoing "Norseman." At one point John Nordholm plays Ping-Pong with a girl. They leave the party in his friend's Chrysler bound for Chicago. Drunken Neil Hovey falls asleep, so John Nordholm drives in a blizzard the entire way, knowing that at the end of the trip is a woman who will marry him. The closeness of Updike's and John Nordholm's experiences shows how Updike fictionalized autobiographical material.

But even when Updike projected himself into an imaginary situation he relied upon material from Shillington. Perhaps intended as an attempt to see his father as an idealistic teacher caught in an ambiguous situation, Updike's story "Tomorrow and Tomorrow and So Forth" concerns note-passing in class. Updike possibly witnessed girls passing notes in Mr. Klopp's social science classes. If so, according to Marvin Waid, he would have remembered that Klopp would demand that the recipient read the note, "so we all know what's in it." In the story, Gloria Andrews passes it while students discuss and then recite in turn the Macbeth soliloquy that gives the story its title. Shillington High English teachers relied upon such rote memorization, and, as previously noted, during Bobby Rhoads' interview he suddenly delivered the Macbeth soliloquy from memory. In "Tomorrow and Tomorrow and So Forth," while a student recites, teacher Mark Prosser intercepts the note Gloria Andrews passes to her friend, Peter Forry.[5] (Of course, Peter Forry's name recalls that of Updike's friend Bill Forry, who had appeared in "The Happiest I've Been.") When Prosser reads the note he discovers Gloria's confession of love for him, and he does not read it aloud. Instead, he lectures her after class on love's various meanings, partly because he wishes to discourage her, but he secretly wants to believe her. Even when other instructors reveal that Gloria has lied before, he clings to the memory of her crying when she left the classroom as evidence of her genuine feelings (*ES* [152]–160). The situation resembles another ambiguous scene Updike witnessed in school and recorded in his memoir. When eleven years old and in the sixth grade, Updike was cutting a stencil for *The Little Shilling* when he overheard a conversation of "informal intimacy" between Principal Dickinson and a teacher, Miss Sara Huntzinger. This caused Updike to realize that teachers had a mysterious "after-hours" world (*SC* 16–17). Unlike Prosser, Updike does not dwell on what an eleven year old can't understand, making the boy's naiveté seem preferable to the complexity of adult relationships.

Updike also mined his observations of his family for fictional material. One classmate, Harlan Boyer, witnessed two episodes concerning Updike's father that were incorporated unaltered into *The Centaur*. Harlan Boyer saw the always helpful Wesley Updike assist a student whose car wouldn't start. The teacher "pushed him out the driveway, and where the drive comes out of the alley on State Street it has a crown, and the Buick went into the dip and its bumper went under the kid's back bumper and smashed the grill. That Buick had a smashed grill as long as I ever saw it." In *The Centaur* Updike's father, now named George Caldwell, experiences such rage over the dented grill that he pummels the fictional student with it. Harlan Boyer also noted that Updike told him how his father picked up a hitchhiker, another incident incorporated into *The Centaur* to underline how Wesley Updike's kindness infuriated his son.[6]

Updike often told his classmates at reunions that if he used persons he knew for models, he would blend them with details from other people or from his imagination. In short, he would make composites, merging characteristics of a person with others. Shirley Smith described Updike's practice: "he'd have some character you knew was a person around town, but he'd add one thing that would keep you from identifying the person." This practice no doubt intended to discourage infringement of privacy or even lawsuits. Yet sometimes even with "one thing" added some people could easily identify the actual person who prompted the character. In the case of the persons on whom Updike based "Rabbit" Angstrom, though, the identification eluded the classmates for many years, possibly because Updike preferred to be enigmatic.

So what composites helped to create "Rabbit" Angstrom? At a class reunion Updike, perhaps facetiously, told Jackie Hirneisen Kendall's husband, Carl Kendall, that he himself was the model for "Rabbit," maybe recalling that in high school Joan George had told him, "John, you're definitely a rabbit." Updike had agreed with her, she remembered, adding, "He'd even go around making his nose and ears wiggle"(Sulkis 10). As the chapter on athletics revealed, Updike loved basketball. His vivid descriptions of the feel of the ball and his concrete visualizations of the various shots made by Harry, Mim Angstrom, Skeeter Farnsworth, and "Tiger" in *Rabbit Angstrom* show that Updike retained a kinesthetic memory of basketball long after leaving Shillington. "Rabbit's" animated recounting of the feeling that he can do anything he wants with the basketball, that he is "in the zone," is so convincing that Updike himself might have experienced it (*RA* 58). Yet Updike's *Hi-Life 1950* caption records merely "Basketball 2," so he could hardly have been the exclusive inspiration for the basketball star.

Since Updike's friend Jerry Potts was a star basketball player, it would be reasonable to assume that he modeled for "Rabbit." But Updike told him directly he did not have him in mind. For one thing, Jerry Potts never had the nickname "Rabbit." That name was the moniker of a student in the Shillington High School class of 1948, Richard Hiester. Since Hiester (pronounced "Heaster") naturally prompted his friends to think of Easter rabbits, his nickname was inevitably created. Although Richard Hiester didn't play basketball, "Rabbit" was still apt since he ran track. Updike liked the surname enough to use it in a story, altering the name to "Heister."[7] Finally, Updike identified Bob Arndt as "Rabbit" (Plath xvi), and later broke the news to Jerry Potts (JPC, Letter to Jerry Potts, 20 Feb. 1996).

As he wrote to Jerry Potts, Arndt was a graceful tall player with somnolent eyes, who would be his prime candidate for the prototypical "Rabbit." Updike had a very good chance to see Bob Arndt often. Since Updike's father was the ticket seller for the basketball season of 1947–48, Wesley Updike was allowed two tickets to all the basketball games in Berks County, and Harlan Boyer went along. Together they witnessed the exhilaration of Arndt's play. In the 1946–47 season Bob Arndt amassed 273 points. (Jerry Potts had 209.) Harlan Boyer was not surprised when Updike told him, "I used him as a model of the super athlete," and in 1990 Updike told a reporter that he saw in Arndt a "rabbity" quality (Plath xvi). "Rabbit" Angstrom was thus a composite in Updike's mind of a triad composed of his own experience as a player, a student who was awarded the nickname "Rabbit" because his surname suggested Easter, and Bob Arndt, a star basketball player with "rabbity" grace. The triad struck a chord that has resounded for a long time. Bob Arndt stated that he was "thrilled" to have been made a part of literary immortality, though he disavowed any connection between Rabbit Angstrom and his own life after high school (Bob Arndt to Author Dec. 2010, telephone interview). Rightly so, since Harry "Rabbit" Angstrom has taken his place beside Huckleberry Finn, Jay Gatsby, and Holden Caulfield as an enduring American mythic figure.

Other models Updike used were not intended to draw sly parallels but, as in *The Centaur,* to amuse and even mock. In one instance, Updike mentions a man "who couldn't cut it in medical school and went to dental school," and Dr. Ernie Rothermel, assuming that he was the analogue, "had a fit," according to Shirley Smith who worked for him. Dr. Rothermel may have over-reacted, but some characterizations were too close to be missed. Wesley Updike felt no such compunction about identifying the character he inspired, since, when a friend asked if he was offended by Updike's use of him as a model for George Caldwell in *The Centaur,* he said pointedly, "It's the truth. The kid got me right" (Plath 26).

Updike's use of the imperious supervising principal Charles J. Hemmig as the model in *The Centaur* for the principal Zimmerman (whose mythical analogue in the novel is Zeus) was drawn from reality. According to Bobby Rhoads, Wesley Updike knew that Hemmig, a former girls' basketball coach, would wander into their locker rooms and try to kiss them.[8] Wesley Updike knew that if he were to expose such conduct, his teaching position would be put in jeopardy. His son must have known this too, since *The Centaur* reveals Zeus/Zimmerman seducing a student without fear of detection during one of George Caldwell's lectures. As though issuing a warning to Caldwell, Zimmerman writes Caldwell's obituary in one of the chapters. Updike apparently felt that by ridiculing Charles Hemmig in *The Centaur* he would avenge his father's mistreatment. This literary "ambush" must have seemed the most effective way to protect his father, but by 1963 when the novel was published, Charles Hemmig's failings were well-known. *The Centaur* did not interfere with his winning many awards for community leadership.

Updike apparently enjoyed naming people his friends could identify in his work. In *Self-Consciousness,* he names a great many classmates and teachers. He mentioned watching, as a child, Jerry Potts' sister Mary Jane taking a bath, and he named Jimmy Trexler as the teller of a wartime tall tale (*SC* 38). He combed Fairview Cemetery for names to use in his poem, "A Cemetery High above Shillington" (*Americana* 29–35), and he asked Jerry Potts for help with this project (JPC, 18 Aug. 2008). Updike named Harlan Boyer, his "birthday twin" in "Upon Becoming a Senior Citizen" (*Americana* 29–37). He alerted his friends to the names of real persons he disguised, for example disclosing that he gave one of his teachers, Mrs. Fritz, the fictional name Miss Feitz (JVYC, 19 Nov. 1983).

Since Updike became a virtuoso at portraying women, his classmates naturally wanted to identify the real girls concealed in his work. Updike acknowledged that Georgean Youndt and Jane Becker were used as Julia Reidenhauser and Gloria Gerhartin in the short story, "Lunch Hour" (*LL,* 16–27; JVYC, 11 Mar. 1996).[9] Joan Venne believed that Jouette Eifert was

Elizanne, the girl David Kern kissed in "The Walk with Elizanne" (*MFT* 38–54). Barry Nelson concurred, and he also felt these persons were models in that story: Joan George Zug as Marnie Kauffman, Joan Venne Youngerman as Betty Lou, and James Trexler as Butch Fogel (Barry Nelson, letter to the author, 18 May, 1996). The closely autobiographical "My Father's Tears" suggested to Barry Nelson that "Mr. Wesley's son" was Updike, and Cookie Behn was modeled on Charles McComsey (Barry Nelson, letter to the author, 18 May, 1996). Fred Muth may have inspired the character of Ned Miller in "The Road Home," while Peggy Lutz Roberts might have modeled for Sandra Lang (*MFT* 185–86).

As earlier shown, Updike had Peggy Lutz in mind for "Queenie" in "A & P." She was the senior class May Queen of Shillington High School, and he referred to Peggy Lutz in his memoir as "the queen of girls." Updike admitted — perhaps like Sammy — to loving her "deeply and ineffectually" (*AP* 168).

As chapter five has shown, Updike's feelings for Nancy Wolf were not ineffectual. He alludes to her in several works written from 1958 to 1983 ("The Dogwood Tree" [1962] and *Self-Consciousness* [1989], *The Centaur* [1963] and five short stories). These dates show that for a quarter of a century Nancy Wolfe persisted in Updike's mind. Updike's use of her can be construed from the awakening of love to its failure and its aftermath. In "The Dogwood Tree" Updike recalls an amorous embrace in the woods "when I was seventeen" which nullified the unpleasant walks he had taken with his parents in the same woods (*AP* 159). In a clearly autobiographical short story, "The Blessed Man of Boston, My Grandmother's Thimble, and Fanning Island," the narrator (Updike?) remembers his "delirious" state in preparing for a date with an unnamed girlfriend he had "acquired," with whom he could be somewhat intimate. The context and time suggest the girl was Nancy Wolf (*ES* 96).The other treatments of Updike's romance concentrate on the failure of the relationship from several different directions.

The Centaur shows how a young boy's need for trust develops from sensual love. Although Updike makes Penny an analogue of the goddess Pandora, in a novel redolent of Greek myths it is difficult to miss another analogue: Penny = Penelope, Odysseus's wife and the focus of his journey that makes his travail bearable. In Peter's recurring dream, Penny responds to Peter in the woods, as she had in "The Dogwood Tree." The dream shows him that he loves the girl he had been close to since the fall (*C* 50). Peter describes Penny in sensuous detail: her eyes, eyelids, and nose have a "delicate irresolution" that "held out the possibility of her being worthy of me" (117). And she is quite worthy, for when he entrusts his "secret" to her (his psoriasis), Penny accepts it and thus shows she loves him.

The short story "Flight" focuses on the intervention of outsiders in ending the romance. The narrative takes place in the fall of Allen Dow's senior year (the same time Updike and Nancy Wolf dated) and provides a view of the strain in their relationship (*ES* [52]–66). On a school debating trip, Allen Dow "plays to" Molly Bingaman, a dressy, poised junior. They dance and kiss innocently. The kiss provides him "reassurance" after he loses the debate, as well as the realization that she alone loved him "without advantage." When his mother recognizes that Allen's involvement might spoil his college plans by allowing an infatuation to lead to marriage or worse, he is forced to reject Molly. Updike would remark in an interview that he chose "middleness" to be his subject. Allen Dow certainly suffers for being between his mother's ambition and his sweetheart.

Updike again recounts the breakup in the last pages of the first section of *Self-Consciousness*, but this time he focuses on the fact of separation, not the causes. Updike recalls that "Nora" (Nancy Wolf) gave him "all that a woman does for a man" short of offering her virginity. Yet her "satiny skin and powdered warmth and soft, forgiving voice" were not enough to anchor him to Shillington, and she was well aware of this (*SC* 37–38). Updike recreates the heart-rending moments of their last encounter.

But the story "Elsie by Starlight" (*The New Yorker* 5 July 2004: 80–87) provides a different, erotic, view of the failure of the romance. This story of failed high school love takes place about 1950 since it is "the new half century." Elsie Seidel, a year younger than Owen, resembles Nancy Wolf in three ways: she dresses in the "New Look" style, seems older than she is, and is willing to mold her plump body to his.[10] Though Owen feels she is socially beneath him, he loves her. The sweethearts undress in the car but stop short of intercourse since they realize they have no future.[11]

Though "Elsie by Starlight" was originally published in *The New Yorker*, it was not collected with other stories, but instead was integrated into a novel in 2004 that presents a panorama of relationships (*Villages* 61–77). This may indicate the importance it held for Updike, since he saw how it fit into a larger scheme. When he gave a talk in Philadelphia, a question was asked about the autobiographical aspect of this segment in *Villages*. One classmate in the audience thought Updike seemed quite irritated by the question, because he advised everyone, as he had often reminded interviewers, to "keep in mind that anything I write is fiction and only fiction," though his fiction often has been shown embedded in his personal experience.

Another story, "The Beloved," seems to describe Nancy Wolfe, telescoping their sensual rapport and their parting into two pages. The protagonist, Francis, a would-be actor, recalls a girl of his adolescence who "stepped forward and disclosed to him the treasure he had been accumulating." Thus he becomes "the beloved," who is provided a display of her breasts and a metaphorical maternal appreciation: "she fed him with an impalpable outflowing of herself." Despite this, and though she insists that without him she will die, he tells her bluntly not to wait for him. Yet, as other stories show, she was his beloved; for him she did not die (*HG* 29–30).[12]

Updike returns to the failed romance, but this narrative takes places several years later. Nancy Wolf appears as "Janet" in "The Persistence of Desire," completed July 19, 1958, six months after "Flight," as Updike notes (*ES* [80]–90, 837). Clyde Behn meets Janet accidentally in the waiting room of an eye doctor's office, and Clyde begs her for a tryst. Yet Updike supplies a subtle warning to Clyde that picking up a failed romance is not possible. While waiting for the doctor, Clyde had read in a magazine that the body's cells are changed "*in toto* every seven years" ([81]). Thus Updike signals the reader that you can't go home again, since "you" are a different person every seven years. This detail provides a connection to Updike's relationship with Nancy Wolf. Clyde last saw Janet, "long ago" (89), perhaps seven years ago. Since Updike completed the story in 1958 it can be assumed that the lovers last met in 1951. To further link their meeting to the time of their separation, Janet wears a summer dress, fixing the time of the narrative to late spring or summer, 1951, when Updike had returned to Shillington from Harvard (83). Also, we learn that Clyde Behn is married with children ages one and three. In 1958 Updike had children aged two and four—Elizabeth, born in 1955 and David, born in 1957. This fictionalized depiction of a chance meeting between Updike and Nancy Wolf in 1958 might have been rooted in fact and caused Updike to reflect on their breakup in 1950. While the previous treatments of the failure focused on its irrevocable character, this story ends ambiguously, as Janet gives Clyde a note, but since he has drops in his eyes he can't decipher it. "The Persistence of Desire" suggests that Updike was unready to achieve closure with a major event in his life.[13]

Nancy Wolf is alluded to again in "One More Interview," first published July 4, 1983. This time the persistence of desire packs a visceral punch. When an unnamed actor, while being interviewed, takes his interviewer for a tour of his hometown, he vividly recalls his "girl friend" when he happens to see her home. Ermajean Willis, he "confesses" to his questioner, "was a grade behind me," as of course Nancy Wolf was, and he instantly remembers the exact color of her skin, "Neutral and natural, tinted by nothing, pure trusting female skin beneath her pastel clothes." He feels "swamped by love . . . physically sickened, to think that such a scene had once been real" (*TM* 137–49). The "yes, but" character of life had struck with force. Updike had written that "inner urgent whispers" were primary, but listening to those whispers could be devastating— even when "the social fabric" does not collapse (Plath 33).

The scene had been very real, and Nancy Wolf whispered to him all his life. But this is no surprise, since Shillington was his "being" and everything connected to it was part of his writer's soul. Updike had once vowed that as a writer he intended to explore even the most mundane subject. What could be more mundane than the loss of a high school

sweetheart? And what in Updike's continuous imagining could be simultaneously more poignant, desperate, and symbolic of ecstasy and failure,
of ambiguity and the tragedy of irredeemable choice?

NOTES

1. Of course, the operative word in this remark is the problematic "essential."
Updike hoped his readers knew "the difference between flesh and paper" (Plath 25).
Yet he often creates personas resembling himself in his non-fiction, poetry, and fiction.
In his essay "Updike and I," he puckishly describes the difference between Updike the
writer and Updike the person, expressing surprise "that I resemble him so closely we
can be confused" (*MM* [757]–58). Yet Updike the writer can be traced to Updike the
person in much of his poetry and fiction—consider "Midpoint," with photos of Updike and his family, and his fictional alter egos, Allen Dow, David Kern and John
Nordholm among others. Updike even remarked, perhaps with tongue-in-cheek, "Intellectually I'm not essentially advanced over Harry Angstrom . . . .we're rather similar" (Plath 60). In *Self-Consciousness* Updike draws direct connections between his life
and art, by providing dates, places, and parallels between incidents appearing both in
stories and his life. He quotes twenty-five times from thirty of his works, including
seven novels, fifteen stories, and three poems.
As Martin Amis remarked, "modern fiction tends towards the autobiographical, and
American fiction more than most—and Updike more than any" (Amis, E–18).Perhaps
because Updike felt so keenly nostalgic, he could not avoid being autobiographical. As
he remarked, "I feel nostalgic about almost everything I have experienced—people I
knew, brand-name products I consumed, movies I saw, books I once read, certain tints
of weather" (*HG* 469). So closely did Updike tie his fiction to his life, that he declared
his *Olinger Stories* made an autobiography "impossible" because, "Composition, in
crystallizing memory, displaces it" (*OS* vi).
2. Updike's given name was often pronounced "Chonny," in the Pennsylvania-
Dutch manner. Compare "Charlie" and "Chonny."
3. "The Happiest I've Been" was collected as an "Olinger" story (*ES* [67]–80). The
name "Olinger" expresses Updike's nostalgia for the town of his early years. He explained that the name is pronounced with a "long *O*, a hard *g*, and the emphasis on the
first syllable. . . .The name is audibly a shadow of 'Shillington' . . . a place on the
map . . . . Olinger is a state of mind, of my mind, and belongs entirely to me" (*OS* v).
The name is surely apt, since it puns on "Oh, linger!" It may have been borrowed from
a classmate's married name, Dolores Frederick, later Ohlinger. She was described as a
"beauty" in the caption beneath her picture in *Hi-Life 1950*. Another possible source
for the name might be Harry C. Ohlinger, who died in 1955. He was a weaver and
faith healer who, in Pennsylvania Dutch, cast spells learned from Mammy Bitting of
Shillington (*OJ* 853).
4. Updike confirmed this when revealing that the story took place "in Shillington,
Pennsylvania, when 1952 became 1953" ("How Does the Writer Imagine?" *OJ* 135).
5. Gloria Andrews was renamed Gloria Angstrom when the story was collected in
The Same Door, but rechristened Gloria Andrews in *Early Stories*. This was Updike's
first use of the name "Angstrom." He appears to have wanted to avoid a possible
family connection between Gloria and "Rabbit." Critics have commented on the sig-
nificance of "Rabbit's" surname.
6. Updike explained in an interview, "George Caldwell was assembled from certain vivid gestures and lights characteristic of Wesley Updike." Further, Updike was
"upbraided" by a pupil of his father's for his "outrageous portrait," showing how
readers instantly saw easily through the fiction to the autobiography. Despite this, he
assumed that even when old family "wounds" were his topics he could write without
worrying that he might lose his parents' love (Plath 26).

7. Dr. Gabriel Hiester Jr. was a shareholder in the "Society of the English Library of Reading" in 1803, and his descendants were continuous supporters and benefactors of the library. It is not known whether or not Richard Hiester descended from the line of Dr. Gabriel Hiester Jr. Barbara Hartz Behney declared, "I was engaged to "Rabbit" Hiester!"

8. Updike cites Hemmig's "Roman hands" "In the Cemetery High above Shillington" (*Americana* 34). He later regretted using this phrase.

9. Barry Nelson also found the following models for "Lunch Hour": Mamie Kauffman/Joan Venne Youngerman; Betty Lou/Joan George Zug; Ann McFarland/Mary Ann Stanley Moyer; and Butch Fogel/James Trexler and Barry Nelson (Barry Nelson, letter to the author, 18 May, 1996).

10. Compare her plump body to Ruth Leonard's one hundred and fifty pounds in *Rabbit, Run* for another possible reference to Nancy Wolfe. One might speculate that Rabbit's entanglement and desertion of Ruth resemble Updike's failed relationship with Nancy Wolfe.

Updike was extremely careful with the naming of his characters (De Bellis, 298–300). "Nora" recalls an author Updike was reading in his senior year, James Joyce, since Joyce's wife was the sexually exciting Nora Barnacle. Molly Bingaman of "Flight" again recalls James Joyce, since Molly Bloom of *Ulysses* is Joyce's most famous female character, perhaps modeled on Nora Barnacle. The Homeric parallel of Penelope to Penny in *The Centaur* strengthens the association of Nora, Molly, and Penny to Nancy Wolf.

To protect the persons who modeled for his characters, Updike changed their names, but he left clues to the originals in those names. Phonetic connections bind the fictional characters to the real person. For example: "Nancy" and "Nora" alliterate; Nancy's two syllable name is repeated in "Penny," "Nora," "Janet," "Elsie," and "Molly"; in *The Centaur* and "Elsie by Starlight," the last syllable of the girls' given names echo: Nancy/Penny; Nancy/Elsie; and the first syllables of their last names alliterate in "One More Interview": "Willis," "Wolf." One wonders if the name of Elsie de Wolfe (1865–1950) led Updike to give Nancy Wolf the pseudonym, Elsie Seidel. Elsie de Wolfe's death date might have signaled to Updike the death of his relationship with Nancy Wolf. See my "The 'Extra Dimension': Character Names in Updike's 'Rabbit' Trilogy." *Names* 36 (Mar.–June 1988):29–42.

11. Owen performs oral sex on Elsie, recalling an allusion to a similar act between "Rabbit" Angstrom and Mary Ann. If Mary Ann is similar to Elsie in this regard, then she also is an analogue for Nancy Wolf, who "was the best of them all because she was the one he brought most to" (*RA* 170). *Couples* graphically describes this sex act, and "Midpoint" contains an allusion to it (*CP* 84–85).

12. Ironically, after Francis leaves his girl for an acting career he has a homosexual experience. "The Beloved," has had an interesting history. It was first published in two parts: "Love: First Lessons," *The New Yorker* 6 Nov. 1971:46-47; and "The Beloved," *Transatlantic Review* Autumn–Wint. 1974:19–29. Then it appeared in a special edition, in "slightly different form" as *The Beloved*. Northridge, California, Lord John P, 1982. Finally, it was reprinted in *Higher Gossip* ([25]–40). One can only guess if Updike would have included the story in this collection had he been the editor.

13. As early as 1956 in "Snowing in Greenwich Village," Updike fictionalized marital difficulties in the union of Joan and Richard Maple. "The Persistence of Desire" could be evidence of Updike's early failure of commitment to his marriage because he had not yet come to closure with his first love, Nancy Wolf.

Appendix A: Updike Chronology

1932   An eleventh-generation American (two Updikes fought in the Civil War on opposite sides [*AP* 211n]), John Hoyer Updike is born March 18, in West Reading Hospital, Reading, Pennsylvania, to Wesley Updike, a mathematics teacher at Shillington High School, and Linda Grace Hoyer, who later published stories in *The New Yorker*. They lived with John and Katherine Hoyer at 117 Philadelphia Avenue, Shillington, Pennsylvania, a suburb of Reading. Shillington was the subject of the memoir "A Soft Spring Night in Shillington" (*SC*) and fictionalized as Olinger (*OS* v).

1933   On his first birthday, his parents and grandparents plant a dogwood tree in his honor. It still stands there as of 2012.

1936   Attends public schools in Shillington. Publishes a collage.

1938   Contracts psoriasis while in kindergarten. Begins cartooning while taking drawing and painting lessons from Clint Shilling.

1944   Enters Shillington Elementary School. Updike's paternal aunt Mary gives his family a subscription to *The New Yorker*.

1945   First literary publication, "A Handshake with the Congressman," February 16, in *Chatterbox*, the Shillington High School newspaper. On Halloween, his family and maternal grandparents move eleven miles south of Shillington to Plowville. They live in the sandstone farmhouse originally owned by Linda Updike's father.

1946   Enters Shillington High School (now Governor Thomas E. Mifflin Intermediate School).Writes a murder mystery (published 1994), light verse, and prose.

1948   Contributes weekly to the Shillington High School newspaper, *Chatterbox*. Elected class president. Death of his uncle recorded in "My Uncle's Death," (*AP* 200–09).

1949   First publication other than *Chatterbox*, "I Want a Lamp," a poem, in the *American Courier* X (July 1): 11. Writes and stars in the junior class play, as he will in his senior play. Updike played the father in both plays and quipped that he "fathered" them.

1950   Graduates co-valedictorian and president of the senior class of
       Shillington High School. Updike had contributed nearly three
       hundred drawings, articles, and poems to *Chatterbox*. He
       contributes a great deal to *Hi-Life*, the yearbook, which identifies
       him as "the sage of Plowville," who "hopes to write for a living."
       Enters Harvard on a tuition scholarship, majoring in English.
       That summer, and for the next two summers, Updike works as a
       copyboy for the Reading *Eagle*.

1951   First prose, "The Different One," is published in *Harvard
       Lampoon*. He writes forty plus poems and draws for the *Harvard
       Lampoon*. Discards a novel about two-thirds written called
       "Willow," about a town like Shillington; it forecasts his stories
       about Olinger (Plath165–66).

1952   Named editor of the *Harvard Lampoon*. A story about an ex-
       basketball player, "Ace in the Hole," written for Albert Guerard's
       creative writing class receives an A (*ES* [ix])

1953   On June 26 marries Mary Pennington, a Radcliff Fine Arts senior.
       The New Yorker buys a story and a poem. Updike's grandfather,
       John Franklin Hoyer, dies.

1954   His senior thesis is titled, "Non-Horatian Elements in Robert
       Herrick's Imitations and Echoes of Horace." Graduates from
       Harvard summa cum laude. Wins a Knox Fellowship to attend
       the Ruskin School of Drawing and Fine Art, Oxford, England.
       While there he meets E. B. White, and White's wife, Katharine
       White, fiction editor of *The New Yorker*, offers him employment as
       a "Talk of the Town" writer. *The New Yorker* publishes "Duet
       with Muffled Brake Drums," August 14, and "Friends from
       Philadelphia." The appearance of this poem and story begin his
       lifelong relationship with the magazine.

1955   Begins work as a staff writer for *The New Yorker* (to 1957).
       Updike's grandmother Katherine Kramer Hoyer dies. Daughter
       Elizabeth is born, April 1.

1957   In April, leaves *The New Yorker* and New York for Ipswich,
       Massachusetts. Completes "Home," his second effort at novel-
       writing; it is unpublished. Son David is born January 19, 1957.

1958   Publishes *The Carpentered Hen and Other Tame Creatures* with
       Harper & Brothers. After this, all books will be published by
       Alfred Knopf.

1959   Publishes *The Same Door* and first novel, *The Poorhouse Fair*. *The
       Best American Short Stories 1959* selects "A Gift form the City."
       Wins a Guggenheim Fellowship to support the writing of *Rabbit,
       Run*. His son Michael is born May 14.

1960   Publishes *Rabbit, Run*. *The Poorhouse Fair* wins the Rosenthal Award of the National Institute of Arts and Letters. "Hub Fans Bid Kid Adieu" appears in *The New Yorker*. Daughter Miranda is born, December 15.

1961   *Prize Stories 1961* includes "Wife-Wooing."

1962   Publishes *Pigeon Feathers* and *The Magic Flute* of Mozart, adapted and arranged for young people. *Prize Stories 1962* includes "The Doctor's Wife." *Best American Short Stories 1962* includes "Pigeon Feathers." Publishes *Rabbit, Run* with London firm, André Deutsch. The re-publication includes "emendations and restorations" Updike made while in Antibes, France. This text was later used for the Modern Library edition and for the Knopf reissue; he makes revisions in the novels of the "Rabbit" tetralogy for both the Everyman edition of *Rabbit Angstrom* (1995) and the Fawcett Columbine editions (1996).Teaches creative writing in the summer at Harvard.

1963   Publishes *Telephone Poles and Other Poems* and *The Centaur*.

1964   Publishes *Olinger Stories* and *The Ring of Wagner*, an adaptation for children of Wagner's "Ring" operas. *The Centaur* wins the National Book Award. *Olinger Stories* is a paperback original and has not been republished. Elected to the National Institute of Arts and Letters, the youngest member so honored at that time. Visits the USSR and eastern Europe under the State Department invitation. Receives an honorary degree from Ursinus College.

1965   Publishes *Of the Farm*, *Assorted Prose*, *A Child's Calendar* (twelve poems), and *Verse*, containing his two previous collections, *Carpentered Hen* and *Telephone Poles*. Wins *Le prix du meilleur livre étranger* for *The Centaur*.

1966   Publishes *The Music School*. *Prize Stories 1966* includes "The Bulgarian Poetess," from *The Music School*, which wins the First O. Henry Prize.

1967   *Prize Stories 1967* includes "Marching through Boston." Receives a Doctor of Letters degree from Moravian College.

1968   Publishes *Couples*, and it remains on the best-seller lists for a year. *Prize Stories 1968* includes "Your Lover Just Called."

1969   Publishes *Midpoint and Other Poems* and *Bottom's Dream* (an adaptation for children of *A Midsummer Night's Dream*).

1970   Publishes *Beck: A Book*. *Prize Stories 1970* includes "Bech Takes Pot Luck." The film, *Rabbit, Run* is released, starring Jack Albertson (Tothero), James Caan ("Rabbit"), Anjanette Comer (Ruth), Arthur Hill (Eccles), and Carrie Snodgress (Janice), with the screenplay by Howard B. Kreitsek, and direction by Jack Smight.

1971   Publishes *Rabbit Redux*. Receives the Signet Society Medal for Achievement in the Arts.

1972   Publishes *Seventy Poems* and *Museums and Women and Other Stories*. Appointed Honorary Consultant in American Letters to the Library of Congress (1972–75). Father, Wesley Russell Updike, dies April 16.

1973   Writes "Introduction" to *Soundings in Satanism*. Visits Africa. At Harvard reads the Phi Beta Kappa Poem, "Apologies to Harvard."

1974   Publishes *Buchanan Dying*. *Prize Stories 1974* includes "Son." Receives a Doctor of Letters degree from Lafayette College.

1975   Publishes *A Month of Sundays* and *Picked-Up Pieces*. *Prize Stories 1975* includes "Nakedness." Wins the Lotus Club Award of Merit.

1976   Publishes *Marry Me: A Romance*. *Buchanan Dying* premiers. *Best American Short Stories 1976* includes "The Man Who Loved Extinct Mammals." *Prize Stories 1976* includes "Separating." *Prize Stories 1976* gives Updike the "Special Award for Continuing Achievement." Elected to the American Academy of Arts and Letters. He and Mary Pennington divorce.

1977   Publishes *Tossing and Turning* and *The Poorhouse Fair*, revised edition, with a foreword by Updike. Marries Martha R. Bernhard, September 30.

1978   Publishes *The Coup*.

1979   Publishes *Problems and Other Stories* and *Too Far to Go: The Maples Stories*, a paperback original.

1980   *Best American Short Stories 1980* includes "Gesturing."

1981   Publishes *Rabbit Is Rich,* which wins the National Book Critics Circle Award, the Pulitzer Prize, and American Book Award the following year. *Best American Short Stories 1981* includes "Still of Some Use." *Prize Stories of the Seventies* includes "Separating." Awarded the Edward MacDowell Medal for Literature.

1982   Publishes *Bech Is Back*. On his fiftieth birthday, Knopf issues, with revisions, *The Carpentered Hen*. Receives an honorary degree from Albright College.

1983   Publishes *Hugging the Shore: Essays and Reviews*, which wins the National Book Critics Circle Award for Criticism, the following year. *Best American Short Stories 1983* includes "Deaths of Distant

Friends." *Prize Stories 1983* includes "The City." Receives the Pennsylvania Distinguished Artist Award from Governor Thornburgh in May. Wins the Lincoln Literary Award bestowed by the Union League Club.

1984   Publishes *The Witches of Eastwick*. Edits and introduces *The Best American Short Stories 1984*. Awarded the National Arts Club Medal of Honor.

1985   Publishes *Facing Nature. Prize Stories 1985* includes "The Other." Receives Kutztown University Foundation's Director's Award.

1986   Publishes *Roger's Version*.

1987   Publishes *Trust Me. Best American Short Stories* includes "The Afterlife."

      Receives the Elmer Holmes Bobst award for fiction. The film, *The Witches of Eastwick*, is released June 12. It stars Veronica Cartwright (Felicia Alden), Cher (Alexandra Medford), Michelle Pfeiffer (Sukie Ridgemont), Jack Nicholson (Daryl Van Horne), and Susan Sarandon (Jane Spofford). Michael Cristofer wrote the screenplay, and George Miller directed.

1988   Publishes *S. Prize Stories 1988* includes "Leaf Season." Receives Brandeis University's Life Achievement Award.

1989   Publishes *Self-Consciousness* and *Just Looking*. Receives the National Medal of Arts from President George H. W. Bush. Mother, Linda Grace Updike, dies October 10.

1990   Publishes *Rabbit at Rest. Best American Short Stories of the Eighties* includes "Deaths of Distant Friends."

1991   Publishes *Odd Jobs. Rabbit at Rest* wins the Pulitzer Prize and the National Critics Circle Award. *Best American Essays 1991* includes "The Female Body." "A Sandstone Farmhouse" wins the "First O. Henry Prize," first prize in *Prize Stories 1991*, and is included in *Best American Short Stories 1991*. Wins Italy's Scanno Prize for *Trust Me*.

1992   Publishes *Memories of the Ford Administration. Best American Essays 1992* includes "First Things First." Receives a Doctor of Letters degree from Harvard.

1993   Publishes *Collected Poems 1953–1993. Best American Short Stories 1993* includes "Playing with Dynamite." Wins the Conch Prize for Literature.

1994   Publishes *Brazil* and *The Afterlife and Other Stories. Best American Essays 1994* includes "The Disposable Rocket."

1995   Publishes *Rabbit Angstrom: A Tetralogy* and *A Helpful Alphabet of Friendly Objects*. *Prize Stories 1995* includes "The Black Room." Awarded the Howells Medal from the American Academy of Arts and Letters, and the French rank of *Commandeur de l'Ordre des Arts et des Lettres*.

1996   Publishes *Golf Dreams* and *In the Beauty of the Lilies*. Receives the Ambassador Book Award for *In the Beauty of the Lilies*. Elected to The Society for the Arts, Religion and Contemporary Culture.

1997   Publishes *Toward the End of Time*. Updike begins and ends "Murder Makes the Magazine." Receives the Campion Award.

1998   Publishes *Bech at Bay*. Edits *A Century of Arts and Letters* and contributes the "Foreword" and the chapter, "1938–47: Decade of The Row." *Best American Short Stories 1998* includes "My Father on the Verge of Disgrace." *Best American Essays 1998* includes "Lost Art." Receives the Harvard Arts Medal May 2, and the Thomas Cooper Library Medal from the University of South Carolina.

1999   Publishes *More Matter*.

2000   Publishes *Gertrude and Claudius*. *The Best American Essays of the Century* includes "The Disposable Rocket." Participates in a panel on "The American Short Story" at Florida State University. Receives the Pell Award and The Enoch Pratt Society's Lifetime Literary Achievement Award.

2001   Publishes *Licks of Love*, "Rabbit Remembered," and *The Complete Henry Bech* published. *Best American Short Stories 2001* includes "Personal Archeology."

2002   Publishes *Americana and Other Poems*.

2003   Publishes *Seek My Face*.

2004   Publishes *The Early Stories 1953–1975* and *Villages*. *Best American Short Stories 2004* includes "The Walk with Elizanne."

2005   Publishes *Still Looking*.

2006   Publishes *Terrorist*.

2007   Publishes *Due Considerations*.

2008   Publishes *The Widows of Eastwick*. *Best American Spiritual Writing 2008* includes "Madurai." *Best American Essays 2008* includes "Extreme Dinosaurs."

2009   Dies January 27. *Endpoint and Other Poems*, *My Father's Tears*, and *The Maples Stories* are published. Updike's papers are sold to Harvard University. "The John Updike Society" is formed.

2010   *Hub Fans Bid Kid Adieu* is published by the Library of America, with revised introduction.

2011   *Higher Gossip: Essays and Criticism* is published.

2012   *Always Looking: Essays in Art* is published.

2013   *Selected Poems* (projected).

Appendix B: Updike's Published Writings Set in Pennsylvania

This list will enable Updike readers to see the breadth of his commitment to his home state, while revealing his depth of his feelings for the people and places there. Rooted in the actual, these poems, stories, and essays suggest an ideal Pennsylvania always on Updike's mind, whether directly in his essays and poetry or through an alterego in his fiction. Since some of his works have multiple settings, it seemed appropriate to place them in each locale. A date that can reasonably be surmised is attached in parenthesis. I would like to acknowledge the valuable assistance of my friend, independent scholar, Jack Ruttle in creating this list.

1. SHILLINGTON

a. Essays:

"The Dogwood Tree: A Boyhood." *Assorted Prose*, 152–87. (1932–1945)
Self-Consciousness. (1932–1950).
"Rabbit Angstrom" in *Higher Gossip*, 456. (1932–1945)
Higher Gossip, 469, 470, 474, and 479. (1932–1945)
"A Bookish Boy." *More Matter*, 672. (1932–1945)
"The Old Movie House." *More Matter*, 641. (1933–1938)
"The Art of Mickey Mouse." *More Matter*, 204, 209. (1935–1940)
"Introduction to *The First Picture Book*." *More Matter*, 685. (1935–1940?)
"The Would-Be Animator." *Due Considerations*, 619.(1937)
"Summer Love." *Due Considerations*, 662–63. (1937–1945)
"My Philadelphia." *Due Considerations*, 666–67. (1937–1945)
"Early Employments and Inklings." *Due Considerations*, 665–66. (1938, 1944)
"Hydrophobia." *Due Considerations*, 82. (Before 1938?, 1944 or 1945)
"High Art versus Popular Culture." *Odd Jobs*, 87. (Before 1938?)
"Footnotes to *Self-Consciousness*," *Odd Jobs*, 865. (1938)
"Christmas Cards." *More Matter*, 781; 797–98. (1939–1940)
"Reminiscences of Reading [PA]." *More Matter*, 804–5. (1939–1947)
"Why Write?" *Picked-up Pieces*, 33. (1940?)
"Writers and Progenitors and Offspring," *Odd Jobs*, 833. (1940?)
"Reflections on Radio." *More Matter*, 803.(1940–1950?)

"Fourth of July." *Odd Jobs*, 75.(Before 1941?)

"Three New Yorker Stalwarts." *More Matter*, 781. (1941)

"Remembering Pearl Harbor." *More Matter*, 802. (1941–1945)

"Introduction to *Chip Kidd: Book One*." *Due Considerations*, 622–3. (mid-1940s)

"Why Live in New England?" *More Matter*, 807. (1942?)

"My Uncle's Death." *Assorted Prose*, 200–9. (1942–1948)

[Childhood Reading.] *Due Considerations*, 658–59. (1942–1948)

"A Sense of Change." *Due Considerations*, 23–24. (1942–1948)

"Ernest Hemingway." *Due Considerations*, 109. (1944)

"Cartoon Magic." *More Matter*, 792–3. (1944–1950?)

"Introduction to the 1977 Edition of *The Poorhouse Fair*." *Higher Gossip*, 430–31. (1945)

"A Childhood Transgression." *More Matter*, 799–800. (1945, 1946)

"My Cartooning." *More Matter*, 787. (1945–1948)

"The Boston *Red Sox* as of 1986." *Odd Jobs*, 91. (1946)

"Rabbit Angstrom" in *Higher Gossip*, 450. (1946–1947)

[The Rabbit Novels.] *More Matter*, 817. (1946–1950)

"Foreword to My Own Bibliography." *Due Considerations*, 653. (1946–1950)

"On Literary Biography." *Due Considerations*, 11–12. (1946–1950)

"One Big Interview." *Picked-Up Pieces*, 33. (1948?)

"How Does the Writer Imagine?" *Odd Jobs*, 134–35.

"The Parade." *Odd Jobs*, [13]-17.

"First Wives and Trolley Cars." *Odd Jobs*, [18]-25.

"Women." *Odd Jobs*, 65.

"Mother." *Odd Jobs*, 68–69.

Odd Jobs, 835.

"On His Oeuvre." *Hugging the Shore*, 839–43.

More Matter, 825, 830.

b. *Poems:*

"Found Poem." *Endpoint and Other Poems*, 94–95. (1878)

"Planting Trees." *Collected Poems*,169. (1933)

"Birthday Shopping, 2007." *Endpoint*, 15–18. (1935?)

"Midpoint: Sections 1, 2, and 4." *Collected Poems*, 64–76, 81–95. (1936?–1950)

"Peggy Lutz and Fred Muth." in "Endpoint." *Endpoint*, 26–27. (1938–1950)

"Upon Becoming a Senior Citizen." *Americana*, 37. (1940?)

"The Author Observes His Birthday, 2005." *Endpoint*, 8–10. (1941?)

"In the Cemetery High above Shillington." *Americana*, 29–34. (1943–1950)

"Dutch Cleanser." *Collected Poems*, 143–44. (pre-1945)

"How to be Uncle Sam." *Collected Poems*, 11–13. (1945)
" Hedge." *Americana* , 28. (1946?)
"Frankie Laine." *Endpoint*, 35. (1949)
"Ex-Basketball Player." *Collected Poems*, 4. (1950?)
"Outliving One's Father." *Endpoint*, 54. (1950?)
"Shillington." *Collected Poems*, 15.
"My Mother at her Desk." *Endpoint*, 12–13.

c. Short Fiction:

"My Father on the Verge of Disgrace." *Licks of Love*, 44–59. (1922–50, esp. 1946–1950)
"The Black Room." *The Afterlife*, 263–82. (1930s)
"His Mother inside Him." *The Afterlife*, 234–241, especially 234–35. (1930s)
"Beloved." *Higher Gossip*, 25–40.(1930s–1940s)
"The Full Glass." *My Father's Tears*, 278–80. (1930s–1940s)
"Trust Me." *Trust Me*, 3–12. (1935 or 1936)
"Plumbing." *Early Stories*, 436–41, especially 439. (1935, 1942)
"The Laughter of the Gods." *My Father's Tears*, 66–81. (1936)
"The Blessed Man of Boston, My Grandmother's Thimble, and Fanning Island." *Early Stories* [91]–101, especially 97. (1940?)
"The Guardians." *My Father's Tears*, 55–65.(1940s)
"The Alligators." *Early Stories*, [7]–12. (March, 1942)
"You'll Never Know Dear, How Much I Love You." *Early Stories*, [3]–6. (1942)
"Kinderszenen." *My Father's Tears*, 212–29.(1942)
"Solitaire." *Early Stories*, [505]–09. (1944?)
"Friends from Philadelphia." *Early Stories*, [34]–41. (1947)
"A Sense of Shelter." *Early Stories*, [41]–51. (1949)
"Flight." *Early Stories*, [52]–66. (1950)
"In Football Season." *Early Stories*, [122]–25. (1950)
"The Walk with Elizanne." *My Father's Tears*, 38–54. (1950)
"Elsie by Starlight." *Villages*, 61–77. (June, 1950)
"My Father's Tears." *My Father's Tears*, 193–211. (September,1950)
"The Happiest I've Been." *Early Stories*, [67]–80. (December 29, 1951)
"The Persistence of Desire." *Early Stories*, [81]–90. (1957)
"The Egg Race." *Problems*, 254–68. (1970 class reunion)
"The Other Side of the Street." *Afterlife*, 136–47. (November, 1989)
"His Mother inside Him." *Afterlife*, 234–41. (1989)
"The Brown Chest." *Afterlife*, 225–33. (1989)
"Lunch Hour." *Licks of Love*, 18–27. (1990 class reunion)
"The Road Home." *My Father's Tears*, 170–92. (2000 class reunion)

d. Novels:

> *The Centaur.* (January, 1947)
> *Rabbit, Run.* (1949–50)
> *The Poorhouse Fair.*

2. PLOWVILLE

a. Essays:

> *Self-Consciousness.* New York: Knopf, 1989. (1932–1950)
> "My Philadelphia." *Due Considerations*, 667. (1937–1945)
> "My Uncle's Death." *Assorted Prose*, 200–09. (1942–1947)
> *Odd Jobs* , 866–67. (1945)
> "My Life in Cars." *Due Considerations*, 87. (1945–1950)
> "The Key-People." *More Matter*, 233. (1945–1950)
> "A Case for Books." *Due Considerations*, 69. (1945–1950)
> "The Future of Faith." *Due Considerations*, 11–12. (1946)
> *More Matter*, 777. (1946–1950)
> "The Would-Be Animator." *Due Considerations*, 619. (1947)
> "The Short Story and I." *More Matter*, 763. (1954)
> "Cemeteries." *Picked-Up Pieces*, 60–61. (1969?)
> "Note on 'A Sandstone Farmhouse.'" *More Matter*, 775.
> "Three New Yorker Stalwarts." *More Matter*, 781.
> "Fictional Houses." *Odd Jobs*, [46]–50.

b. Poems:

> "Plow Cemetery." *Collected Poems*, 176–77. (1904)
> "Planting Trees." *Collected Poems*, 169. (1908?)
> "The Solitary Pond." *Collected Poems*, 27. (Winter, 1946)
> "Leaving Church Early." *Collected Poems*, 137–41. (1948?)
> "Packed Dirt, Churchgoing, A Dying Cat, A Traded Car." *Early Stories*, [101]–21. (1948; March 18, 1972)
> "The House Growing." *Collected Poems*, 116. (1972)
> "Fall." *Collected Poems*, 229. (1989)

c. Short Fiction:

> "The Laughter of the Gods." *My Father's Tears*, 66–81. (1930s)
> "My Father on the Verge of Disgrace." *Licks of Love*, [44]–59, especially 59. (1930–1945)
> "His Mother inside Him." *The Afterlife*, 234–241, esp. 238–39. (1940s)
> "The Gun Shop." *Early Stories*, [480]–90. (1945)
> "Harv is Plowing Now." *Early Stories*, [559]–63. (1945?)

"The Laughter of the Gods." *My Father's Tears*, 66–81, especially 70, 74. (1945, 1948)

"Lunch Hour." *Licks of Love*, 21–27, especially, 21–23. (1945–1950)

"Packed Dirt, Churchgoing, a Dying Cat, a Traded Car," *Early Stories*, [102]–21. (March, 1947)

"The Lens Factory." *Higher Gossip*, [41]–45. (1948)

"Early Employments and Inklings." *Due Considerations*, 665–66. (1948)

"Pigeon Feathers." *Early Stories*, [13]–33. (1949)

"The Blessed Man of Boston, My Grandmother's Thimble, and Fanning Island."

Early Stories, [91]–101, especially 96. (1949–v50)

"Flight." *Early Stories*, [52]–66. (1950)

"My Father's Tears." *My Father's Tears*, 193–211. (1950)

"Home" *Early Stories*, [214]–24. (1955)

"A Sandstone Farmhouse." *Afterlife*, 103–35. (1945, 1950, 1989)

"The Cats." *Licks of Love*, 60–84. (1989–90)

"The Brown Chest." *The Afterlife*, 225–233. (1989, 1991)

"The Road Home." *My Father's Tears*, 170–93. (2000)

d. Novels:

The Centaur. (1947)
Of the Farm.

3. READING

a. Essays:

Self-Consciousness. (1932–1950)

Odd Jobs, 836–38. (1940s)

[Childhood Reading.] *Due Considerations*, 658–59. (1942–1948)

"Cartoon Magic." *More Matter*, 792–94. (1944–1950?)

"Foreword to My Own Bibliography." *Due Considerations*, 653. (1946–1950)

"Early Employments and Inklings." *Due Considerations*, 665–66. (1948, 1950)

"Preface." *Due Considerations*, xvii. (1950–1952).

"Foreword to the1982 edition of *The Carpentered Hen*." *Higher Gossip*, 427. (1950– 1952).

Odd Jobs, 871.

"Stevens as Dutchman." *More Matter*,251.

b. Poems:

"Small City People." *Collected Poems*, 174–75.

"Reading [Pennsylvania]." *Americana*, 19.
"Found Poem." *Endpoint and Other Poems*, 94–95.

c. Short Fiction:

"Lunch Hour." *Licks of Love*, 21–27, esp. 21–23. (1945)
"In Football Season." *Early Stories*, [122]–25. (1948)
"The Walk with Elizanne." *My Father's Tears*, 38–54. (1950)
"My Father's Tears." *My Father's Tears*, 193–211, especially 193–95. (1950)
"His Mother inside Him." *Afterlife*, 234–41. (1989)
"The Road Home." *My Father's Tears*, 170–93, esp. 179–91. (2000)

d. Novels:

Rabbit, Run (1959)
Rabbit Redux (1969)
Rabbit Is Rich (1979)
Rabbit at Rest(1988)
Rabbit Remembered (1999–2000)

4. PHILADELPHIA

a. Essay:

"My Philadelphia." *Due Considerations*, 667–68. (1937–45; 1959–1950)

b. Poem:

"Returning Native." *Collected Poems*, 169.

5. PENNSYLVANIA

a. Essays:

More Matter, 825–27.
More Matter, 855.

b. Poems:

"Returning Native." *Collected Poems*, 211–12.
"The Amish." *Collected Poems*, 330.

c. Novel:

Memories of the Ford Administration.

d. Play:

Buchanan Dying.

Appendix C: John Updike's Contributions to *The Little Shilling* and *Chatterbox*

Chatterbox, the high school continuation of the elementary school paper, *The Little Shilling,* was founded in 1926 by Donald Strause, who organized the school paper and staff. Sevellon Van Liew (1928) was appointed editor-in-chief. *Chatterbox* appeared weekly until 1953; afterwards the paper was published yearly. It won the Pennsylvania School Press Association award, 1932–1948. Of course these newspapers are now rare. *The Little Shilling* has survived in very few copies kept by classmates, and it was not kept by libraries. *Chatterbox* also is incomplete in both the Governor Mifflin High School archives and the Reading Public Library. Updike's *Chatterbox*es were sold to Harvard's Houghton Library in 2009 as part of 170 boxes of his papers, but, since access to them is not possible until they are cataloged, they were unavailable at this writing.

Chatterbox is composed of several eight by ten pages stapled together, with a page for creative work called *Pen and Ink.* The student newspapers were hectographed on eight to twelve pages, back-to-back, and distributed on Fridays. *Chatterbox* had a large staff, supervised by Mrs. Thelma Kutch Lewis, Updike's teacher in grades eight through twelve. Updike always called her his "first editor."

He was so precocious that as early as the first grade he was identified as a student of great promise by his teachers, Helen Becker Hartzell and Dorothy Kauffman. He began appearing in *The Little Shilling,* at least as early as 1944; the following year he wrote for *Chatterbox.* Upon entering Shillington High School, Updike rose rapidly on the staff of *Chatterbox.* He is listed under "Artists" (11 May 1945: [3]), then associate editor for 1946–47 (*Chatterbox* 12 Sept. 1946: [3]) and "co-literary editor." Updike became "roving editor," as well as "art editor" (16 Sept. 1948: [5]). He closed his career as associate editor, 1949–50 (6 May 1949).

In 1946 Updike's first fiction appeared, "And One of These Times" (18 Apr. 1946), and his first poetry, "Ode to a Toad" (29 Mar. 1946: 5). His first published book review was James Thurber's *Fables for Our Time* (9 Nov. 1945: 5), his first film review, "Road to Utopia" (10 May 1946: 10).

Like his drawings, Updike's prose and poetry use a wide range of subjects, humor, and technique. By his senior year at Shillington High School, he began writing a good deal of poetry that was closely tied to his aptitude for cartoon drawing. His short fiction is light and includes parodies of detective stories. The compilation of *Chatterbox* contributions has been created by personal visits to the collections in the Reading Public Library and the Governor Mifflin High School archives. Some earlier citations by other compilers have been corrected, and the authority of certain citations given by Alexander Jemal or Stuart Wright have been added when verification is not possible.

In his final remarks in 1950 Updike said, "I want to express my appreciation to anybody who took the time to read my efforts" (*Chatterbox* 31 July 1997: 4). Updike's "efforts" seem effortless and are a delight to eye and ear. Though he treasured his *Chatterbox* pieces to the point of having them professionally bound, Updike never wanted them professionally published. He considered them only apprentice work, and so they are, but they show an unusually high degree of care. They also show a high volume of activity. Updike's *Chatterbox* contributions amount to at least 319 signed pieces (167 drawings, 88 poems, 45 prose works, and 19 stories). Attributed to him are another 22 drawings, 10 poems, and 6 prose works.

Listed items are signed "Updike," "JU," "J. H. U.," or "JHU" unless otherwise noted. In his last two years, Updike used unusual designs for "JU"; these are listed without comment. Updike seems to have signed everything he contributed, but since he may have left some unsigned, these are included in a separate list. The genre of a written piece is given, along with a description of the subjects of most drawings. Since the pages of *Chatterbox* are not always given, page numbers without brackets have been used.

CONTRIBUTION TO THE LITTLE SHILLING

Drawing of a fledgling on a limb. *The Little Shilling* 29 May 1944. Cover. (Signed "Updike.")

CONTRIBUTIONS TO *CHATTERBOX*

"A Handshake with the Congressman," 16 Feb. 1945: 5 (article).
Drawing of a ballplayer, 6 Apr. 1945: 3.
Drawing of a ballplayer, 13 Apr. 1945: 3.
Drawing of a track runner, 27 Apr. 1945: 3.
Drawing of a ballplayer, 4 May 1945: 3.
Drawing of a track runner, 11 May 1945: 3.
Drawing of a football player, 5 Oct. 1945: 3.
Drawing of a football player, 12 Oct. 1945: 3.
Drawing of a football player, 19 Oct. 1945: 3.

Drawing of boy and girl and three witches, 26 Oct. 1945: cover (first cover drawing).

Drawing of a football player on a horse, 26 Oct. 1945: 3.

Drawing of a football player, 2 Nov. 1945: 3.

Drawing of a teddy bear crying, 9 Nov. 1945: 3.

"Fables for Our Times," 9 Nov. 1945: 5 (first review: James Thurber's *Fables for Our Times*; signed: "John Updike 8B").

Drawing of basketball players, 30 Nov. 1945: 3.

Drawing of a butcher, 30 Nov. 1945: 4.

Drawing of basketball players, 7 Dec. 1945: 3.

Drawing of basketball players, 14 Dec. 1945: 3.

Drawing of "5 Classroom Animals," 11 Jan. 1946: 8.

Drawing of a runner, 18 Jan. 1946: 3.

Drawing of a runner, 1 Feb. 1946: 3.

Drawing of a donkey, 8 Feb. 1946: 3.

Drawing of a runner, 15 Feb. 1946: 3.

Drawing of a basketball player tossing a mule, 22 Feb. 1946: 3.

Drawing of a basketball player in the rain, 1 Mar. 1946: 3.

Drawing of a basketball player with angel and devil, 15 Mar. 1946: 3.

Drawing of a hand, ball, and glove, 22 Mar. 1946: 3 (drawing is in two parts).

Drawing of track equipment, 29 Mar. 1946: 3 (drawing is in two parts).

"Ode to a Toad," 29 Mar. 1946: 5 (first poem).

Drawing of a *Chatterbox* member, 29 Mar. 1946: 8.

Drawing of a baseball player, 5 Apr. 1946: 3.

Drawing, 5 Apr. 1946: 7.

Drawing of a diver, 18 Apr. 1946: 2.

Drawing of a runner, 18 Apr. 1946: 3

"And One of These Times," 18 Apr. 1946: 7 (first fiction).

"Tired," 18 Apr. 1946: 7 (article).

Drawing, 18 Apr. 1946: 9.

Drawing, 18 Apr. 1946: 9.

Drawing of a runner, 26 Apr. 1946: 3.

Drawing of a baseball player, 3 May 1946: 3.

Drawing of a track player, 10 May 1946: 3.

"A Present for Mother," 10 May 1946: 5 (fiction; signed: "John Updike 8B").

"Road to Utopia," 10 May 1946: 10 (first film review).

Drawing of stick figures of all sports, 31 May 1946: 3.

Drawing of schoolboys with football, 12 Sept. 1946: 3 (Updike is now "Literary Editor").

"School Daze," 12 Sept. 1946: 5 (poem; Updike signs his grade rank, 9D).

Drawing of a huge football player stomping on another, 20 Sept. 1946: 3.

"The Last Mohican (a moving poem saga)," 20 Sept. 1946: 5 (poem).

Drawing of a football player, 27 Sept. 1946: 3.

Drawing of a football player, 4 Oct. 1946: 3.

"The Kid from Brooklyn," 4 Oct. 1946: 5.

Drawing of a chicken laying a victory egg, 11 Oct. 1946: 3.

"The Joke," 11 Oct. 1946: 5 (poem).

Drawing of a statue of a football player, 17 Oct. 1946: 3.

Drawing of a football player on horseback, 25 Oct. 1946: 3.

"The Big Sleep," 25 Oct. 1946: 5 (film review).

Drawing of a football player with butterfly net, 1 Nov. 1946: 4.

"A Halloween Story," 1 Nov. 1946: 5 (fiction).

Drawing of a bear lifting a football player, 8 Nov. 1946: 3.

"Why Do You Like the Movies?" 8 Nov. 1946: 5 (mock interview).

Drawing of a tall basketball player and small referee, 15 Nov. 1946: 3.

Drawing, 15 Nov. 1946: 5.

Drawing of a pilgrim and a hunter returning with a pheasant, 27 Nov.
    1946: cover (two-color cover drawing).

Drawing of two female basketball players, 27 Nov. 1946: 3.

Drawing of a superman, 6 Dec. 1946: 3.

Drawing, 13 Dec. 1946: 3.

Drawing, 20 Dec. 1946: 3.

"Christmas Presents," 20 Dec. 1946: 5 (poem).

Drawing, 10 Jan. 1947: 3.

"The Wicked Lady," 10 Jan. 1947: 5 (film review).

Drawing of a basketball player with an ax chasing a bird, 17 Jan. 1947:
    3.

Drawing of a basketball player pushing another out of second place,
    24 Jan. 1947: 3.

"Sing Hoo's Last Case," or "Pardon me, Your Corpse is Showing," or
    "No Checkee, No Washee," 24 Jan. 1947: 5 (first installment of a
    four-part murder mystery).

Drawing of a dog at a grave, 31 Jan. 1947: 3.

"Sing Hoo's Last Case," 31 Jan. 1947: 5 (second installment of the
    murder mystery).

Drawing of a baseball player petting a leopard, 7 Feb. 1947: 3 (Wright
    has "1946").

"Sing Hoo's Last Case," 7 Feb.1947: 5 (third installment of the murder
    mystery).

Drawing of Cupid aiming an arrow at a student, 14 Feb. 1947: cover.

Drawing of a basketball player pushing another player, 14 Feb. 1947:
    5.

"Sing Hoo's Last Case," 14 Feb. 1947: 7 (conclusion of the murder
    mystery).

Drawing of boxers, 21 Feb. 1947: 3.

Drawing of John Henry, 28 Feb. 1947: 5.

"John Henry," 28 Feb. 1947: 5 (poem).

Drawing of a basketball player, 7 Mar. 1947: 3.

Drawing of a female basketball player, 14 Mar. 1947: 3.

"Movie Reviews," 14 Mar. 1947: 5 (reviews "Cross My Heart," "Radio Take it Away," and "The Michigan Kid." Taylor has "1946").

"Gentleman from Spain," 4 Apr. 1947: 5 (article about Ponce de Leon).

Drawing of Casey, 4 Apr. 1947: 9.

"Casey at the Bat Again and Again," 4 Apr. 1947: 9 (poem response to a poem on the same subject by Fred Muth).

Drawing, 11 Apr. 1947: 5.

Drawing, 11 Apr. 1947: 6.

"It Happened in Brooklyn," 11 Apr. 1947: 7 (film review).

Drawing, 18 Apr. 1947: 2.

Drawing, 18 Apr. 1947: 4.

"The Bubble Bursts," 25 Apr. 1947: 2 (editorial).

Drawing, 25 Apr. 1947: 2.

"Odd Occupations I: Jackals," 25 Apr. 1947: 5 (article).

"Odd Occupations: II: Cellophane Wrappers," 2 May 1947: 5 (article).

Drawing, 2 May 1947: 2.

Drawing, 9 May 1947: 2.

Drawing, 29 May 1947: 2.

Drawing of nine graduating seniors, 29 May 1947: 10.

Drawing of a schoolboy, 11 Sept. 1947: 2.

"Welcome," 11 Sept. 1947: 2 (editorial).

"My Story," 19 Sept. 1947: 2 (editorial).

"Achoo!" 26 Sept. 1947: 2 (editorial).

Drawing of a sneezer, 26 Sept. 1947: 2.

"A Bouquet," 3 Oct. 1947: 2 (editorial).

Drawing of man with a bouquet, 3 Oct. 1947: 2.

"Another Bouquet," 10 Oct. 1947: 2 (editorial).

Drawing of man with a bouquet, 10 Oct. 1947: 2.

"Three Steps in the Right Direction," 24 Oct. 1947: 2 (editorial).

Drawing of a schoolboy, 24 Oct. 1947: 2.

"The Spirit of Halloween." 31 Oct. 1947: 2 (editorial).

Drawing of a boy running from a policeman, 31 Oct. 1947: 2 (editorial).

"AEW and Two Formulas," 7 Nov. 1947: 2, (editorial, "AEW" means "American Educational Week").

Drawing of schoolboy and school, 7 Nov. 1947: 2.

"Bouquet Number Three," 14 Nov. 1947: 2.

Drawing of four football players and bouquet, 14 Nov. 1947: 2.

"We Give Thanks," 26 Nov. 1947: 2 (editorial).

Drawing of schoolboy saying, "Gee," 26 Nov. 1947: 2.

"'That Was My Seat,'" 5 Dec. 1947: 2 (editorial).

Drawing of a quarrel over a seat with typewriter held aloft, 5 Dec. 1947: 2.

Drawing of a singer with guitar who sings, "Ah loves to see thet evenin' sun go down," 5 Dec. 1947: 2.

"My Readers' Reactions Up to Date," 12 Dec. 1947: 2 (editorial).

"Peace on Earth," 19 Dec. 1947: 2 (editorial).

Drawing of a person yelling, "They're horrible!" 12 Dec. 1947: 2.

Drawing of a burly basketball player who checks off a win, 19 Dec. 1947: 2.

"Bouquet Numbers 4 to 7 Inclusive," 9 Jan. 1948: 2 (editorial).

Drawing of four bouquets falling from the sky, 9 Jan. 1948: 2.

Drawing of a tall basketball player holding the ball out of reach of a shorter one, 9 Jan. 1948: 2.

Drawing. 16 Jan. 1948: 2.

Note. 16 Jan. 1948: 2 (Updike now "relinquishes" the post of editor to William Bergman.)

Drawing of FDR and his dog. 30 Jan. 1948: 2.

"Three Great Men," 6 Feb. 1948: 2 (editorial tribute to Washington, Lincoln, and Edison).

Drawing. 6 Feb. 1948: 2 (caricatures of the men in previous entry).

Drawing of a shy boy and girl, 13 Feb. 1948: cover.

"Thief in Our Midst," 13 Feb. 1948: 2 (editorial).

"Why Not Movies," 20 Feb. 1948: 2 (editorial).

"Bouquet Number 14," 27 Feb. 1948: 2 (editorial).

Drawing of a boy with schedule, 27 Feb. 1948: 2.

Drawing, 5 Mar. 1948: 2.

Drawing, 12 Mar. 1948: 2.

"Easter and Spring," 25 Mar. 1948: 2 (editorial).

Drawing of a student saying, "Ho Hum," 25 Mar. 1948: 2.

Drawing of one student pushing past another, 2 Apr. 1948: 2.

"The Artists," 23 Apr. 1948: 2.

Drawing of a super athlete flexing his bicep, 23 Apr. 1948: 2.

Drawing, 23 Apr. 1948: 3.

"Something New," 30 Apr. 1948: 2 (editorial).

Drawing of a spacecraft. 30 Apr. 1948: 2.

Drawing of a huge athlete who points a gun at two woeful students, 30 Apr. 1948: 3.

"The Election," 7 May 1948: 2 (editorial).

Drawing of the startled face of a person, 7 May 1948: 3.

"Wars Will Come," 7 May 1948: 5 (poem).

"Farewell," 21 May 1948: 2 (editorial).

Drawing of a door being slammed, 21 May 1948: 2.

Drawing of a baseball player, 21 May 1948: 7 (pagination for this issue is confused).

Drawing, 21 May 1948: 6.

Drawing, 16 Sept. 1948: 3.

"History Does *Too* Repeat," 16 Sept. 1948: 5.

Drawing, 24 Sept. 1948: 3.

Drawing, 1 Oct. 1948: 3.

"Voice from the Past," 8 Oct. 1948: 5 (editorial).

Drawing, 15 Oct. 1948: 3.

"Pep Talk to the Student Body," 15 Oct. 1948: 5 (article; this issue was incorrectly dated, "October 5, 1948." It should be October 15, 1948).

"What is Your Q. Q?" 15 Oct. 1948: 8 (article).

"Lines on the Muhlenberg Game." 15 Oct. 1948: 5 (poem).

"Interview with a Schooblin [sic]." 22 Oct. 1948: 8 (mock interview.)

Drawing, 22 Oct. 1948: 3.

Drawing, 29 Oct. 1948: 3 (Wright has "29 Nov.")

Drawing, 5 Nov. 1948: 5.

"The Disobedient Brother," 5 Nov. 1948: 7 (poem).

Drawing, 12 Nov. 1948: 3.

"The Commentator," 12 Nov. 1948: 5 (poem).

"Whodun It?" 12 Nov. 1948: 5 (poem).

Drawing, 24 Nov. 1948: cover.

Drawing, 24 Nov. 1948: 4.

Drawing, 24 Nov. 1948: 5.

Drawing, 23 Dec. 1948: 5.

"Christmas 1948," 23 Dec, 1948: 10 (poem).

"It Might be Verse," 7 Jan. 1949: 5 (poem; Wright has "7 Jan. 1948").

Drawing,7 Jan. 1949: 3.

Drawing, 14 Jan. 1949: 3.

Drawing, 21 Jan. 1949: 3.

Drawing, 28 Jan. 1949: 3.

"Laugh, World, Laugh," 28 Jan. 1949: 5 (poem).

"Complaint," 4 Feb. 1949: 5 (article).

Drawing, 25 Feb. 1949: 3.

"Hamlet Reviewed (An orgy of superlatives)," 25 Feb. 1949: 5 (film review).

"Throw Away Those Record Books: I've Hit the Extra Double Bonus," 4 Mar. 1949: 4 (article).

"P. S. to Last Week's Editorial," 11 Mar. 1949: 5 (poem).

"Homework (to the Tune of 'The Money Song')," 11 Mar. 1949: 5 (poem).

Drawing, 18 Mar. 1949: 4.

"Dear Aqua and White." 25 Mar. 1949: 8 (reprinted in *Chatterbox* 30 Aug. 1980: 1).

Drawing, 25 Mar. 1949: 4.

Drawing of man with mirror, 25 Mar. 1949: 8 (reprinted: *Chatterbox* 30 Aug. 1980: 1).

Drawing, 14 Apr. 1949: 4.

Drawing, 14 Apr. 1949: 5.

"The Season of Mud," 14 Apr. 1949: 7 (poem reprinted: *Chatterbox* 11 Nov. 1949: 8).

"Ode to the Seniors," 14 Apr. 1949: 7 (poem).

Drawing, 14 Apr. 1949: 12.

Drawings of musicians, conductor, floor sweeper, 14 Apr. 1949: 13.

Drawing of an exhausted player, 14 Apr. 1949: 14.

"On Baseball," 22 Apr. 1949: 5 (poem).

"Apology," 22 Apr. 1949: 5 (poem).

"Typing Turmoil," 28 Apr. 1949: 8 (poem).

"Box Score Blues," 28 Apr. 1949: 8 (poem).

Drawing, 6 May 1949: 4.

Drawing of "ekes." 6 May 1949: 8.

"Ode to Eke," 6 May 1949: 8 (poem).

"The Rise and Fall of the Sunday Newspaper," 23 May 1949: 8 (poem).

Untitled, 15 Sept.1949: 8 (editorial with lyrics).

Drawing, 15 Sept. 1949: 2.

Drawing, 23 Sept. 1949: 2.

"Inscription upon Tombstone," 30 Sept. 1949: 8 (poem).

Drawing, 30 Sept. 1949: 2.

Drawing, 30 Sept. 1949: 8.

Drawing, 7 Oct. 1949: 2.

"Reflections of a Clock Watcher in Trig Class," 7 Oct. 1949: 5 (poem).

"Drawing," 7 Oct. 1949: 6.

"Out of Fashion," 7 Oct. 1949: 8 (poem).

Untitled, 7 Oct. 1949: 8 (poem, which Updike attributes to "Wilma Wifflepeiphre").

Drawing, 14 Oct. 1949: 2.

"Home-Made Epitaphs," 14 Oct. 1949: 8 (poem).

Drawing, 28 Oct. 1949: 2.

"To a Pair of Gone Glasses," 28 Oct. 1949: 8 (poem; Wright has "To a Pair of Glasses").

Drawing of a man seeking his glasses. 28 Oct. 1949: 8 (poem; Wright has "To a Pair of Glasses").

Drawing of a person saying "Bah" to the seasons, 4 Nov. 1949: 2.

Drawing, 4 Nov. 1949: 8.

Drawing, 11 Nov. 1949: 2.

"The Season of Mud," 11 Nov.1949: 8 (poem).

Drawing, 23 Nov. 1949: 2.

"Ballad Before the Newsreel (with a curtsy dropped to Ogden Nash)," 23 Nov. 1949: 10 (poem).

Drawing, 23 Nov. 1949: 10.

"Experience—the Best Teacher?" 2 Dec. 1949: 2 (editorial).

Drawing of a man dropping a match in a barrel marked "Danger," 2 Dec. 1949: 2.

"Notes on Treatment of Typists—to F.M.," 2 Dec. 1949: 8 (poem).

"A Sad Sad Song," 2 Dec. 1949: 8 (poem).

Drawing of five sad students being led in a cheer, 9 Dec. 1949: 2.

Drawing of a man sipping poison through a straw, 9 Dec. 1949: 8.

"True Confession," 9 Dec. 1949: 8 (mock attack on "FM"—Fred Muth).

"Verses One through Five," 9 Dec. 1949: 8 (poem).

Drawing, "Christmas—1949," 22 Dec. 1949: cover.

"A Christmas Carol for Cynics," 22 Dec. 1949: 10 (poem).

Drawing, 6 Jan. 1950: 2.

"Greetings, Etc.," 6 Jan. 1950: 8 (poem; Wright dates this issue errone-
ously as Jan. 7).

Drawing of Santa Claus, 6 Jan. 1950: 8.

Drawing, 13 Jan. 1950: 2.

"Amoeba," 13 Jan. 1950: 6 (poem; Wright has Jan. 10).

"Apologia: The Plight of a Feature Writer," 13 Jan. 1950: 6 (article;
Wright has Jan. 10 for this issue).

"Comment on a Common Indecency," 13 Jan. 1950: 6 (poem).

"Felis Domestica: Finis," 13 Jan. 1950: 6 (poem).

Drawing, "This Wasn't My Idea," 13 Jan. 1950: 6.

"Dead," 13 Jan. 1950: 6 (poem).

"Diamonds," 13 Jan. 1950: 6 (poem).

"Department of Amplification and Abomination," 13 Jan. 1950: 8 (article).

Drawing of sleepy students, 13 Jan. 1950: 8.

"Acceptance of Minority Views," 20 Jan. 1950: 2 (editorial).

Drawing of a finger pointing at a person, 20 Jan. 1950: 2.

"From a Lemming," 20 Jan. 1950: 6 (poem).

Drawing of a lemming typing, 20 Jan. 1950: 6.

"The Moment Called Now," 20 Jan. 1950: 6 (poem).

Drawing of *Life* magazine, 27 Jan. 1950: 8.

"The Mags (a series) I, Life," 27 Jan. 1950: 8 (poem).

Drawing of a hook, 27 Jan. 1950: 8.

"Too Busy," 27 Jan. 1950: 8 (poem).

"Department of Definition and Further Word from my Lemming," 27
Jan. 1950: 8 (it is signed "Imogene").

Drawing, 3 Feb. 1950: [2].

"Let's See What We Can Do," 3 Feb. 1950: [2] (editorial).

"The Mags II—Collier's," 3 Feb. 1950: 8 (poem).

"Transit Unions Reject Arbitration (headline)," 3 Feb. 1950: 8 (poem).

Drawing of stick figures trudging below newspaper headline "Strike
continues," 3 Feb. 1950: 8.

"I. The Movies," 10 Feb. 1950: 2 (editorial).

"The Mags II—National Geographic," 10 Feb. 1950: 8 (poem).

"Obituary," 10 Feb. 1950: 8 (poem).

Drawing of persons gathered at a death bed, 10 Feb. 1950: 8.

"Valentine to the Hydrogen Bomb," 10 Feb. 1950: 8 (poem).

"II—Radio and TV," 17 Feb. 1950: 2 (article; Wright lists this as "II. The Movies").

"The Boy Who Makes the Blackboard Squeak," 17 Feb. 1950: 6 (poem reprinted in *National Parent-Teacher Magazine* Feb. 1950).

"On the Last Day of the Season," 17 Feb. 1950: 8 (poem about basketball which names several players, Barry Nelson and Jerry Potts among them).

Drawing, 17 Feb. 1950: 8.

"The Mags IV—*The New Yorker*," 17 Feb. 1950: 8 (poem).

"Winter (a dirge)," 24 Feb. 1950: 8 (poem).

Drawing of the god of the winds, 24 Feb. 1950: 8.

"From a Lemming (a final word)," 24 Feb. 1950: 8 (poem, signed "Imogene," a pseudonym Updike used in replying to Fred Muth, who fashioned himself "Arthur").

"A Solid Geometry Student Looks at Learning (a triple cinquain)," 24 Feb. 1950: 8. (poem; Wright has "Leary" for "Learning").

"The Mags V—Saturday Evening Post (one of a series)," 24 Feb. 1950: 8 (poem).

Drawing, 3 Mar. 1950: 2.

"Dept. of Omitted Lines," 3 Mar. 1950: 8 (Wright notes: "Erratum" for "On the last Day of the Season" 17 Feb. 1950: [8]).

"Logic," 3 Mar. 1950: 8 (poem).

"The Mags VI—Esquire," 3 Mar. 1950: 8 (poem).

Drawing of person reading *Esquire*, 3 Mar. 1950: 8 (placed above "The Mags VI—Esquire").

"Time Is Circular in Shape," 3 Mar. 1950: 8 (poem).

"& They Lived Happily Ever After," 1 Apr. 1950: 2 (poem).

"An April Fool," 1 Apr. 1950: 2 (poem).

"Ode to Code," 1 Apr. 1950: 2 (poem).

"Philosophical Thought," 1 Apr. 1950: 2 (poem).

"To a Serutan," 1 Apr. 1950: 2 (poem).

"Whimsy," 1 Apr. 1950: 2 (poem).

"Ode on a Pin Ball Machine," 14 Apr. 1950: 10 (poem; Wright has "to" a Pin Ball Machine).

Drawing of a boy with bags of nickels, 14 Apr. 1950: 10.

Drawing of a boy with empty bags, 14 Apr. 1950: 10.

"The Mags VIII—Time (with a feeble stab at Timestyle," 14 Apr. 1950: 10 (poem).

"Sonnet on Chaucer," 14 Apr. 1950 10 (poem).

"A-Headin' fer the Break (a ballad of misery)," 21 Apr. 1950: 2 (poem).

Drawing of student writing, 21 Apr. 1950: 2.

"Wednesday Night Church Service," 21 Apr. 1950: 2 (poem).

"While Awaiting Service in a Shoe Store," 21 Apr. 1950: 2 (poem).

Drawing of a man in stocking feet looking angry, 21 Apr. 1950: 2.

Drawing of man with yo-yo, 28 Apr.1950: 8.

"Move Over, Dodo," 28 Apr.1950: 8 (poem, reprinted in *Songs of Youth*. Los Angeles: American Poetry Society, 1950. 111; *Chatterbox* 12 May 1950; and *Florida Magazine of Verse* XI.1 [Nov. 1950]).

"Yo-Yo Champ," 28 Apr. 1950 8 (poem).

Drawing of a huge spirit of a graduate from college with high school graduate below him, 12 May 1950: cover.

Drawing of a graduate wending his way from high school to "some other school," 12 May 1950: 15.

"Audience Particpiation [sic]: Everybody Sing!" 12 May 1950: 16 (poem).

"Child's Question," 12 May 1950: 16 (poem; on reverse of previous page 15; reprinted in "View from the Catacombs," *Time* 26 Apr. 1968: 73).

"Ha Ha Sam Spade You Slay Me," 12 May 1950: 16 (poem).

"Haunted House," 12 May 1950: 16 (poem; on reverse of previous page 15).

Drawing of seven seniors, including Barry Nelson, 12 May 1950: 17.

Drawing of seven seniors, including Updike and Fred Muth, 12 May 1950: 18.

"Department of Utter Confusion," 12 May 1950: 20 (drawing of seven seniors, including three sets of twins).

Drawing of a student leaving Shillington High School, while another enters; Updike provides a short goodbye, 12 May 1950: 21.

"Move Over, Dodo," 12 May 1950: 21 (poem).

"On FM," 12 May 1950: 21 (poem).

"Frank Advice to a Young Poet," 12 May 1950: 22 (poem).

Drawings of George Bernard Shaw and two others poets,12 May 1950: 22.

Drawing of a large, ghostly student in cap and gown who follows a much smaller student out of Shillington High School, with various images of wickedness alongside the steps, 23 May 1950: cover.

"Last Look," 23 May 1950: 2 (editorial).

"1950 Class Song (To the tune of 'Auld Lang Syne')," 23 May 1950: 2 (poem; reprinted in *Hi-Life* Shillington, Pennsylvania: The Senior Class of Shillington High School, 1950. 70).

UNSIGNED AND ATTRIBUTED CONTRIBUTIONS

(Only attributed are indicated.)

Drawing of two ballplayers, 29 Mar. 1945: 3.

Drawing of a football player, 21 Sept. 1945: 3.

Drawing of a football tackler, 28 Sept. 1945: 3.

Drawing of a football player and a bear, 2 Nov. 1945: 3.

Drawing of two basketball players, 21 Nov. 1945: 3.

Drawing of a basketball player, 11 Jan. 1946: 9.

Drawing of a beaten face, 25 Jan. 1946: 3.

"Our Comments on the Movies," 6 Dec. 1946: 5 (review of "Captain Kidd" and "The Dancing Masters").

"Let's Go to the Movies," 24 Jan. 1947: 8.

Drawing, 31 Oct. 1947: cover.

Drawing, 31 Oct. 1947: 2.

"Bouquet Number Three," 14 Nov. 1947: 2 (unsigned, but almost certainly by Updike).

Drawing, 19 Dec. 1947: cover.

"Daisy Chain," 23 Jan. 1948: 2.

Drawing, 23 Jan. 1948: 2.

"FDR," 30 Jan. 1948: 2.

Drawing, 6 Feb. 1948: 3.

Drawing, 13 Feb. 1948: 2.

Drawing, 20 Feb. 1948: 2.

Drawing, 27 Feb. 1948: 3.

"Impressions of the Wilson Game," 5 Mar. 1948: 2 (editorial).

Drawing, 5 Mar. 1948: 3.

Drawing, 8 Oct. 1948: 3.

Drawing, 11 Feb. 1949: 3.

Drawing, 18 Feb. 1949: 3.

"To the Juniors," 28 Apr. 1949: 8 (poem attributed to Updike and signed "Anonymous." Under the poem is printed: "Note: In answer to the genius of that junior, J U, we print the above poem contributed by a member of the SENIOR class").

"A Meal in a Cafeteria," 18 Mar. 1949: 5 (attributed to Updike by Alexander Jemal).

"Dear Aqua and White." 25 Mar. 1949: 8 (poem attributed to Updike by Alexander Jemal).

Drawing, 6 May 1949: 3.

"To Fred," 4 Nov. 1949: 8 (poem attributed to Updike because of his mock feud with Fred Muth, also an associate editor).

"Gloom," 9 Dec. 1949: 8 (attributed to Updike by Alexander Jemal. Not found).

"The Awful Latin Language," 13 Jan. 1950: 5 (attributed).

"Why," 20 Jan. 1950, [n. p.] (attributed).

"Golden Rules," 27 Jan. 1950, [n. p.] (attributed).

"My Play," 10 Feb. 1950, [n. p.] (an essay and playlet possibly by Fred Muth).

"The Mags IX—Quick," 21 Apr. 1950: 6 (poem unsigned but undoubtedly by Updike).

Drawing, "Prominent Seniors," May 12, 1950: 11 (includes Joan Venne).

Drawing, "Prominent Seniors," May 12, 1950: 12. (includes Jackie Hirneisen).

COMMENTARY ON UPDIKE IN *CHATTERBOX*

Listed with other classmates as "Walt Disney II," 7 Mar. 1947: 8.

"Frosh to Trip Light Fantastic Toe," 18 Apr. 1947: 1, 6 (Updike is listed
as master of ceremonies).

"Comparing Stars," 9 May 1947: 8 (Updike is identified as a good at
drawing, but no Perry Como).

"Birthday Greetings," 3 Mar. 1948: 8 (Updike is listed with other classmates as having a March birthday).

"Two S. H. S. Artists Win Awards," 18 Feb. 1949.

"Try-Out Staff to Edit Chatterbox," 4 Mar. 1949.

"Invitations Enliven Evening," 4 Mar. 1949.

"Little Excerpts and Exhortations," 18 Mar. 1949 (includes the remark,
"Ask John Updike sometime how he got his cut lip, or else see
Peggy Lutz").

"Vocal Music Department Plans an Evening of Music," 28 Apr. 1949: 1
(Updike served as the interlocutor in a minstrel show).

"Chatterbox Staff Announcement Made Public to Students," 6 May
1949 (announcement of Updike's new position as associate editor
of *Chatterbox*).

"Preview Presented by Vocal Groups," 6 May 1949 (description of
Updike's acting as the interlocutor in boys' glee club minstrel
show).

"Thespians of Senior Class Present, Meet Me in St. Louis," 23 Nov.
1949: 1, 6 (Updike is listed as a character in the play).

"My Grievances [.] to JU," 23 Nov. 1949: 7 (Fred Muth, who initials his
article "F. M.," notes he will take no more abuse and writes a poem
"To J. U." with this first stanza:

> A hypocrite unequaled
> Is my dear friend J. U.
> He dissects on his Feature Page
> The Articles I do.)

A note on the end of the "feud" with Fred Muth, 9 Dec. 1949: 5.

"Speaker to Be Chosen for Debating Team," 13 Jan. 1950 (Updike
named as a student in the debate team tryouts).

"Seniors Plan for Class Meeting." 13 Jan. 1950: 4 (Updike as a class
officer is mentioned as discussing a class gift at the meeting).

"Seniors Select Class Motto." 27 Jan. 1950: 6 (Updike was named
among seniors choosing the motto).

"Amulet to Induct Nineteen Members Next Week." 10 Feb. 1950: 1 (Amulet was Shillington High's National Honor Society).

Hirneisen, Jacqueline. "Little Excerpts and Exhortations." 10 Feb. 1950: 3 (Includes a short joke about Updike's prowess in mathematics).

"Amulet Inducts New Members." 17 Feb. 1950: 4.

"Poem by John Updike Appears in P. T. A. Magazine." 17 Feb. 1950: 1 ("The Boy Who Makes the Blackboard Squeak" appeared in *P. T. A.* in February, 1950).

"Artists Attend Exhibition; Updike Wins Award." 17 Feb. 1950(On Feb. 15 Updike had won an award for the best cartoon in the Scholastic Regional Exhibition of Art at Gimbel Brothers in Philadelphia. During this program he gave a talk on five distinctive types of art students).

"Shillington Plays Host to Debate," 24 Feb. 1950: 4 (Updike argued: "Resolved: That the President of the United States Should Be Elected by the Direct vote ofthe People").

"Students Present Exchange Program," 3 Mar. 1950: 6 (announces that Updike will provide a chalk talk on types of Muhlenberg High School students).

"Seniors Select Class Song; Updike Writes Words," 10 Mar. 1950 (the poem was printed in *Hi-Life*, p. 70).

"Seniors to Replace Faculty in Senior Day Activities," N. d. (Updike replaced his father, Wesley Updike).

"Commencement Speakers Revealed; Three Co-Valedictorians Named," 17 Mar. 1950 (Updike, Fred Muth, and Ann Weik all had straight A averages).

"Seniors Participate in Discussion on Junior Town Meeting," 17 Mar. 1950: 1 (Updike was scheduled to speak March 22 at Central Catholic High School in Reading, on the topic, "Do the traditional Academic subjects Prepare for Effective Living?" The program was broadcast on station WRAW March 26).

"Seniors Win Scholarships," 23 May 1950: 1.

Appendix D: Updike's Classmates, Faculty, and Administrators

THOSE MENTIONED IN THESE CHAPTERS

Shillington High School numbered one hundred and eighteen students, sixty girls and fifty-eight boys. There are seventy-three survivors as of February 6, 2012, and all but nine still live within Berks County. Since copies of *Hi-Life*, the 1950 yearbook, are rare, I have copied the yearbook's profiles because they tell much about those students that otherwise might be lost to history. The descriptions provide the flavor of the times and help to bring Updike's classmates to life. None of them are signed. In "Flight," the character Adam Dow, one of Updike's alter egos, remarks, "I was in charge of the yearbook write-ups." Joan Venne remarked that Updike "really did care about his classmates." The following line was written on Updike's deathbed: "Dear friends of childhood, classmates, thank you" (*Endpoint* 26).

Names of the deceased students are *italicized*.

SHILLINGTON HIGH SCHOOL ADMINISTRATION AND FACULTY LISTED IN *HI-LIFE*, 1950

Administration:

Charles J. "Jack" Hemmig (Jan. 1, 1893–June 22, 1989) graduated from Shillington High School in 1911, earned his B.S. and M.S. at the University of Pennsylvania and Columbia University. After returning from World War I, Charles Hemmig taught Elementary school. He coached girls' basketball 1920–21 for Shillington High, then originated plans to purchase land and build a new school. The project was completed in 1926. He then became Supervising Principal of Shillington High School, retiring in 1952. Charles Hemmig was chairman of the "Fiftieth Anniversary of Shillington," and authored *Fifty Years of Progress, 1908–1958*. A chaplain for the Keystone Fire Company in 1959, he taught Sunday school classes for sixty-seven years and also organized the Shillington Businessmen's Organization. He made the popular decision to have Shillington High School play its football games in Albright College stadium. Charles Hemmig was named "Outstanding Citizen of Shillington" in 1961.The City of Reading proclaimed January 18, 1975, Jack Hemmig Day, and later inducted him into the Berks County Sports Hall of Fame as coach, manager, promoter, and leader in sports. Updike saw him as a shrewd educator and booster, and declared, "no one was ever more enthusiastic about Shillington." Hemmig gave financial advice to John Hoyer, hired Updike's parents, and recommended their son for a full scholarship to Harvard (*Story* 70–71, 95, 99–100). Updike included him in his poem "In the Cemetery High above Shillington"(*Americana* 29–35).

Luther Weik attended Wyomissing High School, earned his B.S. at Lebanon Valley College in 1925, and began teaching chemistry at Shillington High School that year. He also taught guidance and driver's education. At the University of Pennsylvania Luther Weik accumulated university credits in school administration, driving to Philadelphia with Wesley Updike. He received the M.S. degree at the University of Pennsylvania. During World War II, high school principal Myrtle Snyder joined the WAVES, leaving the position open for Luther Weik. (The students enjoyed the fact that Luther Amos Weik's three initials spelled "LAW.") He was business manager of the Shillington School District, involving physical facilities and transportation. Luther Weik retired in 1968. Since he boasted a good tenor voice, he appeared in minstrel shows and sang in the choir at the United Church of Christ, where he was the Sunday school teacher of the ladies' class for many years. He was an enthusiastic member of the Lions Club, Masonic Lodge, and Toastmasters. He adhered to the motto: proportion your time properly among work, church, and community. At Wesley Updike's funeral, Updike noticed Luther Weik's tears (Message from Ann Weik Cassar to the Author, 30 Jan. 2010,e-mail).

Among Board of School Directors were:

Dr. Lewis Rothermel
Don C. VanLiew

Among Faculty:

Carlton F. Boyer taught art. He attended Kutztown High School. He received his B.S. at Kutztown State Teachers College and attended the Pennsylvania Museum School of Art. Carlton Boyer did paintings for private and public Shillington patrons, as well as restaurant murals. Updike took Carlton Boyer's art class.

William H. Firing taught physical education to all grades and coached football. He attended Birdsboro High School and received his B.S. at Albright College.

Russell H. Kistler taught social science. He attended Allentown's Allen High School, received his A.B. at Muhlenberg College and his M.A. at Lehigh University. He taught at Millersville State Teacher's College, Iowa State College, and Temple University.

Thelma Kutch Lewis taught Senior English and German. She attended Shillington High School, received her A.B. at Albright College and her M.A. at Columbia University. Peggy White said of her German instruction, "believe me she drilled us." She supervised Updike in two critical ways: she was his playground supervisor and she was his faculty advisor to *Chatterbox*. Partly because she spent her life in Shillington, she and her husband had close social ties to Linda and Wesley Updike. Updike corresponded with his teacher long after graduation. At one point, he wrote that he wished he had taken her for German and Miss Pennepacker for French, rather than art with Mr. Boyer. (TKL/DSC, Letter to Thelma Lewis, 17 Mar. 1985). Updike asked her advice about poems he would later include in *The Carpentered Hen* and inscribed in her copy a note testifying to her importance. She kept him aware of Shillington things by regularly sending packets of newspaper clippings, which Updike said made him remember his playground days. He recalled in one note a favorite drinking fountain where he played pranks, and in another message he asked whether the flag was hoisted at the playground at 8 or 9 A.M. They met in April, 1957 in New York while she was studying at Columbia University. She kept him current on his classmates, especially the "sweet fellow as well as a mighty bright one," Fred Muth (TKL/DSC, Updike letter to Thelma Lewis, 29 Mar 1999). These were all notices from the lost world of his childhood, Updike wrote, and in another letter he called Shillington his genuine world (TKL/DSC, Updike letter to Thelma Lewis, 12 Mar. 1998). Although she often asked if he would be available for a speaking engagement in Reading, he regularly declined because he preferred a solo reconnaissance than lecture (TKL/DSC, Updike letter to Thelma Lewis, November 1998). Yet he did speak in Reading (April 3, 2000, sponsored by the Junior League).

Florence C. Schrack taught dramatics and English. She attended Boyertown High School, and she earned her B.S. at the University of Pennsylvania. Nancy March Le Van said that Mrs. Schrack was called "Eagle Beak" and was "very strict," always pointing. She taught the Palmer method so rigorously, "she'd grab your shoulder" if you failed to write correctly. Nancy March added that Mrs. Schrack "was a lovely person and the kids took such advantage of her." Updike commented that in the eighth grade Mrs. Schrack taught most of the English grammar he knew and was an energetic drama coach (TKL/DSC, Letter to Thelma Lewis, Oct. 2001). Mrs.

Schrack told Jackie Hirneisen that Updike's "genius" was "recognized in the first grade."

Kathryn O. Showalter taught reading, dramatics, and English to students who were preparing for college. She received her A.B., B.S., and M.S. degrees at the University of Pennsylvania. She had attended Shillington High School and taught at Millersville State Teacher's College. Updike remarked that she taught penmanship by getting students to push and pull with forearm instead of the fingers, though he couldn't master the practice (TKL/DSC, Letter to Thelma Lewis, 1991).

Margaret S. Stamm taught mathematics. She received her A.B. and B.S. at Kutztown State Teachers College and her M.A. at the University of Pennsylvania.

Peggy White taught Latin and English at Shillington High School. When Mrs. Schrack moved to Wyomissing, Peggy White was hired to fill the position.

STUDENTS AND STAFF LISTED IN *HI-LIFE*, 1950

William C. Baer. "Basketball Manager 1, 2; Hi-Life 4; Hi-Y; Stage Crew 2, Chief 3, 4; Track Manager 1, 2, 3. *Mr. Inside in many school activities . . . a healthy boy who looks forward to the day when he can join the Marines . . . Pensupreme sundaes are always good when Bill is around . . . class camera fiend . . . ambitious and industrious.*" William Baer became very active politically in local and Pennsylvania politics.

Jane L. Becker (Wertz). "Chatterbox 3, 4; Chorus 2, 3; Hi-Life 4; Y-Teens 2, 3. *Adamstown's gift to the commercial department . . . amiable, ambitious, alert . . . a compact bundle of energy . . . hard-working typist . . . extremely proud of her Adamstown heritage . . . patron of Steve's, driver of Chevrolets, sower of sweetness and light.*" Jane Becker was part of Joan Venne's "Second Street Gang" which battled Updike's gang. Jane Becker was the first of the class of 1950 to die. Apparently, she was the model for a woman in Updike's story, "Lunch Hour" (*LL* 16–27).

Harlan L. Boyer. "Class Play 3, 4; Football 1, 2, 3, 4; Hi-Y 3, 4; Homeroom President 3; Track 1, 2, 3, 4. *Scotty . . . Cars are his main interest, and he is happiest when driving one . . . black Pontiac . . . Grandpa Prophater of senior class play . . . lover of good food and Dixieland jazz . . . a future jeweler who will study at trade school.*" Harlan Boyer was born in West Reading Hospital the same day and only two hours before Updike. He was a cousin of Dolores and Linda Frederick. During the war he made brass scale-model versions of Japanese and German warships; some are in the Smithsonian. After piloting planes for the Navy, 1953–55, Harlan Boyer graduated from Millersville State College with a master's degree in January, 1959. He also went to Temple University graduate school. Harlan Boyer stayed at Millersville as supervisor for Special Education for twenty-three years. He was a guidance counselor in the Schuylkill Valley School District until his retirement in 1992. He built a plane in his garage in 1980, and later farmed on his two acres. In 1961 Harlan Boyer's father took his jewelry business to Shillington. Noted for his fine work, his father made jewels for Queen Elizabeth and Eleanor Roosevelt. He ran a jewelry store in Shillington until his death in 1972, the same year Wesley Updike died. Harlan's mother came from Glasgow. She was also gifted and made a charm bracelet of "pages" that folded into a book, with events in her life on each of the silver pages ("Craftsman"). Updike included Harlan Boyer in his poem, "Upon Becoming a Senior Citizen" (*Americana* 37).

Harlan Conrad . "Band 1; Basketball 3; Chorus 2, 3; Football 2, 3, 4; Hi-Y 3; Treasurer 4; Homeroom Vice-President 4; Track 2, 3. *He was off to a good start in football this year but was benched by a broken wrist . . . colorful shirts and socks . . . Gregg Street . . . H. C. would like to become an M.D. . . . a good egg with all the seasonings.*"

Richard L. Daubert. "Basketball 2, 3, 4; Track 1, 2, 3, 4. *In basketball, a deadly guard; in track, a peerless pole-vaulter . . . swims like the proverbial fish . . . peeved when shoes were thrown into Porky . . . indispensable to the Second Street Gang . . . a little of the Old Nick.*" Richard Daubert came to Shillington High School in seventh grade.

Robert D. Daubert. "Baseball 2, 3, 4; Football 1; Homeroom Treasurer 2; Secretary 3, 4; Track 1, 2, 3, 4. *This peppy twin is right on the ball when it comes to basketball and track . . . Aqua King of the Porky . . . enjoys English . . . People who can tell Bob from Dick mystify us.*"

Jouette Eifert (Chick). "Band 4; Class Play 3, 4; Hi-Life 4; Hockey 3; Student Council Secretary 4; Y-Teens 2, 3, 4. *Jo . . . a lovely lady with a peaches and cream complexion, strikingly black eyes, and a whimsical air . . . a lilting laugh . . . feels the world is a lot of fun, and the feeling is mutual.*"

William A. Forry. "Class Treasurer 3; Class Play 3, 4; Student Council 3; Torch 2, 3. *The self-appointed girl hater of the class . . . vast repertoire of jokes . . . a fanatical Chrysler connoisseur, Bill dreams of a souped-up New Yorker . . . one of our leading actors . . . an extrovert who often indulges in introspection.*" Bill Forry was Updike's childhood friend. After returning from the Korean War he married Doris (Wolfe) April 26, 1955. He worked for twenty-five years as a stationary engineer at The Toledo Hospital. He died on December 21, 2011.

Mahlon M. Frankhauser. "Band 1; Class Play 3, 4; Football 2, 3; Hi-Life 4; Hi-Y 3, 4; Orchestra 1; Track 1, 2, 3, 4. *Mahlon is our class radical (he claims to be merely 'liberal') . . . a star miler who has difficulty avoiding both women and pastry . . . dances, dresses well . . . never backs from an argument . . . has all the equipment a good lawyer needs."* Mahlon Frankhauser was a close friend of Jouette Eifert.

Dolores F. Frederick (Ohlinger). "Band 2, 3; Chorus 2; Class Play 3, 4; Torch 2, 3. *Happy-go-lucky Freddy is always ready for an argument . . . her blue Chevy sees lots of service . . . the Bowmansville beauty recreates by dancing or swimming . . . convertible hair-do . . . Garver's habitué . . . hopes to enter nursing as career."* Dolores Frederick, a cousin of Harlan Boyer, met Updike in 1946 in the ninth grade. Her married name, Ohlinger, may have kindled in Updike's mind the idea of using the sobriquet "Olinger" for Shillington.

Joan L. George (Zug). "Band 2, 3, 4; Class Treasurer 1, 2, 4; Class Play 3, 4; Homeroom President 1, 2, 3; Student Council 1, 2; Y-Teens 2, Vice President 3, President 4. *Pudge is an attractive lass with a charming personality . . . her true loves are food and Kenhorst boys . . . art is tops . . . would like to fill a fashion designer's shoes."* Joan George and Updike went to Philadelphia with their art class for art shows. She was married for twenty years to Nelson Zug, a clarinetist, and Updike recalled that when she mentioned her husband, her face expressed her happiness (JVYC, 11 June 1985). Since Updike was divorcing in 1975, he escorted Joan George to the reunion that year. She was suffering from cancer when Updike visited her in the hospital during his return to Shillington for the fifty-fifth reunion in 2005.

Jack E. Guerin. "Class Play 3, 4; Hi-Life 4; Hi-Y 3, Secretary 4; Homeroom President 1, Treasurer 2; Secretary 3; Student Council 1, 3. *Jack is the energetic, irrepressible redhead always involved in activity— good or bad . . . old Stephen's grad . . . American Casualty's favorite son . . . smooth dancer, competent thespian, future dentist . . . a young man with personality plus."* Jack Guerin was Updike's closest friend, next to Fred Muth. He worked as a buyer for Met-Ed and in public relations for the Three-Mile Island installation. He later went into business building home swimming pools.

Emerson W. Gundy. "Class Play 4; Football 2, 3; Hi-Y 2, 3; Track 3. *A prominent Morgantown roader . . . Emerson and his Ford are just about inseparable . . . dead eye with a shotgun . . . basketball and nighttime ice skating on Green Hills Lake . . . held down Fred's lines in senior class play."* Emerson Gundy is Updike's second cousin, since Updike's mother Linda Hoyer Updike was a first cousin of Emerson's mother. He joined Shillington High School in the ninth grade and rode with Updike and his father every day until he was sixteen. Since Emerson was from the farming area near Shillington, he thought girls mocked his Pennsylvania-Dutch accent, though Jackie Hirneisen said she never noticed it, and she was from Adamstown where Pennsylvania Dutch was spoken. In the caption the phrase, "Held down Fred's lines" might refer to lines Fred Muth wrote for the class play. Emerson Gundy danced waltzclog in *Meet Me in Saint Louis*, directed by Francis R. Gelnett. Mrs. Florence Schrack is said to have "loved him" in this role. He worked in summer stock theater in Green Hills, doing bit parts and backstage work, and he acted with Bella Lugosi in *Dracula*. He met such stars as Signe Hasso and John Carradine. Emerson Gundy's mother, like Linda Updike, graduated from Kutztown University. Emerson and Marlene Gundy purchased the Updike farm from Updike in 1990.

Clarence H. Hall. "Chorus 1, 2, 3, 4. *Clint has no patience with folks who ask if he is older than Milton . . . Marine Reserver . . . German seems to fascinate Bing . . . boisterous singer . . . easy to get along with . . . conscientiousness will take him far.*"

Milton A. Hall. "Baseball Manager 3; Chorus 1, 2, 3, 4. *Milt found an outlet for his excess energy in the Marine Corps Reserve . . . an earnest basketball player . . . veteran Conradman . . . Perry gets a big kick out of Shakespeare . . . more quiet than Clarence, just as likeable.*"

Barbara L. Hartz (Behney). "Basketball 2, 3; Hockey 3, 4; Track 3; Volleyball 2, 3. *Hartzie is another of our athletic females . . . stars especially in hockey and basketball . . . hearty, good-natured laugh . . . might like to further develop her talent at art school . . . a grand kid and swell sport.*" Barbara Hartz lived at 107 Philadelphia Avenue, a few doors from Updike. She noted, "Both of my uncles were coaches." Barbara Hartz was engaged to Richard "Rabbit" Hiester, of the class of 1947. Barbara's uncle rented Stephen's Sweet Shop. Later she ran a stained glass company. She sent a stained glass panda to President Richard Nixon on his successful negotiations with China in 1972.

Jacqueline J. Hirneisen (Kendall). "Amulet 3, Secretary 4; Chatterbox 4; Cheerleading 2, 3, 4; Class Secretary 1; Class Play 3, 4; Court 3, 4; Hi-Life 4; Hockey 2, 3,4; Homeroom Secretary 1, Vice-President 2, 3; Torch 1, 2, 3; Y-Teens 2, 3, 4. *Jackie runs the gamut of adjectives from attractive to zealous . . . combines intellectual acuteness and athletic prowess . . . took leading roles in both class plays . . . the blondest streak in school . . . Shillington High's gift to the business world.*" Jackie Hirneisen moved to Shillington when she was in the fifth grade. In 1943 Updike wrote poems to her, lightheartedly expressing his affection for her.

Joseph R. Jasinski. "Band 1, 2, 3, President 4; Basketball 2; Torch 2, 3. *Jazz . . . a young man with a horn . . . able band president . . . Joe is seldom caught without a witty retort . . . prefers veal cutlets . . . swimming, ice skating and basketball . . . plans to continue music at Lebanon Valley College.*"

Peggy A. Lutz (Roberts). "Chatterbox 4; Cheerleading 1, 2, 3, 4; Class Secretary 3, 4; Class Play 3, 4; Hockey 2, 3, 4; Homeroom Secretary

2; Student Council 1; Y-Teens 2, 3, 4. *Peg is pep personified . . . captained our lively cheerleading squad . . . a sportswoman who above all prefers hockey . . . navy fan . . . sparkling smile, dancing eyes, irrepressible personality . . . a knockout who's going to be tough to forget."* Peggy Lutz was the May Queen. She married Tjaden Roberts of the class of 1948 after graduation. At the reunion of 2005 Peggy Lutz, afflicted with Parkinson's disease, told Updike he was a terrible writer. He found her enchanting still.

Richard W. Manderbach. "Class Play 3; Homeroom Secretary 2, 3. *Mandy follows up his jokes with a sober stare . . . usually in a Plymouth . . . curliest hair this side of a wire-haired terrier . . . expansive smile . . . extensive sideburns . . . Rex hopes to become a mechanical engineer."* Richard Manderbach, nicknamed "Mandy," moved to Shillington from Reading when he was twelve in 1945. After graduating from Penn State University, he became an electronics engineer with Western Electric in Allentown, Pennsylvania.

Nancy March (Le Van). "Band 1, 2, 3, 4; Basketball 4; Chatterbox 3; Class Play 3, 4; Hi-Life 4; Hockey 3; Homeroom President 1, Secretary 4; Orchestra 1, 2, 3, 4; Volleyball 4; Y-Teens 2, 3, 4. *Nan . . . never lacking a remark . . . staunch member of Loyal Lovers of Loos . . . Her interpretation of Mrs. Waughop's lines sparked the Senior Class Play . . . witty, wise, and well-liked . . . intends to work as a fashion artist."* Nancy March, who writes religious poetry, knew Updike from the first grade. She played the flute in a trio that included Mary Ann Schmehl (piano) and Ann Weik (cello).

Charles F. McComsey. "Chorus 2; Swimming 2, 4; Track 1, 2, 4. *Mac seems unusually serious of late . . . fond of fishing, hunting and trapping . . . finds homework a dull chore . . . summertime duck picker . . . His thoughtful nature is only partially cloaked by a fun-loving exterior."* In track he threw the shot put, and he was so strong he could carry Richard Manderbach on his shoulders for hours. He told jokes, often obscene, according to Richard Manderbach. Once, he was threatened with a paddling by Principal Dickinson, which scared him so much he raced down the steps and crashed into Supervising Principal Charles Hemmig. As Tony Van Liew remarked, "that was the end of him." For this and other things, Charles McComsey was sent to parochial school and, according to Richard Manderbach, was "held back three years." Yet, to the surprise of many, Charles McComsey graduated from Teacher's College and became the track coach at Conrad Weiser High.

D. Frederick Muth. "Amulet 3, President 4; Chatterbox 1, 2, 3, 4; Class Play 3; Hi-Y 3, 4; Torch 1, President 2. *Owner, manager, employee of Shilco Stamp Co . . . Report cards can be beautiful . . . wit so dry it crackles . . . Latin scholar . . . chronic Oldsmobile driver . . . twinkle in eye, smile on lips . . . a young man who is going places."* Ann Weik and

Fred Muth appeared in the yearbook photograph as "most studious couple," and, with Updike, were commencement speakers upon graduating. Fred Muth was Updike's best friend from the time they met in first grade. Like Updike he was an only child. As Jackie Hirneisen remarked, "Together with John they were dynamite." Jack Guerin commented, "If it weren't for John, Fred would have been the most intelligent in the class," but Joan Venne remembered that she had to correct Fred Muth's poor writing in handwriting class. Ann Weik recalled her participation in the Big Little Books sessions at Fred Muth's house "with Updike and Larry Essick." Said to be in love with Jane Becker, he was in her Jeep when she hit a bump on Waverly Street, and, since seatbelts had yet to be invented, he was tossed from the car but was uninjured. His father, Dawson H. Muth, was the first judge from Shillington on the Berks County bench of the Orphans Court, serving there twenty years. Eventually following his father into law, Fred Muth practiced in Shillington and Reading. Milton Hall remarked that Fred Muth was, "One of the few I knew who had common sense and never looked down his nose." Funny and warm, Fred Muth did not let juvenile diabetes, contracted at age twelve, hold him back. Writing about him in 2006, Updike recalled how Fred Muth faced diabetes with courage, and that it was a fortunate friendship (AWCC, Postcard to Ann Cassar 23 Oct. 2006). He died at 74 in 2006, prompting Shirley Smith to say, "That really destroyed me." Updike immortalized Fred Muth in "Endpoint," as one who taught him "smarts," and he poignantly recalled how, at the end of his life, the disabled Fred Muth politely fetched Updike's coat. Fred Muth was a classmate who provided him "heaven" at the "start" ("Peggy Lutz, Fred Muth" *Endpoint* 26).

Barry R. Nelson. "Baseball 3; Basketball 2, 3, 4; Chatterbox 4; Class Treasurer 3; Football 1, 2, 3, 4; Hi-Life 4; Olympus 3, 4; Student Council 2, 3, 4; Torch 2. *"Busy—that's Barry . . . this three-fold sport star finds time to serve the school in a dozen sundry ways . . . pleasing personality could tame a tiger . . . full of humor (?)* [sic] *. . . future M.D . . . has what it takes, plus."* From Adamstown, Barry joined Shillington High School in the ninth grade. He met Updike while working on *Chatterbox*. At Stephen's Luncheonette he tried to warn Updike not to put "tons and tons and tons of salt on his burgers," but to no avail. Barry taught journalism at Governor Mifflin High School, and he later became the school's principal. His journalism class produced a slide show of Updike's life in Shillington. He wrote "Updike Terrain," showing the places used for inspiration in *The Centaur*, a very valuable source study. Of Updike he remarked, "He put Shillington on the map, there is no doubt about that" (Posten).

Benarda A. Palm. "Chatterbox 4; Chorus 3; Class Play 3; Hi-Life 4; Y-Teens 2, 3, 4. *Benny . . . unfailingly high spirits . . . loves to play, coach, and watch all manner of sports . . . constant companion of Ginnie . . . a conscientious worker . . . vigorous laugh (some call it horsey) . . . hopes to become a teacher.*" Benarda Palm graduated from Kutztown University and taught in Reading for over thirty years.

Edward P. Pienta. "Football 2, 3, 4. *Pazoot is Kenhorst bred . . . We almost lost this stalwart to the Navy but our luck held . . . a locker room warbler who will imitate Al Jolson at the drop of* [a (ed.)] *tambourine . . . Where there's Ed, there's fun.*"

Mary Ann Schmehl. "Amulet 3, 4; Band 4; Court 2, 3; Chief Justice 4; Hi-Life 4; Homeroom Secretary 1, 2; Orchestra 1, 2, 3, 4; Torch 1, 2; Y-Teens 2, 3, 4. *Schmehlie instrumentalizes not only upon the piano but also on the viola and glockenspiel . . . ambitious and conscientious, she assumes much responsibility . . . never too harrid* [sic] *to laugh at a joke . . . has urge to become a librarian.*" Mary Ann Schmehl was one of six valedictorians. She married Bill Ehst.

Shirley F. Smith (Berger). "Cheerleading 2, 3, 4; Class Play 4; Hockey 2, 3, 4; Homeroom Secretary 1; Volleyball 2, 3, 4. *Proven—Good things come in small packages . . . Shirl seems enthusiastic about everything . . . hard-hitting hockeyette . . . wowed 'em as Tootie in the senior class play . . . Kenhorst may well be proud of this home grown product.*" Shirley Smith took the straight secretarial track. She was in Wesley Updike's Homeroom for four years. Updike signed his name in her yearbook with a nickname he rarely used. Jackie Hirneisen was her best friend. She later worked for Dr. Ernie Rothermel, the Updikes' family dentist. She said that in 1950 her husband played second base for the St. Louis Cardinals baseball team, managed by Berks Country native, George "Whitey" Kurowski.

Mary Ann Stanley (Moyer). "Cheerleading 1, 2, 3, 4; Class Play 3, 4; Hockey 2, 3, 4; Homeroom President 1, 3; Y-Teens 2, 3, 4. *Swoosh! There goes Stan, with exactly 8.2 seconds to make homeroom . . . Well, after all, she does live one whole block away . . . cheered and played mamma to the class plays between trips to Stephen's . . . stately grace.*" Mary Ann Stanley recalled, "For my thirteenth birthday on Victory in Japan Day [August 14, 1945], Updike brought me two mysteries by Erle Stanley Gardner" (Posten A2). She captured the coveted role of Mrs. Smith in the senior play, *Meet Me in Saint Louis,* a play by Sally Benson, originally published in *The New Yorker.* She also played the wife in *The Divine Flora,* a comedy by Florence Ryerson and Colin Clements. Since Mr. Smith was played by Updike in the former play, and her husband in the latter, some called Mary Ann Stanley "Updike's first wife." Updike admitted that he always felt a little married to her. He remembered her stage presence thirty-five years later (JVYC, 11 June 1985), and she is alluded to in "In

Football Season" as the character Mary Louise Hornberger (*Early Stories*, [52]–66). Mary Ann Stanley worked for a district judge and sold real estate.

James M. Trexler. "Band 1, 2, 3, 4; Class Play 3, 4; Homeroom President 1; Orchestra 1, 2, 3, 4; Swimming 1, 2, 3, 4. *The Fords really roll when Jim's driving . . . dialect jokes . . . just naturally full of mischief . . . 'Tex' suited Trex to a T . . . The Big Boy and his tuba gave the band an extra something.*" After high school he and Charlie McComsey went to Colorado where they worked in sugar mills and drove trucks. He served in the Air Force and met Charlie McComsey, who was also in the service, in London. James Trexler was the sales manager for thirty-five years of Heizmann Tool Makers, later Columbian Cutlery, Inc.

John H. Updike. "Amulet 3, Vice-President 4; Basketball 2; Chatterbox Artist and Associate Editor 1, 2, 3, 4; Class President 1, 4; Class Play 3, 4; Debating 4; Hi-Life 4; Homeroom President 1, Secretary 2, Vice-President 4; Torch 1, 2, 3. *Uppy doubles as poet and cartoonist . . . fathered both class plays . . . calls Stephen's home . . . pet hate: ketchup . . . love dat Buick! . . . basketball and pinballing big sports interest . . . The sage of Plowville hopes to write for a living.*"

D. Anthony VanLiew. "Torch 1, 2, 3. *Tony . . . rabid Dodger fanatic . . . not a good man to have in a china shop . . . 'Bah!' . . . Spider had plenty of headaches as ad manager . . . claims his favorite dish is watermelons and fried chicken (!) . . . finds television wrestling hilarious.*" Tony Van Liew first met Updike in kindergarten. After Updike left his summer work at the Reading *Eagle*, Tony Van Liew filled the vacancy, and he later worked as copy editor. He did title searches as well, and once saved his company a great deal of money.

Joan P. Venne (Youngerman). "Band 1, 2, 3, 4; Class Play 3; Hi-Life 3, 4; Homeroom Secretary 1, 2; Student Council 1; Y-Teens 2, 3, 4. *Joanie . . . As head majorette, she had the whole band in back of her . . . a gracious hostess . . . The Venne homestead never wanted for visitors . . . Stardust . . . Oh, those New York Yankees! . . . one in whom you can confide.*" Joan Venne arrived in Shillington in July 1941, and entered Shillington Elementary School in the fourth grade; there she met Updike, since their last names put them next to each other alphabetically. He promptly wrote her a love letter. For the next nine years they were close friends in school, and their friendship lasted all his life. Joan Venne was a colonel in a children's "army" called Junior Commandos that mimicked the armies fighting in World War II. "We would march once a week to 225 Lancaster Avenue to do bandages in a finished basement." She and Updike dated casually, and at one point he sent her a valentine; another time he sent her a poem. Together, she said, they had "so much fun." She watched him doodle caricatures of students during English class, and, after showing them to her, he would toss them away. She would retrieve them, and he would ask why she did so. Updike later remarked that Joan Venne was a great audience for his jokes (TKL/DSC, Letter to David Silcox, 31July 2007). She worked with him on *Chatterbox* and *Hi-Life*, but she didn't appear for the yearbook photos of those publications. Joan Venne went to Webber College near Lake Wales, Florida. Although it was a "finishing school" Joan Venne insists, "I didn't get finished." Afterwards she worked for fifteen years in fashion sales promotion at Pomeroy's Department Store in Reading, where Linda Updike had sold drapery in the 1930s. She was best friends with Joan George (Zug), while she worked in retail sales. Later she worked for Lit Brothers department store as a special event coordinator, and she worked for the Pennsylvania Welfare department. She was Updike's constant correspondent, and of her closeness to him she remarked, "I always felt only his wives knew him better than I did" (Posten A2).

Marvin Waid. "Band 1, 2, 3, 4; Orchestra 1, 2, 3, 4. *The little man with the big smile . . . Marv is enemy number one of English grammar . . . one of our Loos Lovers . . . We wonder what that Chevy truck has more of, horse power or rattles . . . future contractor.*" Marvin Waid met Updike in first grade and was with him through their senior year.

Ann M. Weik (Cassar). "Amulet 3, 4; Band 2, 3, 4; Chatterbox 1, 2, Associate Editor 3, Chief Editor 4; Class Play 3; Orchestra 1, 2, 3, 4; Torch 1, 2; Y-Teens 2, 3, 4. *The only letters lower than A on Ann's report card are those in her name . . . explosions in chemistry lab . . . We don't know whether to call this versatile miss a female Faraday, a petite Piatigorsky, or a small-town Swope.*" "Swope" was an allusion to Herbert Bayard Swope, a *New York World* newspaper editor and reporter, and it was meant as a witty comment on Ann Cassar's work on the school paper. She still clearly remembers that on the first day of kindergarten she wore a pale blue and white checked gingham dress, sewed by her mother, and she had Shirley Temple curls as well. Since her father was principal of the school, Ann considered herself, along with Updike, one of the "teacher's brats."

Georgean Youndt. "Chorus 2; Hi-Life 4; Y-Teens 2, 3. *One of our lovely Adamstown belles . . . Honey found Shakespeare delightful . . . green Studey . . . habitué of Stephen's . . . The Blush has unchangeable opinions on almost any subject . . . says her ambition is to get out of school.*" Doris Gerhardt, a character in "Lunch Hour" is modeled on her (LL 16–27).

EARLIER GRADUATES ASSOCIATED WITH UPDIKE MENTIONED
IN THIS BOOK

Robert Arndt graduated from Shillington High School in 1947. His unitalicized caption in *Hi-Life* reads "Big Stoop . . . Athletic . . . Wolfing . . . Proud of 'Pop's Car' . . . Yearns to be a bachelor (Ha! Ha!) . . . Peeved by stuck-up girls . . . Roast beef . . . Embarrassed when pronouncing big words . . . Winter and midnight, ah! . . . Fondness for Kindergarten not yet surpassed by other grades." Robert Arndt played clarinet in the band and once performed a clarinet duo with Bevan Waid. He starred in basketball, and Updike watched him during the season of 1946–47 and noted, "there was something very pale and rabbity about him" (Plath xvi).

Myrtle Council graduated from Shillington High School in 1941. A member of the Woman's Club (established 1938), she served as President of the Pennsylvania Federation of Woman's Clubs, 1984–1986 (*Shillington Story* 92). Myrtle Council worked in the fleet post office in New York City in the "WAVES." (A division of the U.S. Navy for women during World War II, WAVES is an acronym for "Women Accepted for Volunteer Emergency Service.") A leader of the Shillington High School Alumni Association, she edited *Berks County Women,* written by Irene Reid. She served as secretary to the guidance counselor at Shillington High School and still edits the Alumni newsletter, also called *Chatterbox* (*Story* 96). Myrtle Council was voted to the Pennsylvania Honor Roll of Women in 1996.

Roma Greth went to Shillington High School only in ninth grade. A member of an informal group of writers from the Reading area that met in the 1970s, she was a friend of Linda Updike. She published many plays and murder mysteries, and since Linda Updike influenced her son, Roma Greth may have had a distant influence on Updike's idea of what a writer should be.

Richard "Rabbit" Hiester graduated from Shillington High School in 1941. His unitalicized caption in *Hi-Life* reads "'Go peddle your papers.' . . . Embarrassed when he lost his wallet at the Kenhorst Fire Hall . . . Hates to see a woman crying over a man . . . Usually found eating or loafing . . . 'Rabbit' wanted to be the millionaire of the class of '47." Though on the track team, Hiester did not play basketball. Clearly earned the nickname "Rabbit" because "Hiester" sounds like "Easter," and coupled to his track ability, "Rabbit" was the obvious choice. Members of the Hiester family had lived in the Reading area since the eighteenth century and were instrumental in the success of the Reading Public Library (Heizmann 14).

Reverend Victor Kroninger graduated in 1949. He went through elementary school and Shillington High School with John Updike. At seventeen he was pictured in a national magazine on his Indian motorcycle with a seventy-six-year-old neighbor. Originally planning to be an obstetrician, he changed to the ministry when a close friend and minister drowned. He accepted a church in Robesonia eight years after ordination in 1964. At the Nazareth Speedway on June 9, 2001, he rode for the Twelfth Annual Bike for Hunger (Trapani B1, B4.) He was notorious for long sermons, and Wesley Updike once said after a service, "Vic prays too long. We all tell him, but he won't cut it short" (JVYC, 16 April 2004). He helped clear the weeds near a fence where the pigeons were buried in Updike's story, "Pigeon Feathers." Reverend Kroninger's father baptized John Updike and confirmed him at Grace Evangelical Lutheran Church, Shillington. Since his father was famous for his "hell fire and damnation" sermons, he may have modeled for Reverend Fritz Kruppenbach of *Rabbit, Run*.

William "Bill" Le Van graduated from Shillington High School in 1946. He married Nancy March, class of 1950. He went to Albright College and then to dental school. He continues to work as a dentist.

Jerry "Pottsie" Potts graduated from Shillington High School in 1948. Updike always felt accepted in his home, though he was admonished when he spied on Jerry's sister Mary Jane while she was given a bath (*SC* 26–27). Jerry Potts and his sister attended Albright College after Shillington High. He was stunned when his girlfriend Joyce Erb was killed in a horse riding accident in 1951. When Shillington High School was being converted into Governor Mifflin High, Jerry Potts rescued memorabilia, including chalk and the chalk troth from the homeroom of Wesley Updike. He also retrieved pieces of the asbestos tiles from the chicken coop on the Updike Shillington property. Jerry Potts has been a member of Shillington Borough Council and the Governor Mifflin School Board for twenty-four years.

Eddie Pritchard graduated in 1945 from Shillington High School. Five years older than Updike, he bullied Updike, who was only four or five years old, by calling him "Ostrich," after Walt Disney's 1937 character "Ollie Ostrich." To Eddie Pritchard, Updike had a ridiculously long neck. Updike carried the scars from that experience quite deeply into his life (*SC* 79, 103, 124; *AP* 175–76). After Eddie Pritchard died in 1986, Updike jokingly wrote to Joan Venne that death was the proper punishment for having called him "Ostrich" (JVYC). Updike immediately withdrew the remark.

Robert Rhoads was a roofball buddy of Updike's. He dated Joyce Erb in high school. He later succeeded his father as pastor at Immanuel United Church of Christ, 1969, after serving as assistant pastor.

Reverend Robert I. Rhoads officiated at Dr. Ernie Rothermel's funeral. He retired in 1995.

Ernest M. Rothermel, D.D.S. was the son of Dr. Lewis Rothermel, former board president of Shillington High School. Ernest's father was the Updike family physician. He graduated from Shillington High School in 1927, the New York Military Academy in 1928, Franklin and Marshall College in 1931, and Temple University Dental School in 1935. Dr. Rothermel's office faced the GM Educational Center on Lancaster Avenue. He married Myrtle Potteiger, a gym instructor at Shillington High School. One of his two sons, L. Philip Rothermel, was the second husband of Priscilla Hendricks. She was "Miss Shillington" of 1958, "Miss Pennsylvania" of 1960, and a finalist in the 1960 "Miss America Pageant." She was named Shillington's "Outstanding Citizen" of 1960. Her father, Howard L. Hendricks, was superintendent of Governor Mifflin Joint School System. Ernie Rothermel's brother, Robert L. Rothermel, graduated from Shillington High School and had three children, Judith, Kimberly, and a son, David D. Rothermel, who graduated from Lehigh University and now owns a successful cabinet business.

LATER GRADUATES LINKED TO UPDIKE

Joan Borner (Conrad) graduated in 1951. She attended an art class with Updike and sat with him on the train several times when the class went to Philadelphia to see art shows. She married Harlan Conrad and has two children, Michael and Allyson. Joan Borner worked for Bell Telephone and lives in Shillington.

Nancy Ann Wolf (Jauss) was born on November 22, 1933, in Shillington, Pennsylvania, daughter of Chaplain Earl E. Wolf and Mary Elizabeth Stephens. She lived with her grandparents in a second floor apartment on State Street near Brobst while attending Shillington High School, where she sang in recital, March 30 (*Chatterbox* 24 Mar. 1950). After studying at the Wyomissing Institute of Fine Arts, she graduated from Shillington High in 1951. Her grandfather was a deacon of the Baptist church. Nancy Wolf dated Updike during his senior year, and they continued a correspondence after he left Shillington. She graduated in 1955 from Lebanon Valley College and married David H. Jauss, Jr. in 1955 or 1956 in Reading. She was a longtime member of Messiah Lutheran Church of Harrisburg where she served as past president of the Lutheran Church Women, and was an active member and soloist in the church choir. She died on Valentine's Day, 2009, less than three weeks after John Updike.

PROFILES OF 1950 SHILLINGTON SCHOOL FACULTIES

Shillington Elementary School

In grades three through six students were divided into two groups: "A" (college preparation) and "B" (business, secretarial) But if grades improved, a "B" could become an "A." Mixing of the groups was discouraged (*SC* 14).

Raymond Dickinson was the principal of the elementary school, and he taught the "A" section of sixth grade. Gray-haired and handsome, he was a strict teacher.

Carleton F. Boyer taught art to students from elementary through twelfth grade. He attended Kutztown High School, earned his B.S. at Kutztown State Teachers College, and attended the Pennsylvania Museum School of Art. Carlton Boyer did murals for Shillington restaurants. Updike took Carlton Boyer's art class. (See Chapter Seven, *Chatterbox:* Cartooning and Drawing.)

Miss Grill taught fourth grade, 4A, and singing. She attended Kutztown High School, earned her B.S. at Kutztown State Teachers College.

Sara Louise Huntzinger (Sprecher) taught sixth grade, 6A. Her sister-in-law, Mrs. Mary E. Shupp Huntzinger, described her as a dedicated teacher, superintendent, and administrator, who "was proud" that Updike was one of her pupils (Letter to John Updike from Mrs. Mary E. Shupp Huntzinger, 6 Oct. 2006. In Mrs. Huntzinger's possession).

Ruth Richards taught fifth grade and chorus. She was married to J. Allen Richards (see below).

Miss Tate taught first and third grades. Updike describes her as very tall and "wonderfully comical" when she dressed at Halloween as a girl with dabbed-on freckles and a big Band-Aid on her knee (*SC* 13).

Junior High

Ann Weik (Cassar) (SHS '50) has generously allowed me to use the following description of the school:

There was little delineation between junior high and senior high. Same building and use of classrooms and facilities, teacher overlapping, same administration and support staff. The name on the outer wall was "Shillington High School." The band and orchestra were divided into junior high grades 7 to 9 and senior high 10 to 12. The curriculum was quite different in 7th and 8th from the succeeding grades. The subjects in 7 and 8 were mostly required by everyone. Arithmetic, English, Guidance (taught by my father [Luther A. Weik, ed.]), science, music, art, industrial arts, home ec, gym class, and no languages. In ninth grade there were choices between college prep and non college prep, secretarial subjects for the girls, and industrial arts related courses for the boys. In ninth grade the courses for College Prep were part of a four-year plan starting with Latin, Algebra, English, probably General Science, Social Science, Art if desired, and private music lessons, Chorus, Band and Orchestra. John would not have participated in any musical activities. We had classes on how to use the library as well as study hall in there sometimes (Message to the author, 19 December 2010, e-mail).

Faculty and Staff

Wesley Updike taught mathematics. (See, Chapter One.)

Other Shillington High School Students and Faculty Not Mentioned in this Book

Mary A. Achey (Cooke) "Homeroom president 1, Secretary 3, Volleyball 3. *Peggy is a peppy Pennwyngal . . . motorcycle riding! . . . waxes ecstatic over 'Grand Ole Opry' hillbilly music . . . proudest possession is Eddy Arnold's autograph . . . thrilled on first airplane ride . . . Tennessee bound . . . future navy nurse."*

June F. Bachman (Stoudt). *"Juney . . . a fun-loving football and basketball fan . . . has no patience with baseball . . . favorite pastimes are eating, flirting, and listening to good music . . . dark hair, stunning eyes, immaculate grooming . . . thinks nursing would be an interesting career."*

Marilyn M. Barth (McCombe). "Hi-Life 4; *Lyn is one of our commercial students . . . They tell us she really rattles off typing assignments . . . calls Morgantown Road home . . . reticent in class . . . post-graduation exercise: finding a position in an office."*

Richard R. Barthold. "Basketball 3; Class President 2, 3; Football 1, 2, 3, 4; Homeroom Treasurer 3, President 4; Swimming 3; Track 1, 2, 3. *Barty is an all-around guy and athlete . . . twice elected class president . . . hitch-hiked to and from Canada . . . Can he eat spaghetti! . . . This husky end's big desire is to become an S. H. S. alumnus."* Illustrating Updike's sensitivity to his classmates, when Richard Barthold's father was ill, Updike asked about him.

Robert W. Bausher. "Baseball 2, 3; Basketball 2, 3, 4; Football 1, 2, 3, 4; Hi-Y 3; Homeroom Vice-President 2. *We wonder why the football players call their quiet, reserved co-captain 'Lover Boy' . . . Bud is a plugger who has shown us remarkable versatility in sports . . . plans to work with his father in the roofing business."* Robert worked for Edwards Business Supply. His wife, Doris Whitehead, who was one year behind him in high school, worked at Governor Mifflin School for thirty-three years.

Margaret L. Bowman (Gechter). "Y-Teens 2, 3, 4. *The young lady apparently still operates on the theory that children should be seen and not heard . . . long curly hair, smiling brown eyes . . . Love of flashy jewelry contradicts her undemonstrative nature . . . home ec.student.*"

Donald R. Brendel. "Band 1, 2, 3, 4; Basketball 1, 2; Orchestra 1, 2, 3, 4; Tennis 1, 2. *This Petrilloman tootles a sweet clarinet and sax . . . commutes to and fro school on Transit Company rattler . . . claims he is losing weight, though his belt denies it . . . a great future in music.*"

LeRoy E. Brendle. "Torch 1, 2. *'Passionate' is too pale a term to describe his affection for the St. Louis Cardinals . . . also finds stamp collecting and mystery stories exciting . . . amused by the class of 1950 . . . considering the fate of a lawyer.*"

Gloria M. Ciemiewicz (Hain). "Chorus 2. *Sissy gets a kick out of twirling for the Temple Drum Corps, and enjoys nothing more than competition from the West Reading Corps . . . quiet, thoughtful . . . gets along well in business class . . . considers becoming a waitress.*"

Doris A. Craley (Novak). "Homeroom Secretary 1. *Suzzy always informs the second period English class when it is 9:45 with a well-timed ker-choo . . . giggly . . . operates an L. C. Smith (whatever that is) . . . aims to get married come June.*"

Donald M. Davis. "Baseball 2; Football 2, 3, 4. *The big gridman was sidelined by a sudden injury . . . often seen in attendance at the Shillington Theatre . . . enjoys baseball as spectator and participant . . . prefers practical courses over theory . . . strong and usually silent.*"

Robert L. Davis . "Band 1, 2, 3; Baseball 1, 2, 3; Football 1, 4; Hi-Y 1, 2, 3, 4; Orchestra 1, 2, 3. *Bob is a sports enthusiast who rates baseball high . . . an expert swimmer . . . His personality has been described as 'persistent' . . . engaging smile . . . God's gift to the junior girls . . . aims to further education.*"

Irene A. Dietrich (Harrold). "*Renie comes from Grill . . . a passion for wrestling matches contradicts her quiet nature . . . a conscientious General student who always had her homework . . . ever ready with a smile and a helping hand.*"

Norman J. Dysput. "Band 2, 3; Football 2. *Dissy is the big boy with the big, big voice . . . a valuable man to have in a cheering section . . . Norm never wearies of praising his Dad's Cadillac . . . a true-blue Kenhorstian and proud of it.*"

John C. Eckenroth. "Track 2, 3, 4. *John hails from the metropolis of Gouglersville . . . track is this easy-going boy's prime sports interest . . . steadfast friend . . . we detect a liking for the simple pleasures of life . . . allergic to girls . . . hopes to own a chicken farm.*"

Ralph E. Eckenroth. "*Ecky is an Alleghenyville product . . . usually grinning . . . his Dad's '40 Pontiac, he claims, has earned enough tickets to paper his bedroom . . . found the General Course so general he is uncertain of his future calling.*"

Patricia L. Eisenbise (Deal). "Chatterbox 1, 2, 4; Cheerleading 2, 3, 4; Chorus 4; Class Play 3; Debating 3, 4; Hi-Life 4; Hockey 2; Torch 2, 3; Y-Teens 2, 3, 4. *Pat is a forthright girl who is not afraid to say what she thinks, and she thinks a great deal . . . can't help giggling . . . This effervescent cheerleader just dotes on apples . . . Albright bound.*" Patricia Eisenbise was, according to Joan Venne, a "self-conscious" cheerleader. She would measure her nose against Joan Venne's to see whose was bigger. Patricia Eisenbise double-dated to the junior prom with Updike and Joan George Zug. Her date was Larry Yocum.

Frances E. Emerick (Bergman). "Chorus 2, 3, 4; Hockey 3, Co-captain 4; Track 3; Volleyball 2. Co-captain 3; Basketball 3, 4. *Frankie hails from Gouglersville . . . a regular passenger on Elmer's bus . . . the girl athletic wonder of the class . . . high good humor . . . enjoys long walks . . . wants (cross my heart) to be a lady wrestler.*"

Larry R. Essick. "Chatterbox 2; Hi-Y 3, 4; Swimming 2; Track 1. *We wonder if Acid ever relaxes . . . after a strenuous school day, Mighty Mite (among other things) nurses hamsters, prepares firecrackers, practices magic tricks, seeks uranium and whips cream at the Penn . . . compressed dynamite.*"

George E. Fessle. "Baseball 3, 4; Basketball 2, 3, 4; Homeroom Executive Committee 3. *Fegley doesn't let the change of seasons interfere with his year-round affair with basketball . .eats to live, lives to eat . . . an uninhibited joker . . . horn-rimmed glasses give him a Harold Lloydish look.*"

Rebecca J. Flail (Van Liew). "Chorus 2, 3; Volleyball 3, 4. *Beckie has one of the most reserved and placid personalities of our class . . . thrilled at driving a blue 1948 De Soto, or meeting Peter Lawford . . . might become a wealthy potato chip heiress.*"

Betty J. Gaston (Ludwig). "Chorus 2, 3; Class Play 3; Homeroom Treasurer. *Betty Spends much of her spare time in front of the Kenhorst and Temple Drum Corps . . . big, cat-green eyes . . . our only entry in the Miss Reading Fair contest . . . a future Reading housewife.*"

Robert S. Groome. "Chorus 3, 4; Tack 1, 2. *Groomie is a taciturn gent who places action before diction . . . plays a mean piano . . . hard-working patron getter . . . active member of male chorus . . . would like to labor in an automobile paint shop after graduation.*"

Kenneth R. Herzog. "Basketball 2, 3, 4; Chatterbox 2, 3, 4; Football 2, 3, 4; Hi-Y 3, 4; Homeroom Vice President 2, 4; Track 1, 2, 3. *Big Ken . . . a powerful pile of muscle . . . a year-round athlete who feels nothing beats football . . . swallowed two front teeth in the Lititz-Shillington game. Tho what? . . . Henry's smile could eat a banana sideways.*"

LeRoy D. Hill. "Baseball 2, 4; Basketball 2. *Hilly is a sports enthusiast who rates basketball high . . . mathematician . . . proud of his Colonial Hills' heritage . . . a big boy who likes to pilot his Dad's Buick . . . plans on attending Wyomissing Polytech.*"

LeRoy I. Hill. "Baseball 2, 3. *Leroy I . . . hard to beat at basketball and baseball . . . not heard from very often . . . a good deal of wit lurks under Monk's shy exterior . . . prefers drafting or mechanical engineering as a future vocation.*"

Nancy E. Hoffman. "*Nancy knits argyle socks in her spare time . . . efficient switchboard operator . . . faithful member of the SSSS (Society for Shillington Sports Spectators) . . . always in earnest . . . will make some lucky employer an excellent secretary.*"

Sara J. Horning (Ebersole). "*One of the lassies we imported from the country . . . a bilinguist who feels right at home with Pennsylvania German . . . two deep dimples set off her pleasing smile . . . on the Maple Grove softball team . . . future secretary.*" Like Peggy Lutz Roberts, Sara died on Dec. 4, 2008.

Catherine M. Johns (Fletcher). "*The air forces come high on Cathy's list . . . can be found at Eshie's after school hours . . . pleasant, kindly, conscientious . . . Her excellent work in bookkeeping shows promise of a fine secretary some day.*"

Mildred F. Kachel (Moyer). "Chatterbox 4; Chorus 3; Hi-Life 4. *Milly can never be caught with her smile down . . . spends much time dancing at Maple Grove . . . hails from Knauers . . . proud of her driver's license . . . Cooking ability qualifies her as a fine future homemaker.*"

Doris J. Keffer (Wenrich). "Chatterbox 1; Chorus 2; Homeroom Treasurer 2. *One of the first to earn her driver's license . . . Her air of quiet reserve is quickly dropped at football and basketball games . . . wrestling matches and television also excite her . . . Montrose's gift to hospital patients.*"

Frederick L. Kirlin. "Band 1, 2, 3, 4; Orchestra 1, 2, 3, 4; Track 3. *Fred feels lost without a toothpick in his mouth . . . California hamburgers are unbeatable, says he . . . beats time in the West Reading Drum Corps . . . rather taciturn . . . day dreamer . . . music should take this tall percussionist far.*"

Leverne C. Kohl. "*Kohlie doesn't have much to say . . . never drives to school twice in the same truck . . . an advanced Latin student . . . Working for father consumes much leisure time . . . would like to become a forrester* (sic)."

Shirley J. Kuser. "Class play 3. *If the way to a man's heart is through his stomach, Shirl doesn't need a road map—she loves to cook . . . giggles extensively, blushes readily . . . enjoys roller skating . . . favorite classes are home ec. and '50.*"

William R. Lesher. "Hi-Y 3, 4; Homeroom Vice President 3; Track 3. *Bill . . . friendly easy going . . . an old hand at the Berkshire Knitting Mills . . . one of the few car owners of the class (it's a Ford) . . . frequents the Dairy Maid . . . has the ingredients of a fine dental technician.*"

Grace B. Ludwig (Bricker). "Basketball 3; Chatterbox 4; Cheerleading 2; Chorus 2, 3, 4; Hi-Life 4; Hockey 4; Track 3; Volleyball 3. *Book-*

keeping keeps Grace plenty busy . . . ever-present rooter at football and basketball games . . . loves to play any sport . . . fun-loving . . . cheerful chorus member . . . always willing to lend a hand."

Mary E. Malone (Bishop). *"Gregarious, vivacious Bib easily fitted in and became one of us . . . slick dancer . . . a red-hot rooter for the Cleveland Indians . . . Chambersburg bred . . . likes gay parties . . . We think she will make an excellent secretary."* When Updike attended the 1980 reunion, the registration slip asked, "Whatever happened to Mary Malone." He wrote a witticism on it stating she became a celebrity singer.

June D. Mays. *"Hockey Manager 2, 3, 4. Juney has a personality as pleasant as the morning sun . . . was a conscientious manager of the hockey team for three years . . . never without a kind word . . . hard worker . . . Just ask June for chewing gum."*

David H. Mervine. *"Baseball 2, 4; Homeroom Vice-President 3. Skip likes basketball, baseball and seeing the St. Louis Cardinals win . . . an expert auto mechanic and gasoline dispenser . . . This moody Montrosian operates a '35 Plymouth . . . His sly comments reveal a knowing nature."*

Wilbur K. Mohn. *"Baseball 1, 2. Mooney yeans to own a Ford of his own some day . . . steady rooter for the Adamstown Hatters . . . not the talkative type . . . Cal's bus . . . after school days are over he plans to be a truck driver."*

William S. Moore. *"Bill finds he likes woodshop best . . . Favorite pastime centers around fall and a well-stocked hunting ground . . . attended Reading Business Institute . . . plans to don the blue and white of the Navy after graduation."*

William J. Moser. *"Baseball 2, 3, 4; Football 4; Swimming 3, 4. The babysitter of our class . . . Billy is easy to like . . . bravely bore his battle scars from the football front . . . one of our few natural blonds . . . notorious party thrower . . . all wolf and a yard thick."* Updike remembered him as a very sweet person (JVYC, 13 Apr. 1998).

Roy J. Ninzeheltzer. *"Baseball 3. Ninzie . . . a prominent Morgantown roader . . . Slim has a mighty wide stride . . . one of the least diminutive people we know . . . babies his '39 Pontiac . . . laughs loud and often . . . beautiful crop of hair . . . future stone mason."*

Peter P. Novak. *"Baseball 1; Class Vice-President 3, 4; Class Play 4; Court 4; Football 1, 2, 3, 4; Hi-Y 2, 3, 4; Olympus 3, 4; Track 2, 3, 4. Pete's sad, thoughtful eyes contradict his aggressive play on the gridiron . . . When this bonecrusher blocks, they stay blocked . . . The brute can also cook, and admires sentimental songs . . . wishes to play pro football, and then coach."* Updike jested that his wife Martha wanted to dance with Pete Novak at the 1995 reunion. That was unlikely, since he was a notorious drinker (JVYC, 2 Apr. 1993).

Samuel C. Nunemaker. *"Basketball 1, 2, 3. Sambo can often be found on the business end of a fishing rod or shotgun . . . perpetual grin . . . pro*

basketball player (or is it semi-pro?) . . . views girls with great disinter-
est . . . thought typing terrific."

Mary C. Orff. "Band 1, 2, 3, 4; Basketball 3; Chatterbox 1, 2, 3, 4; Hi-Life
4; Hockey 3, 4; Orchestra 1, 2, 3, 4; Student Council 4; Torch 1, 2, 3;
Track 3; Volleyball 2, 3. *Mary fairly bubbles with school spirit . . . never
misses a sporting event . . . ever cheerful . . . thinks chem. lab. is fun . . .
Wilson College bound, and then to become a doctor . . . a sincere hard
worker who will make her mark."* Born in Philadelphia, Mary Orff's
straight As from first grade to twelfth made her one of six valedictorians. She also played the French horn. Ann Weik recalls that the
Orffs held a higher status than her other friends and families:
"They had a live-in maid, (I remember the little silver bell on the
table), and had lace tablecloths and sterling silver for all meals. My
first taste of beef filet was at their house." The Orffs also owned a
pipe organ. Ann Cassar recalled, "During the war we met at
Mary's and had 'The Junior Commandoes.'" Her older brother,
Clark Orff, a sixth-grader, was killed by a car when getting off a
Reading trolley at Waverly and Lancaster Avenue, across from
Shillington High School property and directly in front of her home.
Mary Orff witnessed this tragedy. Since her brother intended to
become a doctor like his father, Mary decided to fulfill her father's
dream. So, she went to Wilson College, and then Temple University Medical School. She interned at Reading Hospital. Mary Orff
always wanted to become a surgeon; however, at that time women
were discouraged from seeking such positions (Message to the author from Ann Weik Cassar, 27 Dec. 2009, e-mail).

Georgene C. Painter (Stehman). "Basketball 1, 2, 3, 4; Hockey 1, 2;
Homeroom President 2. *Sparkling smile matches a captivating personality . . . 'Cut it out' . . . Little Miss Dimples carries on a nation-wide
correspondence . . . seldom has to raise her voice . . . easy, charming
manner . . . plans to be a happy homemaker."* Georgene appeared in the
Queens Court. She married former football player Donald "Burch"
Stehman of the class of '48 and had four children.

Richard T. Phillips. "*Dick came to us from Readingtown this year . . . curly
hair and pink shirt created quite a furor among feminine circles . . .
basketball and golf excite his sporting blood . . . Chief of Test Tube Crack-
ers in lab."*

Christine E. Rabzak (Budgy). "Chorus 2; Hi-Life 4; Y-Teens 2, 3, 4.
*Chris is a demure and pleasant Kenhorst indigene . . . Art is by far her
favorite subject . . . 'You know' . . . enjoys going for long walks in the
country . . . efficient worker . . . intends to take up nursing."*

Jeanette A. Reiter (Born). "Chatterbox 4; Chorus 2, 3; Class Play 4; Hi-
Life 4; Homeroom Secretary 2; Student Council 3, 4. *Financial secretary for the Student Activity tickets . . . Her thoughtful, serious nature*

often finds place for a smile and a joke . . . rendered Kate's lines in senior class play . . . a housewife's life for her."

Virginia M. Remp (Machemer). "Chorus 3; Y-Teens 2, 3, 4. *Ginnie spends much of her time in Mohnton . . . Her frequent giggles assure us she can find fun anywhere . . . black hair, brown eyes, soft voice . . . Favorite recreation is dancing . . . always pleasant."*

J. Allen Richards. "Amulet 3, Treasurer 4; Baseball 1, 3, 4; Basketball 1, 4; Homeroom President 1; Student Council 1; Torch 1, Vice President. *Al is so dead a basketball shot they call him Coffin . . . one of our faculty babies . . . big, soulful eyes . . . considers the New York Yankees tops . . . He makes up in heart what he lacks in size."* With Ann Weik Cassar and John Updike, J. Allen Richards was considered a "teacher's brat," one whose parent was a teacher or administrator at the school. But J. Allen Richards was "a double teacher's brat," because his mother Ruth taught the fifth grade and handled the chorus in elementary school, while J. Allen Richards, his father, taught social studies at Shillington High School and coached sports. Notice his name and his father's are identical.

Joan E. Rittenhouse. "Basketball 2; Chatterbox 4; Orchestra 1. *You will be familiar with this gracious waitress if you are a patron of the Shillington Diner . . . enjoys Jeepster driving . . . a laugh-loving lady who should always have fun."*

Frances G. Runge (Kaffine). "Business manager 3; Court 3, 4; Hi-Life 4; Homeroom Vice-President 2, President 4; Y-Teens 2, 3, 4; Torch 2, 3. *Fran . . . proud graduate of Fairview . . . had her hands full as Hi-Life Editor . . . if silence is golden, this busy miss is 24 karet* [sic] *. . . expressive eyes . . . slow shy smile . . . has in mind a nurse's future."*

Donald L Schubel. "Football 3, 4; Homeroom Vice-President 3. *Big Don is one of our rugged linesmen . . . imperturbable . . . coming from Joanna, Don is our champion, long-distance commuter . . . How does he squeeze into that little Ford? . . . Favorite Subject—lunch . . . girls? Spell it."*

Donald H. Schwartz. "Band 2, 3; Football 4; Hi-Y 3, 4; Homeroom Vice-President 1; Orchestra 2, 3; Student Council 2.*This big boy is both a Marine and football hero . . . 'I got plenty monies' . . . A sheep in wolf's clothing who wears girls like boutonnieres in his lapel. . . . thrilled when* [sic] *discovered meaning of 'nnupt.'"*

Janet E. Shadler (Neuheimer). "Basketball 1; Chorus 3; Y-Teens 2.*Jan would like to find a nice office job waiting at the end of school . . . calls Reading home . . . ardent listener to local disc jockey programs . . . a giggle box in a perpetual good humor."*

Janet C. Smith (Craley). "Chorus 2, 3; Homeroom Treasurer 1. *Smitty . . . placid as a quiet pond, pleasant as a summer stream . . . Jan is envied for her long blonde, naturally wavy hair . . . feels friendship is the greatest possession . . . a hard worker who will succeed as a nurse."*

Stewart F. Sonen. "Chorus 1. *Stut has reduced beating the clock to an exact science . . . He and his removable teeth liven up any class room . . . Ask him how it happened . . . How he drives! . . . plans to be a factory-trained mechanic."*

Barbara L. Stackhouse (Martin). "Y-Teens 2, 3. *Bobbie . . . enjoys many things, among them ice skating, Pepsi Cola and 'Smoke Gets in Your Eyes' . . . An unfailingly good nature accentuates a genuine liking for people . . . will make a tireless secretary."*

Mae B. Stafford. "Track 1; Volleyball 1. *Philadelphia's loss proved to be Shillington's gain . . . staunch navy* [sic] *supporter . . . big, round eyes and a questioning look . . . Her glasses were novel . . . hopes to become* [a] *social science instructress, via West Chester State Teachers College."*

Judith E. Sterner (Meck)."Chatterbox 3, 4; Y-Teens 2. *It is hard for Judy to stop grinning . . . amiability itself . . . thrives on French Fries and cheeseburgers . . . There has never been a song the equal of 'Jealous Heart' . . . likes to pilot that '40 Chevrolet."*

Barbara J. Stoudt (Brightbill). "Hi-Life 4; Y-Teens 2, 3. *Babs shares companionship and love of motorcycle riding with Janie . . . chocolate ice cream . . . 'Oh, if I only had a car' . . . came to us on the Pennwyn lend-lease . . . hoedowns are super . . . Tennessee bound."*

Walter R. Stoudt. "Band 4; Class Play 4; Football 1; Hi-Life 4; Hi-Y 3, 4; Stage Crew 2, 3, 4; Swimming 2. *Gook . . . one great big lump of activity . . . hard working stage manager . . . phenomenal patron getter (two year total—312) . . . Latent musical talent emerged with that big bass drum . . . Pensupreme kitchenman . . . All he wants is out."*

Patricia A. Stover (Steinfurth). "Chatterbox 3, 4; Class Play 3; Y-Teens 2, 3, 4. *One more example of Kenhorst's good neighbor policy . . . hair of gold, eyes of blue . . . conscientious feature page typist . . . ready smile . . . football fan . . . Shyness does not conceal her natural vivacity . . . hopes to work as* [sic] *secretary."*

Barry C. Styer. "Baseball 1, 2; Basketball 2. *Barry is a Gouglersville native . . . likes the fast game of basketball . . . loves to eat, lives to eat . . . pinball pro . . . ever present at athletic contests . . . comes equipped with well-oiled horse laugh."*

Betty L. Sweitzer (Jeddic). "Homeroom Secretary 3. *An attractive commuter who goes all out for colorful dress . . . the smile, the dimple, the long black hair . . . hobby—flirting . . . Room 111 after school is her Nirvana . . . she fancies office work after graduation."*

Irene J. Tinus (Dobson). "Class Play 3; Volleyball 2; Y-Teens 2, 3. *Tinnie is proud to be a Temple majorette . . . She says typing is tops . . . vivacious volley ball player . . . counts on becoming a secretary . . . frequenter of Y. W. C. A. . . . . Her smile never seems to fade."*

Mary Jane Tylka (Barasso). "Hi-Life 4. *Janie hails from Angelica . . . the proud possessor of what is undoubtedly the biggest dimple in this local-*

ity . . . loves motorcycle riding and art class, though not at the same time . . . yearns to travel to Tennessee."

*Barbara Wagner (Schwartz)."*Band 4; Basketball 3; Cheerleading 1, 2; Homeroom President 1. *A midget member of the notorious Second Street Gang . . . Blonde, blue-eyed Babs enjoys all kinds of sports, including driving her dad's car . . . S. S. S. (Steady Supporter of Steve's) . . . pinochle player par excellence."* Updike walked to elementary school with Barbara Wagner and Barbara Yurick. When they died Updike felt another part of his childhood was gone.

Phyllis L. Walk. "Chatterbox 3; Chorus 3; Class Play 3; Y-Teens 2, 3. *Phyl without a smile is like a sky without a sun . . . enjoys playing taxi to her careless comrades . . . happily spectates at football games and stock car races . . . eager to become a Bell operator."*

H. Christian Weisman. "Band 1, 2, 3, 4; Class Play 3; Football 1, 2, 3, 4; Hi-Y 2, 3, President 4; Orchestra 1, 2, 3, 4; Student Council 4; Track 1, 2, 3, 4. *Who can remember when Chris had long hair? . . . sincere, hard worker . . . pillar of strength in our stone-wall line . . . FFF (Faithful Followers of Firing) . . . hard to dislike . . . Man can he pound those drums!"* Although his first name was "Howard," he was always called Chris. He was a faithful follower of Firing (FFF) because Chris played football under William H. Firing for four years.

Mark R. Wenrich. "Band 1, 2, 3, 4; Chatterbox 1; Homeroom President 1, 3, 4; Orchestra 1, 2, 3, 4; Student Council 3, 4. *Mark is not as some think, Doctor Ibach; he just works there . . . tootles the trombone in band and orchestra . . . never without a wisecrack and an angelic stare . . . member of the unforgettable German band."*

Neil F. White. "Chatterbox 2, 3, 4; Court 3; Football 2, 3, 4; Hi-Y 3, 4; Homeroom Treasurer 4; Track 1, 2, 3, 4. *Neil operates on the assumption that the whole world's a joke . . . has the rugged physique necessary for chemistry lab . . . Snaps from center were always true . . . hits top form in the locker room . . . on it."* He and his wife Barbara Farris graduated from Albright College.

Carl B. Witwer. "Basketball 3. *It is easy to see why they call him Silent Wit . . . summers in the Pensupreme kitchen . . . Girls tend to bore him . . . good listener . . . tireless sports fan and tough to match in basketball."*

Richard E. Witwer. "Band 1, 2, 3, 4; Orchestra 1, 2, 3, 4. *Butch is usually on the other side of the counter at Ibach's . . . hamburger lover . . . The band won't seem the same without his red-hot trumpet . . . He plans on becoming a navy* [sic] *man."*

Betty L. Yerger. *"Bet is practically a permanent resident of the Adamstown Athletic Association . . . declares deep felt admiration for chicken potpie . . . slick dancer . . . cringes before the dreaded words, 'And now for your homework assignment'!"*

Margaret L. Young (Wenger). "Chatterbox 4; Class Play 3; Hockey 3; Homeroom Secretary 3; Y-Teens 2, 3, 4. *We are never sure whether Peggy is laughing with us or at us . . . She insists she loves to eat, though her figure belies it . . . Pet Peeves: people . . . considering the fate of the medical secretary.*"

Barbara J. Yurick (Novak). "Basketball Manager 3; Class Play 3; Hockey 2, 3, 4; Homeroom Treasurer 2; Secretary 4; Y-Teens 1, 2, 3, 4. *Babs . . . a cute, perky blond . . . hockey player, football fan . . . worst mistake was to get Stinky inscribed on her class hat . . . likes to bake, but finds housework bothersome . . . burning ambition — to make lots of money.*" Updike walked to elementary school with Barbara Yurick and Barbara Wagner. He felt his childhood expiring when they died.

Anna G. Zimmerman (Amole). "Band 2, 3, 4; Chatterbox 4; Orchestra 1, 2, 3, 4; Y-Teens 2. *Short but sweet . . . This diminutive music lover enjoys hearing Bach through to bebop, but makes little noise herself . . . Infrequent smiles show fun-loving disposition beneath a placid exterior . . . thrilled by the Philharmonic Orchestra.*" Anna Zimmerman played the oboe.

Elizabeth L. Zimmerman (Ziegler). "Band 4; Orchestra 1, 2, 3, 4; Y-Teens 2. *At the end of the list, in the rear of the room . . . Zimmie is not known for her taciturnity . . . 'You bet' . . . spaghetti . . . counts on becoming a telephone operator . . . Bet finds much to grin at.*"

Shillington School Teachers and Administrators

Shillington Elementary School

In grades three through six, students were divided into two groups, "A" (college prep) and "B" (business, secretarial). But if grades improved, a "B" could become an "A." Mixing of the groups was discouraged (*SC* 14).

Mr. Brobst was Principal.

Mr. Raymond Dickinson. See above.

Carleton Boyer. See above.

Kathryn Brobst (Hartman) taught sixth grade from 1941–43. She taught Updike reading and science, and reported that he excelled in both. Perhaps because he stuttered, he was shy, and never volunteered an answer, or when called upon, kept his responses short. He preferred doing science experiments alone, and he played by himself.

Mrs. Eisenberg was the advisor to *The Little Shilling.*

Olive Fritz taught first, fourth, and fifth grades. Her best friend was Kathryn Brobst (Hartman).

Marie Goodman taught fourth grade.

Miss Grill. See above.

Helen Becker Hartzel taught kindergarten and first grade. Miss Becker was invited by Updike to be Snow White (*SC* 13). While in her kindergarten class, Updike experienced an attack of measles, which later caused psoriasis (*SC* 42).

Miss Hollenbach taught third grade.

Sara Louise Huntzinger (Sprecher). See above.

Dorothy N. Eberly taught second grade.

Miss Landis taught kindergarten.

Ruth Richards taught fifth grade and chorus. She married Allen Richards. (See below.)

Miss Tate. See above.

Junior High School

(see comments by Ann Weik above)

Faculty and Staff

William M. Brunner taught industrial arts to all grades. He attended Kutztown State Teachers College.

William H. Firing. See above.

Mrs. Ruth Heffner was the librarian. She taught office practice, advanced business, and bookkeeping. She attended Boy's High School, Reading, and she received her B.C.S. at Rider College.

Virginia Kleppinger taught seventh grade.

W. Walter McElroy taught English. He attended Warwick Township High School, Chester County, and he received his B.S. at West Chester State Teachers College and his M.S. at the University of Pennsylvania.

John H. Schrack taught geography and Latin. He earned his B.S. at Kutztown State Teachers College and his M.Ed. at Duke University.

OTHER SHILLINGTON HIGH SCHOOL ADMINISTRATION AND FACULTY LISTED IN *HI-LIFE*, 1950

Board of School Directors:

Russell W. Klopp
Elwood A. Leininger
Stanley A. Moorehouse
Dr. Lewis Rothermel
Don C. VanLiew
Ivan F. Zendt, Jr.

Faculty:

Eleanor Baum taught health and physical education. She attended Oley High School, and she received her B.S. at Ursinus College.

Ruth J. Blatt was the librarian. She attended Muhlenberg Township High School, and she received her B.S. at Kutztown State Teachers College.

William M. Brunner. See above.

Grace Conrad taught music. She attended Reading High School, and she received her B.S. at West Chester State Teachers College.

Dorothy N. Eberly practiced dental hygiene, and she attended R. D. H. Easton High School and the University of Pennsylvania.

William H. Firing. See above.

Elizabeth B. Freed taught commercial subjects. She attended Allentown High School, and received her B.S. at Cedar Crest College.

Paul F. Freed taught mathematics and student drivers training. He attended Allentown High School and received his B.S. at Muhlenberg College.

Harold W. Fries taught physics. He attended Reading High School and received his B.S. at Franklin and Marshall College.

Francis R. Gelnett taught commercial subjects. He attended Selmsgrove High School, and he received his B.S. at Susquehanna University, and his M.S. at Bucknell University. Francis Gelnett taught eighth grade at Shillington High School, then at Union City for five years before going into the Navy. Gelnett left teaching in 1963 and went into "the orchestra business" until the late 1970s. He was married in 1972. (His wife, Mona, enjoyed bragging, "I danced with Updike!") He was the 1950 class sponsor and later told Updike, "Your class was the great class." Updike sent Gelnett a "blow-by-blow" description of the Shillington High School fifty-fifth reunion, and he, past 90 years of age, responded with a long letter, recalling the "show-stopper" that was the "Me and My Shadow" act Updike had written, with its lyric: "'I go into a booth to telephone/ It wouldn't be crowded if I could leave my shadow at home.' Ah, youth!"

Ruth L. Heffner. See above.

Russell H. Kistler. See above.

Paul B. Klopp taught social science. He attended Shillington High School, and he received his B.S. at Franklin and Marshall College.

Kenneth Kohl taught industrial arts. He attended Shillington High School, and he received his B.S. in social science at Kutztown State Teachers College.

Bessie S. Leiby, R.N was the school nurse. She attended Reading High School, and she received her A.A. at Mars Hill College, Reading

Hospital, School of Nursing, and her B.S. at the University of Pennsylvania.

Edmund J. Lewis taught drivers training and general science. He attended Carbondale High School, and he received his B.S. at East Stroudsburg State Teachers College and his M.Ed. at Temple University.

John G. Loos taught instrumental music. He attended Reading High School, and Ernest Williams School of Music, University of Pennsylvania. He received his B.S. at Lebanon Valley College.

W. Walter McElroy. See above.

William A. Morrow taught biology. He attended Reading High School, and he received his B.S. at Lafayette College. William Morrow was in charge of the band, whose members nicknamed him "Catfish" because of his moustache.

Estella R. Pennepacker taught Latin and French. She attended Shillington High School, and she received her A.B. at Albright College.

J. Allen Richards taught social science and was the director of athletics. He attended Robsesonia High School, and he received his A.B. at Lebanon Valley College, Interstate Commercial College, and his M.A. at Columbia University.

Joyce M. Ruth taught home economics, social science, and health education. She attended Reading High School, and she received her B.S. at Albright College.

John H. Schrack. See above.

Norman W. Shrawder taught English. He attended Wernersville High School, and he received his B.S. at Kutztown State Teachers College.

Lois W. Swoyer taught home economics. She attended Williamsport High School, and she received her B.S. at Albright College.

Anna C. Taylor taught English and general language. She attended Womelsdorf High School, and she received her A.B. at Wilson College.

Peggy White. See above.

Works Cited

"Alice McDermott Wins a Top Award for Fiction." *New York Times* 20 Nov. 1998: B8. Print.

Amis, Martin. "Updike: Life under a Microscope." Reading (Pennsylvania) *Eagle* 4 Oct. 1987: E-18. Print.

Astor, David. "Updike Is Honored by Cartoonists." *Editor & Publisher* 15 Dec. 1990: 36. Print.

Bailey, Peter J. "'The Bright Island of Make-Believe': Updike's Misgivings about the Movies." *The John Updike Review* 1.n.1 (Fall 2011): 69–87. Print.

Bragg, Melvyn. "Forty Years of Middle America with John Updike." *South Bank Show* BBC. London Weekend Television. June, 1990. Video.

Britton, Burt. *Self-Portrait*. New York: Random, 1976. Print.

Broer, Lawrence R. Ed.*Rabbit Tales*. Tuscaloosa, Alabama: U of Alabama P, 1996. Print.

Bruccoli, Mary. Ed.*The Dictionary of Literary Biography Documentary Series*. Vol. 3. Detroit, Michigan: Gale, 1983. 251–320. Print.

Callaway, John. "John Callaway Interviews John Updike."WTTW Chicago. 26 Nov. 1981. Video.

Cassar, Ann Weik. Message to Author. 25 May 2005. E-mail.

———.Message to Author. 30 Jan. 2010. E-mail.

———.Message to Author. 19 Dec. 2010. E-mail.

Chatterbox. Shillington High School. 1945–50. Print.

Cobblah, Elizabeth Updike. "Reflection on Dad." John F. Kennedy Library Tribute to John Updike. 7 June 2009.

Corbett, Burl N. "Linda Updike: A Tribute to a Very Special Woman." Reading (Pennsylvania) *Eagle* 22 Oct. 1989: E-20. Print.

De Bellis, Jack. "'The Awesome Power': John Updike's Use of Kubrick's *2001* in *Rabbit Redux*."In Jack De Bellis, ed. *John Updike: Critical Responses to the "Rabbit" Saga*. Westport, Connecticut: Praeger, 2004. 83–94. Print.

———. "'It Captivates . . . It Hypnotizes': Updike Goes to the Movies." *Literature/Film Quarterly* 23.3(1995): 169–87. Print.

———."The 'Extra Dimension': Character Names in Updike's 'Rabbit' Trilogy." *Names* 36 (Mar.–June 1988):29–42.

———. *The John Updike Encyclopedia*. Westport, Connecticut: Greenwood Press, 2000. Print.

———. *John Updike Remembered*. Ed. Jack De Bellis. Tuscaloosa, Alabama: U of Alabama P, date to be announced.

———."Linda Grace Hoyer." *American National Biography*. New York: Oxford UP, 1996. Print.

———."Oedipal Angstrom." *Wascana Review* 24 (1989): 45–59. Print.

Dudar, Helen. "John Updike: The Art of Whittling Fantasy out of Paper." *The Attentive Eye*. Ed. Peter Goldman. Philadelphia, Pennsylvania: Xlibris, 2002:19–31. Print.

Ecenbarger, William."Tracing Updike's Roots." Philadelphia *Inquirer* 10 Oct. 2008: A1.

"Famous Only Children." *People Magazine* 29 Oct.1990: 7. Print.

Fichtner, Margaria. "The Private John Updike."Miami(Florida)*Herald* 30 Jan. 1994:1. Print.

Greiner, Donald."John Updike." *American Poets since World War II*. Detroit, Michigan: Gale, 1980: 327–34. Print.

Greth, Roma. "Mother & Son: A Pair of Only Children as Professional Writers." *Historical Review of Berks County* Spg. 2000: 64–65. Print.

Hagan, Chet. "John Updike: Berks County's Most Honored Writer Now Challenges the New Millennium."*Historical Review of Berks County* Spg. 2000: 57–60, 62–63. Print.

Hartman, Susan Beth. "The Role of the Berks County Setting in the Novels of John Updike." Diss. U of Pittsburgh. 1987. Print.

"The Harvard Freshman Register 1954."*The Register*. Cambridge: Harvard Yearbook Publications, 1950. Print.

Heer, Jeet. "Dear Orphan Annie: Why Cartoon Characters Get All the Best Mail." *Boston Globe* Sept. 2002: Ideas. Print.

Heizmann, Louis J. *The Library that Would Not Die: The Turbulent History of the Reading Public Library*. Reading, Pennsylvania: The Reading Public Library, 1971. Print.

Hi-Life 1946. Shillington, Pennsylvania: The Senior Class of Shillington High School, 1946. Print.

Hi-Life 1950. Shillington, Pennsylvania: The Senior Class of Shillington High School, 1950. Print.

Hoerr, Dorothy Lehman. "Shillington Native, World-renown Author John Updike."*Berks County Living* May–June 2005: 48. Print.

Hoyer, Linda Grace."Church Attendance in Olden Times." Robeson Lutheran Evangelical Church. 1970. Unpublished. Print. (Note: Linda Updike published under her maiden name.)

———. *Enchantment*.Boston: Houghton Mifflin, 1971. Print.

———. The Linda Hoyer Updike Collection. Reading Public Library. Reading, Pennsylvania.

———. *The Predator*. New York: Ticknor & Fields, 1990. Print.

Huntzinger, Mrs. Mary E. Shupp. Letter to John Updike 6 Oct. 2006. In Mrs. Huntzinger's possession.

Jemal, Alexander J. "John Updike Collection." Unpublished catalog. Typescript. 2009. Print.

Kreider, Dusty. "The Class of 1950 at Shillington High School Remembers John Updike and He Remembers Them." *Susquehanna Magazine* 3 (Jan. 1978): 18. Print.

Lewis, Thelma Kutch. Letters from and to John Updike. In the Thelma Kutch Lewis and David Silcox collection. Alvernia University. Reading, Pennsylvania. Print.

Mandelbaum, Paul, Ed. *First Words: Earliest Writing from Favorite Contemporary Authors*. Chapel Hill: Algonquin Books of North Carolina, 1993. Print.

Miller, Larry. "C. F. Boyer—Retiring Teacher." Reading (Pennsylvania) *Eagle* 30 April 1969. Print.

Nelson, Barry. "The House on Philadelphia Avenue." Unpublished typescript. Fourteen pages, plus two pages of deeds and one page of photos. April 1999. Print.

———."John Updike at Shillington High School." No date. Unpublished typescript. October, 2002. Print.

———. Letter to the author, May 18, 1996.

———."The Updike Terrain." Reading, Pennsylvania. Typescript. Eleven pages. 1996. Print.

Peters, Lisa A. Jauss. Telephone interview. 12 Aug. 2009.

Plath, James. *Conversations with Updike*. Jackson, Mississippi: U P of Mississippi, 1994. Print.

Posten, Bruce R. "Berks-born Author John Updike Dies." Reading (Pennsylvania)*Eagle* 28 Jan. 2009: A2.

———."Craftsman Weaned on Self-reliance." Reading *Eagle* 25 Sept. 2010. Website edition.

Potts, Jerry. Letters from and to John Updike. Jerry Potts Collection.

Pritchard, William H. *Updike: America's Man of Letters*. South Royalton, Vermont: Steerforth Press, 2000. Print.

"Remembering Updike." Reading (Pennsylvania) *Eagle* 15 Mar. 2009: E-1. Print.

The Shillington Story: 100 Years in the Making. Shillington, Pennsylvania: Shillington Centennial Committee, 2008. Print.

Silcox, David. Letters from and to John Updike. In the Thelma Kutch Lewis and David Silcox collection. Alvernia University. Reading, Pennsylvania.

Sulkis, Ellen. "Berks County Game: Find Yourself in John Updike's Books." *The Sunday Bulletin* (Philadelphia) 21 Nov. 1965: 10.

Taylor, C. Clarke. *John Updike: A Bibliography.* Kent, Ohio: Kent State UP, 1968. Print.

Thomas, Heather. "For Linda Updike, Reclaiming the Farm Came before Writing." Reading (Pennsylvania) *Eagle* 17 Jan. 1982: 25. Print.

Trapani, Beth E. "Pastor Revs up Fun." Reading (Pennsylvania) *Eagle* 23 July 1994: B-1, B-4.

Updike, David. "A Toast to the Visible World: Remembering John Updike." Eulogy read at the New York Public Library's *Tribute to Updike,* March 19, 2009.

Updike, John. *Americana.* New York: Knopf, 2001. Print.

———. *Assorted Prose.* New York: Knopf, 1965. Print.

———. *Bech: A Book.* New York: Knopf, 1970. Print.

———. *Bech at Bay.* New York: Knopf, 1998. Print.

———. *The Beloved.* Northridge, California: Lord John Press, 1982. Print.

———. *The Carpentered Hen and Other Tame Creatures.* New York: Harper & Brothers, 1958. Print.

———. *The Centaur.* New York: Knopf, 1962. Print.

———. *Collected Poems, 1953–1993.* New York: Knopf, 1993. Print.

———. *Concerts at Castle Hill.* Northridge, California: Lord John Press, 1993. Print.

———. *Due Considerations: Essays and Criticism.* New York: Knopf, 2007. Print.

———. *The Early Stories, 1953–75.* New York: Knopf, 2003. Print.

———. *Endpoint and Other Poems.* New York: Knopf, 2009. Print.

———. Foreword. *The Complete Book of Covers from* The New Yorker *1925–1989.* Knopf: New York, 1989: v–vii. Print.

———. *Higher Gossip.* New York: Knopf, 2011. Print.

———. *Hub Fans Bid Kid Adieu.* New York: The Library of America, 2010. Print.

———. *Hugging the Shore: Essays and Criticism.* New York: Knopf, 1983. Print.

———. Interview. Sydney, Australia. *Morning News* 23 July 2006. Print.

———. *In the Beauty of the Lilies.* New York: Knopf, 1996. Print.

———. *Jester's Dozen.* Northridge, California: Lord John Press, 1984. Print.

———. "John Updike: 'Rabbit' Books 'Pleasing to Write.'" Roanoke *Times* 7 Feb. 2005. Print.

———. Letter from John Updike to Mrs. Linda Updike. 1950.

———. Letter to *The Boston Globe* 27 Oct. 1994. Print.

———. *Licks of Love.* New York: Knopf, 2000. Print.

———. *Midpoint.* New York: Knopf, 1965. Print.

———. *More Matter.* New York: Knopf, 1999. Print.

———. *My Father's Tears.* New York: Knopf, 2009. Print.

———. *Odd Jobs.* New York: Knopf, 1991. Print.

———. *Of the Farm.* New York: Knopf, 1965. Print.

———. *Olinger Stories.* New York: Vintage, 1964. Print.

———. *Picked-Up Pieces.* New York: Knopf, 1968. Print.

———. "Rapt by the Radio." *Diamonds Are Forever: Artists and Writers on Baseball.* Ed. Peter H. Gordon, with Sydney Waller and Paul Weinman. San Francisco: Chronicle Books, 1987: 102. Print.

———. "Reminiscences of My Cartoons." *Hogan's Alley* Spring 1996: 124–34.

———. "Seeing Norman Rockwell." *The Wilson Quarterly* 15 (Spg. 1991): 136. Print.

———. *Self-Consciousness.* New York: Fawcett, 1990. Print.

———. *Self-Consciousness.* New York: Knopf, 1989. Print.

———. *Trust Me.* New York: Knopf, 1987. Print.

———. *Villages.* New York: Knopf, 2004. Print.

"View from the Catacombs." *Time* 26 Apr. 1968: 66–68; 73–75. Print.

Weber, Bruce. "'As Good a Writer's Mother as One Could Ask For.'" *The New York Times Book Review* 14 Jan. 1990: 11. Print.

Wright, Stuart. "John Updike's Contributions to *Chatterbox.*" *The Bulletin of Bibliography* Dec. 1985: 170–77. Print.

Youngerman, Joan Venne. Interview.

Zanganeh, Lila Azam. "Updike Redux." *Flagler Live* 22 Nov. 2010. Print.

Index

Achey, Mary A. (*later* Cooke), 147
acrostic poems, 60–61, 84
administration, high school, 131, 132
Afterlife, 9
Albright College: students aiming for, 20; Wesley at, 11
Andrews, Gloria, 91, 98n5
Angstrom, Gloria, 98n5
Angstrom, Harry "Rabbit", 89, 92–93
Angstrom, Janice, 71
Angstrom, Mary, 17
Angstrom, Mim, 93
anxiety of middleness, 6
Arndt, Robert (Bob), 93, 143
art training, 73–79; with Carleton Boyer, 76, 77–78, 132, 146; with Clint Shilling, 4, 26, 74, 77; Philadelphia trips for, 69, 78
Asthma, 47n9
athletics. *See* sports

Bachman, June F. (*later* Stoudt), 147
Baer, William C.v, 134
Barth, John, 29n24
Barth, Marilyn M. (*later* McCombe), 147
Barthold, Richard R., 147
baseball, 51–52
basketball, 52, 75, 92–93
Baum, Eleanor, 158
Bausher, Robert W., 147
Becker, Elsie Kachel, 11
Becker, Helen (*later* Hartzell), 117, 157
Becker, Jane (*later* Wertz), 94, 134, 138
Becker, Orville, 11
Behn, Clyde, 97
Behn, Cookie, 94
Behney, Dick, 53
Betty Lou, 94
Bingaman, Molly, 95, 99n10

Bitting, Mammy, 98n3
Blatt, Ruth J. (*later* Shrawder), 158
board of school directors, 132, 157
Borner, Joan (*later* Conrad): on John's appearance, 33; John's opinion of, 69; as movie-goer, 68; on Nancy Wolf, 70; as playmate, 65; profile of, 145; on Wesley's teaching, 13
Bowman, Margaret L. (*later* Gechter), 147–148
Boyer, Carleton F., 76, 77–78, 132, 146
Boyer, Harlan L.: at basketball games, 93; on car joyriding, 61; on clowning, 60; clowning by, 59; hiking trips of, 45; on John's appearance, 34; on John's cartooning, 73; on John's sports participation, 50, 52; on John's writings, 21; on Linda, 8; as model, 94; profile of, 134; at Stephen's Luncheonette, 45; on stuttering, 34–35; on teachers, 12; on Wesley's kindness, 92; on Wesley's teaching, 12
Brazil, 63n6
Brendel, Donald R., 148
Brendle, LeRoy E., 148
Brobst, Kathryn (*later* Hartman), 156
Brobst, Mr. (elementary principal), 156
Brunner, William, 157

Caldwell, George, 16, 62n2, 63n8, 89, 92, 94, 98n6
Caldwell, Peter, 16, 25, 30n31, 39n3, 63n8
Caniff, Milton, 74
cars: black 1936 Buick, 15, 29n28, 63n8; clowning with, 61–62; as inspiration, 91; John hit by, 2, 61
cartooning, 73–79

The Centaur: classmates reading, 19, 21, 22; clowning in, 62n2, 63n8, 64n9; inspiration for, 4, 16, 24, 30n31, 30n33, 45, 47n7, 81n13, 91, 94; models for, 90, 95, 99n10; reading focused in, 46

Chafetz, Hope, 71

Chatterbox: cartooning and drawing for, 73–79; description of, 117; detective story written for, 42; female contacts and, 66, 67, 69; John's contributions to, 117–130; literary pranks in, 60; poetry for, 78–79, 83–85; prose for, 85–86; signing methods for, 19; writings for, 42

Children's Activities, drawing published in, 73

Ciemiewicz, Gloria M. (*later* Hain), 148

classmate profiles, 134–142

class reunions, xx–xxi, 22–23, 63n5, 158

Clayton, Alfred, 64n9

clowning and pranks, 57–62; by Wesley, 12–13, 14

comics, inspiration from, 73–74

Conrad, Harlan, 42, 135, 145

Cooper, Lane, Professor, 5

Cornell University, Linda and Wesley at, 1

Council, Myrtle, 6, 8, 9; on John's boyhood friends, 3; on John's relationship with father, 15; on John's sports participation, 51, 54; on movie theater, 43; profile of, 143; on Wesley's teaching, 13

Couples, 19; classmates reading, 22; models for, 99n11; notes for, 80n4

Craley, Doris A. (*later* Novak), 148

Daubert, Richard L., 42, 52–53, 135

Daubert, Robert D., 8, 67; on cartoons, 76; as gang member, 42; on John's vocabulary, 37; on John's writings, 21; Peggy Lutz relationship with, 70

Davis, Donald M., 148

Davis, Robert L., 148

debating team, 36–37, 67, 69

Dedman, Johnny, 45

Depression, effects of, xxi, 3, 15

Dickinson, Raymond, 91, 138, 146

Dietrich, Irene A. (*later* Harrold), 148

Disney influence, 73, 73–74, 79, 79n1

dogwood tree, at Shillington home, 1, 27

Dow, Allen, 27n3, 30n42, 39n3, 72n2, 95, 131

Drawing, 73–77; poetry with, 78–79

Duryea, Charles, 24

Dysput, Norman J., 148

Eberly, Dorothy N., 157, 158

Eckenroth, John C., 148

Edison, Joan, 90

Eifert, Jouette (*later* Chick), 68, 94, 135

Einstein, Aaron, 25

Eisenberg, Mrs. (*Little Shillington* advisor), 75, 156

Eisenbise, Patricia L. (*later* Deal), 149

Elizanne, 94

Emerick, Frances E. (*later* Bergman), 149

Endpoint: classmates reading, 21; John comment on, 22

Erb, Joyce, 144

Essick, Larry, 139, 149

faculty members: elementary school, 146, 156–157; high school, 132–134, 157–159; junior high, 157

Farnsworth, Skeeter, 92

Farris, Barbara (*later* White), 155

Fegley, Berry Fehl, 55n11

Feitz, Miss, 94

females, as models and inspiration, 65–71

Fessler, George E., 149

Firing, William H., 13, 132, 149, 155

Flail, Rebecca J. (*later* Van Liew), 149

Fogel, Butch, 94, 99n9

Fool's Hill drawing, 12

football, 53–54, 75

Forry, Peter, 91

Forry, William A. (Bill): in card games, 44; as gang member, 42; hiking trips of, 45; on John's vocabulary, 37; as model, 91; in poetry, 84; profile of, 131

Frankhauser, Mahlon M.: in card games, 44; as gang member, 42; as model, 91; profile of, 135

Frederick, Dolores (*later* Ohlinger), 36, 134; as model, 98n3; profile of, 135–136

Frederick, Linda, 134

Freed, Elizabeth B., 158

Freed, Paul F., 158

Fries, Harold W., 158

Fritz, Olive, 94, 156

Games, 41–46

Gaston, Betty J. (*later* Ludwig), 149

Gelnett, Francis R., 136, 158

George, Joan L. (*later* Zug) (Pudge), 68, 149; as playmate, 65; profile of, 136; at prom, 71n1; on Rabbit, 92

Gerhartin, Gloria, 94

Gertrude and Claudius, 19, 64n9

girls, as models and inspiration, 65–71

golf, 54, 55n11

Goodman, Marie, 156

Grace Evangelical Lutheran Church, 2, 11

Gray, Harold, 74

Greth, Roma, 6, 13, 143

Grill, Marie, 146

Groome, Robert S., 149

Gruber, Miriam, 22

Guerin, Jack E., xx, 38; in card games, 44; on clowning, 58; on dating scene, 69; on Fred Muth, 139; as gang member, 42; on John's popularity, 38; on John's stuttering, 34–35; on John's vocabulary, 37; on Linda's attitude toward sports, 54; profile of, 136; on smoking, 45

Gundy, Emerson W., 14, 36; buying Plowville farm, 28n14; on John's writings, 20; profile of, 136

Hall, Clarence H., 59, 137

Hall, Milton A., 12, 38; clowning by, 59; on Fred Muth, 138; on John's popularity, 68; on John's vocabulary, 37; on Peggy Lutz-John relationship, 69; profile of, 137; on stuttering, 34

Harrison, Thelma, 72n6

Hartman, Kathryn Brobst, 4, 41

Hartz, Barbara L. (*later* Behney), 67; on Carlton Boyer, 78; on Clint Shilling, 77; engagement of, 99n7; games played with, 41; as gang member, 42; on John's appearance, 34; John's cartoon for, 74; on John's sports participation, 51; on John's writings, 21; on Nancy Wolf, 70; as playmate, 65; in reading sessions, 44; relationship with Updike family, 4; on stuttering, 35; on Wesley's teaching, 13

Harvard University, 23; clowning trick at, 60; drawing opportunities at, 73; interests listed on application, 47n7; John appearance at, 67; selection of, 8

Heffner, Ruth, 157

Hemmig, Benneville H., 25, 30n38

Hemmig, Charles J., 6, 8, 12, 25; clowning and, 59; collision with McComsey, 138; as model, 94; profile of, 131; Wesley difficulties with, 58

Hendricks, Howard L., 145

Hendricks, Priscilla, 145

Herzog, Kenneth R., 149

Hiester, Dr. Gabriel, Jr., 99n7

Hiester, Richard "Rabbit", 93, 137, 143

Hi-Life (yearbook): classmate profiles in, 134–142, 147–156; classmates ambitions in, 20; cover design of, 77; drawings for, 77; earlier graduate profiles in, 143–145; female contacts and, 67, 69; John appearance in, 77

Hill, Leroy, 53

Hill, LeRoy D., 149

Hill, LeRoy I., 149–150

Hirneisen, Jacqueline J. (*later* Kendall), 8; on Emerson Gundy, 136; on Fred/ John relationship, 138; as gang member, 42; hiking trips of, 44, 45; on John's appearance, 67–68; John's drawing for, 74; on John's intelligence, 35; on John's popularity, 38; on John's relationship with father, 15; on

John's writings, 21; as model, 71, 90; on models used by John, 92; as movie-goer, 68; as playmate, 65; poems written to, 67; profile of, 137; on psoriasis, 35; in Sunday activities, 45; on Wesley's teaching, 14

Hoffman, Nancy E., 150

Hollenbach, Miss (elementary teacher), 157

Hook, John F., 18

Hornberger, Mary Louise, 140

Horning, Sara J. (*later* Ebersole), 150

Houck, Karl and Caroline, 90

Hovey, Neil, 91

Hoyer, John Franklin (grandfather), 1, 18–19, 22; burial in Plow Cemetery, 28n13; discouraging Linda's writing, 5; Hemmig stock sales to, 131; John reading cartoons to, 74; selling farm, 6; selling Shillington home, 6

Hoyer, Katherine Ziemer Kramer (grandmother), 1, 17, 34; buried in Plow Cemetery, 28n13; carnival invitation for, 41; John's relationship with, 65; marriage of, 18

Huntzinger, Mary E. Shupp, 11, 13, 146

Huntzinger, Sara (*later* Sprecher), 91, 146

Hydecam, William and Dorothea, 26

inspirations, 89–97

In the Beauty of the Lilies, inspiration for, 26, 47n7, 71

Jasinski, Joseph J., 42, 59, 137

Jauss, David H., Jr., 145

Johns, Catherine M. (*later* Fletcher), 150

Jones, Judith, 66

Kachel, Mildred F. (*later* Moyer), 150

Kauffman, Dorothy, 117

Kaufmann, Marnie, 94, 99n9

Keffer, Doris (*later* Wenrich), 37, 150

Kemp, Karl, 59

Kendall, Carl, 4, 41, 92

Kern, David, xxivn1, 63n6, 72n3–72n4, 94

Kirlin, Frederick L., 150

Kistler, Russell H., 133

Kleppinger, Virginia, 157

Klopp, Paul B., 91–92, 158

Klopp, Russell W., 157

Kobrin, Jerry, 24

Kohl, Kenneth, 158

Kohl, Leverne C., 150

Kroninger, Rev. Victor, 3, 11, 13, 14, 29n20, 41–44, 143

Kruppenbach, Rev. Fritz, 29n21, 143

Krusty the Clown, 80n6

Kuser, Shirley J., 150

Lampoon, 8, 85; drawing opportunities in, 73; editing, 79; pranks in, 64n9

Landis, Miss (kindergarten teacher), 157

Lang, Sandra, 94

Lasch, Christopher, 55n4

Lebanon Valley College, 71

Leiby, Bessie S., 158

Leininger, Elwood A., 157

leisure activities, 41–46

Leonard, Ruth, 99n10

Lesher, William R., 150

LeVan, William (Bill), 12, 143–144

Lewis, Edmund J., 159

Lewis, Thelma Kutch, 8; as *Chatterbox* advisor, 66, 117; on John's sports participation, 51; on John's writings, 22; on literary pranks, 60; as model, 72n6, 90; profile of, 133

The Little Shilling, 91, 117; cartoons for, 74; female contacts and, 69

Loos, John G., 159

Luden, William H., 24

Ludwig, Grace B. (*later* Bricker), 150

Lutz, Peggy A. (*later* Roberts), 38; children of, 72n5; clowning by, 60; death of, xxii; on debating team, 69; in games, 44; as gang member, 42; home of, 26; John's drawing of, 76; John's perception of, 68; John's relationship with, 69–70, 71, 71n1; marriage of, 70; as model, 71, 72n5, 90, 91, 94–95; as playmate, 65;

profile of, 137; smoking by, 45
Lutz, Thelma, 90

McComsey, Charles F. (Charlie), 12,
141; clowning by, 59; as model, 94;
profile of, 138
McCoy, Robert, 64n9
McCoy, Skip, 43
McElroy, Walter, 157
McFarland, Ann, 99n9
magazines, poetry on, 83
Malone, Mary E. (*later* Bishop), 151
Manderbach, Richard W., (Dick,
Mandy),: on Charlie McComsey,
138; on clowning, 57; in games, 44;
as gang member, 42; on Halloween
activities, 42; on John's intelligence,
36; on John's popularity, 38; as
model, 91; profile of, 137–138; sports
participation by, 53; on stuttering,
35; on Wesley's appearance, 11; on
Wesley's teaching, 12, 14
Maple, Richard, 63n8
March, Nancy (later LeVan): on
Florence Schrack, 133; as gang
member, 42; on John's writings, 22;
on Nancy Wolf, 70; profile of, 138; at
Stephen's Luncheonette, 45; on
Wesley's teaching, 12; winning
senior art award, 78
Marshfield, Tom, 55n11
Mays, June D., 151
Memories of the Ford Administration,
64n9
Mervine, David H., 151
Mickey Mouse, as inspiration, 73–74,
79n1
Mifflin, John, 25
Mifflin, Thomas, 25–26
Miller, Dick, 42
Miller, Ned, 94
Minuit, Belle, 5, 28n11
models, 89–97. *See also* individual
persons
Mohn, Wilbur K., 151
Moore, William S., 151
Moorehouse, Stanley A., 157
Morrow, William A., 159
Moser, William J., 42, 151

movies: John's interest and attending
of, 37, 42–43, 67; reviews of, 85; at
Shillington theater, 26, 43
murder mysteries, 86
museums, Reading, 4, 25, 31n43, 77
Muth, D. Frederick (Fred), 36, 38, 133;
in card games, 44; chess games
with, 44; death of, xxii; games
played with, 41; as gang member,
42; John's drawing of, 76; on John's
vocabulary, 37; on John's writings,
20; literary feud with, 60, 61; as
model, 91, 94; in poetry, 84; profile
of, 138; in reading sessions, 44;
sports participation by, 53, 55n9; at
Stephen's Luncheonette, 45; writing
class play, 136
Muth, Dawson H., 138

Nash, Ogden, 84
Nelson, Barry R., xxi; on black Buick,
29n28; car joyriding with, 61;
cartoon collection of, 74; on
cartoons, 75, 76; on *Chatterbox* work,
86; on clowning, 58; on John's
appearance, 34; on John's college
selection, 7–8; on John's intelligence,
36; on John's sports participation,
49–50, 53, 54; on John's writings, 21;
on Linda, 8; as model, 99n9; on
models for writings, 89, 94; on
pinball playing, 78; in poetry, 84;
profile of, 139; at Stephen's
Luncheonette, 45; on Wesley's
appearance, 11
The New Yorker: drawing rejection slips
from, 76; inspiration from, 74
Ninzeheltzer, Roy J., 151
Nordholm, John, 47n14, 89, 90, 91
Novak, Peter P., 151
Nunemaker, Samuel C., 151

Of the Farm: classmates reading, 19, 21;
inspiration for, 31n45
Ohlinger, Harry C., 98n3
Orff, Mary C., 42, 152

Pagoda building, 24
Painter, George C. (*later* Stehman), 152

Palm, Bernarda A. (Benny), 8, 9, 36, 38; on Carlton Boyer, 78; on cartoons, 76; on clowning, 59; on John's relationship with father, 15; on John's writings, 21; on movies, 43; profile of, 140; in Sunday activities, 45; on Wesley's teaching, 11

Pennepacker, Estella R., 67, 133, 159

Pennington, Mary (*later* Updike and Weatherall), 17, 29n21, 30n39; artistic gifts of, 80n3; on John's beard, 39n2; John's paintings and, 81n12; John's pranks on, 60; John's proposal to, 91

Pennsylvania School Press Association award, 84

Penny, 95

Peters, Lisa Jauss, 71

Philadelphia: art class trips to, 23, 69, 78; not featured in writings, 23

Phillips, Richard T., 152

Pienta, Edward P., 12, 22, 140

pinball, 78, 84

Plow Cemetery, 28n13

Plowville farm: commuting from, 37; current status of, 27; Gundy purchase of, 28n14; Linda attachment to, 6–7; Linda raised at, 1; move to, xxi–xxii, 7, 26; selling of, 6, 18

poetry: *Chatterbox*, 83–85; drawing with, 78–79

poorhouse, 19, 26

The Poorhouse Fair, 48n17; classmates reading, 21, 22; clowning in, 63n8; inspiration for, 26, 47n7, 48n18; model for, 19

Potts, Jerry, 3, 12; home of, 26; on John's sports participation, 49, 52, 53; on Linda's attitude toward sports, 54; as model, 93, 94; profile of, 144; sports awards of, 53

Potts, Mary Jane, 68, 94, 144

pranks, 57–62

Pritchard, Eddie, 38, 144

Prosser, Mark, 62n2, 91

psoriasis problem, 2, 20, 35, 39n2–39n3

Pulitzer Prize, 8

"Queenie", 72n4, 94–95

Rabbit, Run: classmates reading, 19, 21; existential anxiety in, 84; inspiration for, 24, 28n15, 29n21, 45; obscenity issues in, 63n6; reading focused in, 46; sports in, 52

Rabbit at Rest: models for, 5, 72n6; sports in, 55n6

Rabbit Is Rich: models for, 72n6; Pulitzer Prize for, 8

Rabbit Redux: inspiration for, 17; obscenity issues in, 63n6; sports in, 55n6

Rabzak, Christine E. (*later* Budgy), 152

Reading (city), as setting for writing, 24–25

Reading *Eagle* and *Times* newspapers, 21–22, 24, 61

Reading Museum, 4, 25, 31n43, 77

Reading Public Library: importance to John, 24, 45; Linda Hoyer Updike Collection in, 9

Reich, Sam, 43

Reidenhauser, Julia, 94

Reiter, Jeanette A. (*later* Born), 152

Remp, Virginia M. (*later* Machemer), 153

reunions, xx–xxi, 22–23, 63n5, 158

Rhoads, Robert I., 13, 20; on Hemmig's interactions with students, 94; on John's intelligence, 36; on John's writings, 21; on Linda, 8; Macbeth soliloquy by, 91; profile of, 144; on psoriasis, 35; reciting in class, 62n1; on stuttering, 34; on Wesley's teaching, 12

Richards, J. Allen (father), 11, 146, 159

Richards, J. Allen (son), 153

Richards, Ruth, 146, 153, 157

Riehm, George, 25

Rittenhouse, Joan E., 153

Roberts, Tjaden ("Jady"), 70, 137

Robeson Evangelical Lutheran Church, 18

Robinson, Joey, 31n45

roofball, 49–51

Rothermel, Dr. Ernest, 27, 93–94, 140, 145

Rothermel, Dr. Lewis, 145, 157
Rothermel, Mrs. (teacher), 35
Rothermel, Robert L., 145
Runge, Frances G. (*later* Kaffine), 153
Ruskin School for Drawing and Fine Art in Oxford, 81n12
Ruth, Joyce M., 159
Ruth, Miss (librarian), 24

Schiffner, Miss (piano teacher), 5
Schmehl, Mary Ann (*later* Ehst), 42, 138, 140
school board, 132, 157
Schrack, Florence C., 36, 67, 133, 136
Schrack John, 157
Schubel, Donald L., 153
Schwartz, Donald H., 153
Seidel, Elsie, 96, 99n10
Self-Consciousness, 43, 94, 95, 96
Shadler, Janet E. (*later* Neuheimer), 153
shaped poems, 81n17
Shilling, Clint, 4, 26, 74, 77
Shilling, Samuel, 25, 77
Shillington: description of, 25–27; history of, 25
Shillington home (Philadelphia Ave.): current status of, 27; description of, 18; leaving, 7; Linda unhappiness with, 6
Showalter, Kathryn O., 12, 67; pranks played on, 57–58; profile of, 134
Shrawder, Norman W., 36, 159
Shverha, Joseph, 26, 43
Sing Hoo, 86
Smart, Jane, 71
Smith, Janet C. (*later* Craley), 153
Smith, Shirley F. (*later* Berger): in card games, 44; on car joyriding, 61; on Fred Muth, 138; on John's writings, 21; on models, 92, 94; on Nancy Wolf, 70; profile of, 140; on psoriasis, 35; smoking by, 45; on Wesley's appearance, 11; on Wesley's teaching, 11, 12, 13–14; on yearbook, 77
smoking habits, 45
Sonen, Stewart F., 153–154
sports: drawings of, 75; John's participation and interest in, 3, 26, 37, 49–54
Stackhouse, Barbara L. (*later* Martin), 154
Stafford, Mae B., 154
Stamm, Margaret S., 1, 15, 134
Stanley, Mary Ann (*later* Moyer): as gang member, 42; John's perception of, 68; as model, 91, 99n9; as playmate, 65; profile of, 140
Stehman, Donald, 152
Steinberg, Saul, 74
Stephen's Luncheonette, 27, 45
Sterner, "Fats", 50
Sterner, Judith E. (*later* Meck), 154
Stevens, Wallace, 24
Stoudt, Barbara J., 154
Stoudt, Walter R., 154
Stover, Patricia A. (*later* Steinfurth), 154
Strause, Donald, 117
stuttering, 34–35
Styer, Barry C., 154
Sweitzer, Betty L. (*later* Jeddic), 154
swimming, 44, 47n12
Swoyer, Lois W., 159

Tate, Miss (teacher), 35, 146
Taylor, Anna C., 159
teachers. *See* faculty members; *individual teachers*
Terrorist, 63n6
Thurber, James, 74
Tinus, Irene J. (*later* Dobson), 154
Trexler, James M. (Jim): on cartoons, 76; on clowning, 59; as gang member, 42; as model, 94, 99n9; profile of, 141; on Wesley's teaching, 13
Trexler, Jim and Evvie: on John's writings, 21; on Plowville move, 6
Tylka, Mary Jane (*later* Barasso), 154

Updike, David (son), 14, 30n36, 54, 80n3
Updike, Don (uncle), 19
Updike, Elizabeth (daughter), 17, 80n3
Updike, Hartley Titus (grandfather), 19, 30n40
Updike, John Hoyer: acrostic structures of, 60–61, 84; anxiety of

middleness in, 6; appearance of, 33–34; art training for, 4, 77–78; asthma attack of, 47n9; baptism of, 29n20; birth of, xxi, 1, 24, 28n10, 30n36; cartooning by, 73–77; character of, xxi–xxii; on *Chatterbox* staff, 75–77, 78, 117–130; childhood art work of, 3; childhood games of, 41; childhood writings of, 3; children of, 15, 80n3; church activities of, 29n21; classmates comments on his writings, 19–23; in class play, 140; as class president, 38; at class reunions, xx–xxi, 22–23, 63n5, 158; clowning devices of, 57–62; college selection for, 7–8; confirmation of, 24; dancing lessons for, 4; death of, xix; as debater, 36–37; Disney films influencing, 73, 79n1; divorce of, 15; driver's license and, 26, 61; driving under the influence, 62; editing mother's writings, 8; exhibiting art in Philadelphia, 23, 69, 78; extra-curricular activities of, 36, 67; on farm chores, 7, 26; as fast talker, 34; fear of ghosts, 17; financial management by, 15; first birthday of, 1; games enjoyed by, 43–44; in gangs, 42; girls' and women's interactions with, 65–71; grandparents of, xxi; high school academic achievements of, 36, 39n4; hit by car, 2, 61; identifying with dogwood tree, 27; inspirations for, 89–97; intelligence of, 35–37; kissing girls, 4; leisure activities of, 41–46; letter to Gelnett, 158; literary feud with, 60; on Little Shilling staff, 75, 117, 118; magazines described in poetry, 83; on Mary Malone, 151; memorial in Plow Cemetery, 28n13; memories of Shillington, 10; Mickey Mouse influence on, 73, 79n1; models for, 89–97; mother's typewriter as rival to, 6; move to Plowville, xxi–xxii, 6–7, 26; as movie-goer, 37, 42–43, 67; movie reviews by, 85; museum visits of, 4; 25; music lessons for, 4; as only child, xxi; in parade, 29n19; Pennsylvania surroundings of, 23–27; perception of mother, 9; personal reading program of, 37; poetry combined with drawing by, 78–79; poetry in *Chatterbox*, 83–85; popularity of, 38; proposal to Mary, 91; prose in *Chatterbox*, 85; psoriasis problem of, 2, 20, 35, 39n2–39n3; reading at preschool age, 4; Reading (city) experiences of, 24–25; as Reading newspaper employee, 24–25, 61; Reading Public Library connections of, 24, 46; reading selections of, 46; reading sessions with friends, 44; relationship with father, 14, 16; in school plays, 37; self-portrait of, 80n9; Shillington home of, 6, 7, 18, 26, 27; Shillington setting for, 25–27; signatures used by, 118; similarities to father's life, 15; smoking habits of, 45; sports participation and interests of, 3, 26, 37, 49–54; at Stephen's Luncheonette, 27, 45; stuttering of, 34–35; Sunday activities of, 45, 47n13; swimming adventures of, 44, 47n12; as teacher's brat, 153; teaching at Harvard, 29n24; on typing, 9; as valedictorian, 35–36; visits to Berks County, xix; visualizing future, 42; vocabulary of, 37; wartime activities of, 43; wedding gift to, 17; writings set in Pennsylvania, 109–115; yearbook profile of, 141; on yearbook staff, 77
Updike, Linda Grace Hoyer (mother), 1–10; ambitions of, 1; attitude toward Shillington, 6–7, 26; birth of, 1, 17; on boyhood friends, 3; burial in Plow Cemetery, 28n13; college friends of, 90; cultivating John's arts interests, 4–5; drawing with John, 73; education of, 1, 18; fearing injury in fights, 3–4; John perception of, 9; John's relationship with, 65; on John's sexual orientation, 3; on John's smoking, 45; meeting

Wesley, 1; move to Plowville, 6–7; on Nancy Wolf, 71; papers in libraries, 1; photographing John, 9; planting dogwood tree, 1; psoriasis problem of, 2; relationship to Gundy family, 136; on relationship with girls, 4; on sports participation, 51–52; as substitute teacher, 6; temper tantrums of, 3; wedding of, 1; at Women's Club, 6; writings of, 5–6, 8

Updike, Martha, 151

Updike, Mary (aunt), 19, 74

Updike, Michael (son), 28n13, 54, 80n3

Updike, Miranda (daughter), 80n3

Updike, Virginia Emily Blackwood (grandmother), 19

Updike, Wesley Russell (father), 10–16; appearance of, 11; ballpark named for, 15; at basketball games, xxii, xxivn3; burial in Plow Cemetery, 28n13; chaperoning dances, 68; childhood of, 10; church membership of, 11; classroom antics of, 11–14, 57; in community events, 11; early jobs of, 10–11; education of, 10, 11; funeral of, 132; on John's smoking, 45; leaving Shillington home, 7; meeting Linda, 1; mistreatment of, 94; as model, 89, 92, 94; name causing jeers, 30n32; personality of, 9; planting dogwood tree, 1; on poverty, 15; punishing John, 43; relationship with German woman, 28n16; rumored heart attack of, 22; similarities to son's life, 15; sports participation by, 51, 54; teaching at Shillington High School, 11–14; at University of Pennsylvania, 132; visits from grandchildren, 14; wedding of, 1; yearbook caption for, 15

Ursinus University: Linda degree from, 1; Wesley at, 10

Van Liew, Anthony (Tony), 7; on car joyriding, 61; on clowning, 58, 60; as gang member, 42; on John's sports participation, 51, 52; on John's

writings, 21; on literary prank, 61; Peggy Lutz perception of, 70; playing in "Black Forest", 43; sports participation by, 52; on Wesley's teaching, 12–13

Van Liew, Don C., 132, 157

Van Liew, Sevellon, 117

Venne, Joan P. (*later* Youngerman), 12, 38, 149; on art shows, 78; on boyhood friends, 3; in card games, 44; on car joyriding, 61; Christmas card to, 79; on clowning, 57–58, 60; on Fred Muth, 138; in games, 41, 44; as gang member, 42; hiking trips of, 45; on John's appearance, 33, 67–68; on John's sports participation, 52; on John's vocabulary, 37; on John's writings, 20–21; on Linda influence on John, 9; Linda Updike welcome of, 4; as model, 71, 89–90, 94, 99n9; Nancy Wolf and, 71; as playmate, 65; on Plowville move, 7; profile of, 141; relationship with John, 4; smoking by, 45; on stuttering, 34

Villages: classmates reading, 22; models for, 96

visual arts: cartooning, 73–79; drawing, 73–77; training for. *See* art training

Wagner, Barbara (*later* Schwartz), 42, 155

Waid, Marvin: on cartoons, 76; on clowning, 59; as gang member, 42; on John's writings, 21, 22; in neighborhood adventures, 44; on note-passing in class, 91; playing in "Black Forest", 43; profile of, 141–142; on stuttering, 35

Walk, Phyllis L., 155

Weik, Ann M. (*later* Cassar), 38; on Big Little book sessions, 138; as gang member, 42; on high school English teachers, 67; on high school Shakespearean studies, 87n8; John's drawing of, 76; on John's intelligence, 35; John's perception of, 68; on John's writings, 20, 22; on junior and senior high description, 146; literary uses of, 71; on Mary

Orff, 152; as most studious, 138; in musical trio, 138; profile of, 142; in reading sessions, 44; as teacher's brat, 153; on Wesley's teaching, 14
Weik, Luther A.: in community events, 11; discipline by, 59; profile of, 132
Weisman, Christian, 155
Wenrich, Mark R., 155
White, Nancy, 59
White, Neil F., 42, 155
White, Peggy, 13, 133, 134
Whitehead, Doris (*later* Bausher), 147
The Widows of Eastwick: classmates reading, 22; clowning in, 64n9; inspiration for, 71; obscenity issues in, 63n6
Williams, Ted, 52
Willis, Ermajean, 97
Wilmot, Alma, 71
Wilmot, Rev. Clarence, 30n40
Wilson. Charlie, 21–22
Witwer, Carl B., 155
Witwer, Richard E., 155
Wolf, Nancy Ann (*later* Jauss), 38; death of, xxii; as model, 95–97;

profile of, 145; relationship with John, 70–71
Wolfe, Doris (*later* Forry), 44
women, as models and inspiration, 65–71

Yerger, Betty L., 155
Yocum, Larry, 71n1, 149
Yoder, Wilma Mae, 43
Youndt, Georgean (*later* Bixler): games played with, 41–42; as gang member, 42; on John's appearance, 34; as model, 94; profile of, 142
Young, Margaret L. (*later* Wenger), 155–156
Yurick, Barbara (*later* Novak), 43, 156

Zendt, Ivan F., Jr., 157
Zimmerman, Anna G. (*later* Amole), 156
Zimmerman, Elizabeth L. (*later* Ziegler), 156
Zimmerman (fictional principal), 94